THE SHADOW OF THE PARTHENON

BY THE SAME AUTHOR

Fiction

ACHILLES HIS ARMOUR

THE SWORD OF PLEASURE

THE LAUGHTER OF APHRODITE

HABEAS CORPUS

CAT IN GLOVES

Travel and Biography

THE EXPANDING EYE

KENNETH GRAHAME : A STUDY OF HIS LIFE, WORK, AND TIMES

SIR THOMAS BROWNE

JOHN SKELTON

Classical History and Literature

ESSAYS IN ANTIQUITY

JUVENAL : THE SIXTEEN SATIRES

ARMADA FROM ATHENS : THE FAILURE OF THE SICILIAN EXPEDITION, 415-413 B C

THE YEAR OF SALAMIS : 480-479 B C

ALEXANDER THE GREAT : A HISTORICAL BIOGRAPHY

THE SHADOW OF THE PARTHENON

STUDIES IN ANCIENT HISTORY AND LITERATURE

PETER GREEN

UNIVERSITY OF CALIFORNIA PRESS

BERKELEY AND LOS ANGELES

1972

University of California Press
Berkeley and Los Angeles, California

ISBN 0-520-02322-6
Library of Congress Catalog Card Number 72-87205
Printed in Great Britain

Contents

for Alan and Julie Boegehold

with love, as always

Preface and Acknowledgments

This book forms a companion volume to *Essays in Antiquity* (1960); since the latter work is not only still in print, but depressingly often—from my point of view—the one book I have written which people know and remember, there may be room for a further venture in the same field. As before, with one or two exceptions, none of the studies here presented has previously appeared in anything like its present form; and even the exceptions have undergone very substantial revision. 'The Shadow of the Parthenon' appears here for the first time; and the bulk of its companion-pieces have been so drastically rewritten, recombined and expanded that they, too, can virtually count as new creations. Material has gone into them from a number of widely disparate sources: I have in fact printed no more than about one-tenth of the material at my disposal, preferring to regard a book of this sort as a critical selection and reappraisal of my views over a twelve-year period rather than an untidy holdall for the dusty contents of my bottom drawer.

Lectures, seminar-notes, and reviews or articles which first appeared in *The Times Literary Supplement* account for a good proportion of the raw material fed into my files for reworking and revision. The section on Sappho in 'The Individual Voice' began life as a postscript to my novel *The Laughter of Aphrodite*, was subsequently revised and expanded for publication in the *Cornhill Magazine* and *Horizon* (U S A) and acquired further additions and modifications from several years' lecturing on Greek history and literature. 'The First Sicilian Slave War' was originally published (with full documentation) in *Past and Present* 20 (Nov. 1961), pp. 10–29. 'Juvenal and his Age' is reprinted, with various additions, deletions, and modifications, from the Introduction to my translation of Juvenal for the Penguin

Classics. My Appendix on 'The Date of Archilochus' appears here in print for the first time.

Reading over all this material suggests to me that my views on ancient history, and classical literature, and the academic world in general, may have become a little less rebarbative (but not, I hope, boringly so) with the onset of middle age. When I wrote *Essays in Antiquity* I was a freelance maverick flaying the professors; now the whirligig of time brings in its revenges, and I write (though still not quite adjusted to the condition) as a professor myself. I take comfort, however, from the following passage in Anatole France's *L'Ile des Pingouins*, originally brought to my notice by a correspondent (whether in a spirit of criticism or encouragement I have never quite decided). This, I feel, may appositely stand as an epigraph, not so much to the present book—where it might be taken as implying qualities to which I myself am far from laying claim—but rather to the whole field of historical studies, modern no less than ancient:

> A quoi bon, mon pauvre monsieur, vous donner tant de peine, et pourquoi composer une histoire, quand vous n'avez qu'à copier les plus connues, comme c'est l'usage? Si vous avez une vue nouvelle, une idée originale, si vous présentez les hommes et les choses sous un aspect inattendu, vous surprendrez le lecteur. Et le lecteur n'aime pas à être surpris. Il ne cherche jamais dans une histoire que les sottises qu'il sait déjà. Si vous essayez de l'instruire, vous ne ferez que l'humilier et le fâcher. Ne tentez pas de l'éclairer, il criera que vous insultez à ses croyances. Les historiens se copient les uns les autres. Ils s'épargnent ainsi de la fatigue et évitent de paraître outrecuidants. Imitez-les et ne soyez pas original. *Un historien original est l'objet de la défiance, du mépris et du dégoût universels.*

I would like to think that the situation today is not quite so black as Anatole France painted it—though uneasily conscious of my own kinship, in too many respects, with that hypothetical conformist whom he portrays, *mon semblable, mon frère.* But if

I have managed, in the course of these pages, to displace, with legitimate arguments, even one hallowed but erroneous *idée reçue*, I shall not feel my time has been spent altogether in vain.

My sincere thanks go to Messrs T. C. W. Stinton and W. G. Forrest, whose searching criticisms, published in *Past and Present* 22 (July 1962) pp. 87—92, led me at several important points to modify my conclusions on the First Sicilian Slave War. Mr Forrest has since, all unwittingly, put me still further in his debt with the publication of that brilliant, witty, stimulating and splendidly heterodox book *The Emergence of Greek Democracy*, a dog-eared copy of which has accompanied me through all my Greek travels, and must, inevitably, have left its mark on some of the views propounded here: though to say that its author should not be held responsible for these is no mere empty disclaimer. I am also grateful to my colleagues on the Faculty of College Year in Athens, especially Professor H. D. F. Kitto and Mr A. R. Burn, for many stimulating discussions, and much perceptive criticism of ideas developed in the course of this book. Lastly I would like to name, *honoris causa*, several Cambridge scholars whose wise teaching and counsel put me immeasurably in their debt as an undergraduate, and whose friendship has meant much to me since: Mr G. T. Griffith, Professor W. K. C. Guthrie, Professor G. S. Kirk, Mr S. J. Papastavrou, and Mr F. H. Sandbach. Like all students of ancient history, I also owe a great debt to Professor M. I. Finley.

For permission to reprint material here included my grateful thanks go to the following: Mr Arthur Crook, Editor of *The Times Literary Supplement*, and Times Newspapers Ltd., for parts of 'The Shadow of the Parthenon', 'Clio Reviewed', 'Athens and Jerusalem', 'Myths and Symbols', 'The Individual Voice', and 'Juvenal and his Age'; the Editors of *Horizon* and *The Cornhill Magazine* for part of 'The Individual Voice'; the Editor of *Past and Present* for 'The First Sicilian Slave War'; the Editors of Penguin Classics and Penguin Books Ltd., for the greater part of 'Juvenal and his Age'; Mr Guy Davenport, and the University of California Press, for the translation of Archilochus quoted on pp. 164–65, which appears as no. 262 in his book *Carmina Archilochi: The Fragments of Archilochos*. All other translations are my own: those of Sappho were originally made for *Horizon*.

PETER GREEN

Department of Classics
The University of Texas at Austin
October 1971

The Shadow of the Parthenon

ONE GUSTY March afternoon, a few years ago, I found myself trudging up the approaches to the Acropolis in the company of a well-known British novelist whose habits were more convivial (to say the least of it) than one could ever have guessed from his published work. After an excellent and discursive lunch in the old quarter known as the Plaka, I asked him what he would like to do next. 'See the bloody Parthenon, I suppose', he said. His voice was an interesting blend of helplessness and suppressed resentment. So we plodded our way to the summit of that vast outcrop, eyes half-closed against the stinging, dust-laden wind, passed through the Propylaea, and began picking our way across a wilderness of jumbled marble blocks towards the huge and too-familiar temple, outlined now against a sky of grey scudding clouds. The air was mournful, oppressive; occasional rain-drops plopped heavily groundwards. It was all very different from the travel posters.

A curious expression came over my companion's face. He stopped, blew his nose with a loud trumpeting sound, and stared, briefly. 'Aaargh,' he said. Into that curious noise he injected all the censorious impatience produced by years of peddling Greek culture to lymphatic schoolchildren. Then he found a comfortable block, and settled himself down on it with his back squarely turned to the ostensible object of our visit. Little by little he relaxed, beaming euphorically as he took in the hazed industrial gloom of Piraeus, the squalid proliferation of sugar-cube houses creeping out to embrace the lower slopes of Mount Parnes, the big jets whining down past us on their approach to Ellenikón Airport. His eyes focussed, briefly and mistily, on the middle distance, where a dirty white mushroom cloud ascended from the Eleusis cement-works, symbol of Demeter's final capitulation to the *deus ex machina*. 'Ah', he said at last.

'Now *this* is what I call the right way to look at the Parthenon.' He paused, then added: 'Did you know who invented that phrase about "the Glory that was Greece"? Edgar Allan Poe.'

I knew exactly what he meant. The Parthenon is not only the Western world's biggest cultural cliché; it also casts the longest and most influential shadow. This, I may say, has very little to do with its purely historical or technical aspects. What Professor Broneer discovered about the Mycenaean Acropolis leaves most people as cold as the architectural and financial details of the temple's erection: the kind of sober survey, I mean, which is now provided (along with numerous splendid photographs to leaven the academic lump of a serious text) by Professor R. J. Hopper. Not even Professor Rhys Carpenter's engagingly off-beat theory that there were *two* Parthenons seems to have caught many readers' imaginative fancy. What they see in the Parthenon is a symbol of Greek culture at its apogee: the symmetry, the harmony, the proportion, the splendid creative achievement, the possession for ever. The Taj Mahal and the Pyramids may be just as familiar, and at least as impressive to look at (was it not Rabindranath Tagore who found himself reduced to tears by what he regarded as the barbarian ugliness of the buildings on the Acropolis?) but they do not pressurise one with such an overwhelming assumption of moral and aesthetic superiority.

The essence of that superiority, however, tends to be somewhat elusive, and has a trick of vanishing, like the Snark, if investigated too closely. The editorial manifesto for a new series of classical monographs entitled 'Ancient Culture and Society' contains one very intriguing statement about the contributors: 'In examining the inter-relations of the institutions and thought of the ancient world, the kind of question they ask themselves is not "What was the Parthenon?" but "What was the Parthenon *for*?"' *Quot capita, tot sententiae*: consult any six scholars, independently, as to what the Parthenon was *for*, and the answers, one suspects, will surprise by their variety. The first might say it was for the worship of Athena, the second for the cultural glorification of Athens, and the third for the safeguarding of tribute. The fourth might describe it as a piece of political propaganda to impress foreigners and mop up domestic unemployment. For the fifth it might be the embodiment of Periclean idealism, for the sixth a symbol of imperial hubris. Several might well object that the word 'for', in itself, implied a utilitarian concept which they were not prepared to accept.

The most remarkable thing about what we may loosely term the 'Parthenon myth' has always been its remarkable ability to stifle really damaging criticism. Yet one need only—even with the soberest and most academic scholar—raise an issue like the war in Vietnam, or the present regime in Greece (or Czechoslovakia, depending on temperament) to see impartiality go up in a blaze of angry and committed liberalism—or harden into quite ferociously reactionary conservatism: the twin poles of contemporary classical studies (see below, pp. 47 ff.). The same is true when we back-project our own contemporary concerns, and begin to analyse so thorny a subject as, say, the popularity of the Athenian Empire (that particular row has been sputtering on for over a decade now) or government by the 'best people'. It is virtually impossible for any Western scholar *not* to let his attitudes regarding democracy, freedom of speech, and the whole totalitarian spectrum affect his judgments when writing history. Yet so overwhelming is the *mana* distilled by the Parthenon and everything it stands for, that until very recently fundamental objections to its cultural and political antecedents tended to be stifled at source or buried under a mass of emotionally charged special pleading.

In consequence, when the criticism *does* appear, it is liable to overstate its case with exaggerated vehemence. Just as Kingsley Amis—a by no means insensitive writer—was goaded into snarling about 'filthy Mozart', for much the same reasons, so there are quite a few classicists around today who seem determined to jettison the fifth-century Periclean experiment *in toto*. Such iconoclasts will dismiss the Funeral Speech as a hair-raising collection of frigidly paternalistic apophthegms laced with the worst sort of unthinking self-conceit, to be compared unfavourably, as a summing-up of Athenian aspirations and *mores*, with that rebarbative little pamphlet on the *Constitution of Athens* by an anonymous author most commonly known as the 'Old Oligarch'.[1] For them the Periclean mystique is not only hubristic but also hypocritical, resting on a basis of intellectual and political despotism sanctioned by the vote-catching illusion known as Athenian democracy. Some are even prepared to assert that Attic drama, far from being an unmatchable 'possession for ever' which can only be elucidated, never subjected to criticism, is in fact a wildly over-rated phenomenon, stuffed with the grotesque platitudes pilloried by A. E. Housman in his famous parody, and given its proper due by Aristophanes, who never took kindly to sacred cows of any description. Having gone so far, the extremist may well round off his commination service by concluding that the Parthenon resembles nothing so much as an overblown city bank (which, among other things, it in fact was) and that Athenian philosophy from the late fifth century onwards became a minority creed activated by increasingly extreme political totalitarianism and idealized homosexuality.

Scholars who go apoplectic over such heresies have only themselves to blame for them. For years they had fenced in the whole complex of Greek culture with a kind of all-embracing *cordon sanitaire*, which effectively blinkered their judgment when it came to evaluating ancient history, art, literature or philosophy. Indeed, one of the odder features of the whole classical tradition—seldom accorded the attention it deserves—has always been its special immunity from criticism. For the Middle Ages Aristotle possessed quasi-Scriptural authority; it was not some towering Christian saint or patriarch, but Virgil who guided Dante through Hell. As late as Shelley's day educated Europeans were still so brain-washed by the legend

[1] Preserved among the works of Xenophon, though certainly not by him; perhaps datable to the late 440s, and thus the earliest surviving example of Attic prose—and right-wing propaganda.

that they unquestioningly accepted the ancient Greeks as supermen, giants of a lost Golden Age. The phenomenon has by no means been altogether eradicated today. The number of books which actually *criticize* classical authors or institutions, though larger than it was, still remains extraordinarily small. The special value of *The Greeks and the Irrational* was, precisely, that it blew one aspect of the myth sky-high; yet even so Professor Dodds felt obliged to apologize to his classical colleagues (would he, one wonders, do so today, twenty years later?) for presuming to import the alien tools of anthropology and psychology. The most radical reappraisals are often written by outsiders: Professor Popper's dissection of Plato in *The Open Society and its Enemies* is one obvious example.

Reading a classicist on Homer or Thucydides is, all too often, uncomfortably like listening to a Jesuit expounding the doctrine of the Immaculate Conception—but with one important difference: the Jesuit knows his opponents' arguments, if only for purposes of refutation, whereas the classicist (with honourable exceptions) tends to pride himself on sticking to his own narrow last, rather like the vociferous *ultra*-in-the-street who damns Communism while priding himself on never having read a word of Marx. In these circumstances it is not surprising that serious criticism of Greek and Roman literature (as, say, Dr Leavis or Professor Trilling might conceive it) scarcely exists at all. One notable exception is provided by the American classical quarterly *Arion*. But *Arion* is, at most, a bridgehead. The classics have nearly half a century of revolutionary critical development to catch up on: the thing cannot be achieved overnight, and many traditionalists will argue that it should not be achieved at all. One of the most broadly read and civilized classical scholars of this century, the late Sir Maurice Bowra, who read Pindar and Pushkin, Sophocles and Mallarmé with equal zest, still tended to write as though time, critically speaking, had come to a stop about when T. S. Eliot published *The Sacred Wood*. (Even so, this represented a distinct advance on most of his colleagues, who were still trusting hopefully to Mackail and John Addington

Symonds.) Modern comparisons, it is argued, are invariably misleading: classical literature can only be studied, if not *sub specie aeternitatis*, at least in its own context and on its own terms. There is a good deal of truth in this thesis, but all too often it is made an excuse for abandoning criticism altogether. Behind the reasoned apologia the myth of perfection still exerts its lure.

In Forster's novel *The Longest Journey* Rickie complains to his friend Ansell that 'Cambridge has lost touch with the times'. To which Ansell retorts: 'Was she ever intended to touch them?' This must sum up the attitude of many classicists, even today: the 'possession for ever' stands above and beyond all changing fashions, and thus cannot be criticized, only expounded, since aesthetic judgments rest, ultimately, on mere personal preference. Facts are sacred, opinions suspect. Stick to the knowable, young scholars are told; leave opinionative fancies to the *littérateurs*. A. E. Housman, a unique combination of poet and textual critic, remarked in his *Introductory Lecture* of 1892 that no right-minded man would go to a classical scholar for judgments on literature, and the situation has not radically changed since then. Truly dissentient critics, such as E. R. Curtius, tend to produce shock as well as disagreement. Professor Lesky, in the preface to his *History of Greek Literature*, alludes sorrowfully to 'those utterances on the sinking light of Hellas which many must wish that he [Curtius] had kept to himself': it is rather like some old-fashioned parish priest discussing the Bishop of Woolwich's *Honest to God*. Are we really so poverty-stricken that only the exceptional maverick (George Thomson, a Marxist, in *Aeschylus and Athens*, Eric Havelock with *The Liberal Temper in Greek Politics*, Dodds and Popper with the works mentioned above) can shock us into any radical rethinking of fifth-century Greek literature and history?

For the matter of that, what impulse was it drove generations of humanists to idealize those chilly authoritarian figures Pericles and Plato? Why have we romanticized their aims and achievements, just as Droysen and Tarn romanticized those of Alexander? Oh, those impossible, white-draped, too-noble

Greeks of one's schooldays, living (one unconsciously assumed) in small replicas of the Parthenon—that insidiously all-pervasive symbol—healthy-minded and physically fit, their thoughts far above such mundane things as money, work, or self-advancement, moving through sunlit colonnades talking for ever of the True, the Good and the Beautiful! In this ideal Greece there was never any bad weather (a notion which permanent residence there soon dispels in the most brutal fashion). Somewhere, hazily in the background, women, a lesser breed, would be busy about life's menial tasks, assisted by slaves—who of course were treated with every consideration, if not as friends. In time of war a shining patriotism was expected and freely given. The whole earth was the grave of famous men, who, Spartan and Athenian alike, returned home either with their shields or on them (rhipsaspists like Archilochus and Alcaeus were, after all, only poets, and allowances therefore had to be made for them; besides, what could you expect from two anti-social oddballs of whom one was illegitimate and the other queer?).

Exceptions, as MacNeice reminds us in *Autumn Journal*, nagged at the mind, to be dismissed hastily—raving cannibal Maenads (but that was a Thracian import, which never really came closer home than Thebes), brutal treacheries and cold-blooded massacres, on Corcyra and Melos and elsewhere, Athens' ruthless exploitation and coercion of her subject-allies (but didn't the democratic end justify the means? and wasn't it for their own good in the long run?). Temples built with sweated tribute, noble platitudes masking greed and famine and unemployment, the cut-throat competition for export markets, the average Athenian's strident anti-intellectualism—somehow these things never really registered in one's mind. All one remembered, finally, was the trumpet-call (but not the double-dealing and collaboration) of the Persian Wars, the lofty radical idealism of Pericles, the Golden Mean as exemplified by Sophoclean tragedy, the silver intellect that was Plato; muscular male torsos in marble, steatopygous warriors swooping (rather like

Groucho Marx) round too-well-proportioned red-figure vases. No dirt, no stink, no real cruelty or treachery, no irrational passions except in myth, and surprisingly little sex, which was something, as they say, to be risen above; blue skies, eternal sunlight, nothing in excess—the popular romantic fairy-tale of which our big coffee-table art-books are no more than the last and glossiest apotheosis.

The myth of a Golden Age is endemic to humanity. Jam yesterday, jam tomorrow, but never jam today; if man is not looking forward to the millennium he is looking back to some lost Eden. At least as early as Hesiod's day men spoke with wistful longing of the fabulous reign of Kronos—and perhaps with good reason: a pastoral nomadic existence, in an under-populated world, was vastly preferable to scratching a living, tied to the soil the whole year round, from the barren hillsides of Boeotia. The Greeks did not romanticize their own harsh daily life. 'We live a wretched sum of years, and badly, too', declared Semonides, and his was a common opinion. Better never to be born, and if born, then to die quickly. Tough, unscrupulous fifth-century realists such as Themistocles, Cleon, Alcibiades or Critias—all of whom died violent deaths—might have derived a certain ironic pleasure from the thought that posterity would look back on their century as the Golden Age, and on Athens as the *summum bonum* of intellectual, moral and aesthetic achievement.

Politically speaking, the claim is at least open to serious doubt. The pundits of antiquity knew imperialistic self-aggrandisement when they saw it. Sparta's last appeal to Athens before the Peloponnesian War was: 'Give the Greeks their freedom.' High-handed despotism, even when practised for high-minded motives, was expected of barbarians, but frowned on in Greeks. Yet scholars who should know better are still splashing through the Augean stable of Periclean politics with their whitewash-buckets at the ready. Nineteenth-century imperialism might contrive to view its Athenian forerunner through rose-tinted spectacles; after fifty years of totalitarian ruckus we can hardly be expected to do the same. We are, for instance, reminded *ad nauseam* that Athens was the cradle of free speech and democracy—two concepts about as elusive as the Cheshire Cat's grin. It all depends, I suppose, whether we judge by intentions or results. Democracy, of a sort, certainly came into being at Athens during the sixth century B C; how clearly it was planned for is quite another matter. 'The last temptation is the greatest treason: to do the right deed for the wrong reason.' At the same time (a point less often made) given the general pattern of political institutions then prevalent throughout the Near East, Greek democracy resembles that dog walking on its hind legs which Dr Johnson used as an image for a woman preaching. The wonder is not that it was done well (which it was not) but that it was done at all.

This is a virtue which our overblown eulogies of the Greek achievement as a whole tend to obscure. Supermen are seldom praised for succeeding in a cack-handed way with all the odds against them. A stunning achievement such as that of Salamis is not enhanced—quite the contrary—by glossing over the bad faith, opportunism and collusion that accompanied it. The highminded moral virtues which a scholar such as Dr Ehrenberg professes to find in those tough social reformers Solon and Cleisthenes (see below, pp. 55 ff., 71) simply depreciate their credibility without making us admire them. There is a story that Solon leaked information to certain friends of his which enabled them to make a killing in real estate; and Cleisthenes may well have juggled the redistribution of tribes and demes in such a way as to leave the power of the Alcmaeonidae—his own family —more or less intact. Whether such things are true or not, they can only be regarded as unquestionable nonsense by those with a fundamental ignorance of political realities, and a vested interest in manufacturing plaster saints. Cleisthenes only 'took the people into his *hetairia* [political club]', as Herodotus calls it, to whip up mass support during a bloody factional struggle for power, and after two previous attempts by more conventional means had proved costly failures. This does not alter the value—the lasting value—of what he brought about, but it does make one seriously question his motives in doing so.

Odder still, the period most closely associated in people's minds with Athenian democracy, the so-called 'golden years' before the Peloponnesian War, coincides with Pericles' long period of quasi-dictatorship as First Citizen, when real democratic usage largely went by the board. (It is no answer to say, what is quite true, that Pericles was re-elected annually by Assembly vote; a democracy which turns itself over to a guru, even though voluntarily and in due form, has abrogated its basic function.) After Pericles' death, with the ascendancy of tough rabble-rousers such as Cleon and Hyperbolus, something more like true democracy, warts and all, begins to appear; but this is precisely the point, we are told, at which true 'democracy' declined through abuse and corruption.

The ironic truth, of course, is that while intellectuals were still theorizing about democracy, the urban proletariat was rapidly reaching a point where it could take effective political action in its own right. With the establishment of Athens as a great naval power, the 'sailor rabble' had become a more important factor, politically, than the propertied yeomen who fought in the ranks at Marathon. Pericles was not the last gentleman-radical to wake up one morning and find his ungrateful protegés breathing down his neck with ideas of their own. The tail had begun to wag the dog; and as the melancholy history of fifth-century Athens shows, the dog it was that died. Here is where the modern apologists for Periclean Athens try to have it both ways. They are all for the democratic ideal; but they jib at real democracy in action. Most Western Hellenists can only stomach the democratic formula when it is strictly non-democratic: this is one reason why Pericles has such a powerful appeal for them. But then—as the modern Greek scene makes one painfully aware—real democracy in action leads, more often than not, to chaos and anarchy. Man is free, and can go to the devil in his own way; but unfortunately he tends to need a non-democratic pragmatist to clear up the mess afterwards. Such a pattern has been perennial throughout Greek history; in that sense the present regime, with its piecemeal administrative reforms, public works programme, and legislation for moral uplift, is simply following a well-worn trail blazed by Peisistratus, Critias and the Four Hundred.

If Greece was, in fact, the cradle of democracy, one can only surmise that some mischievous goddess left a changeling in the crib. The best that can be said for the popular leaders of the late fifth century is that they just managed to defeat the right-wing *putsch* which their own stupidity and corruptness had provoked (Papandreou was not so lucky). Otherwise they present a depressing picture of hysteria, greed, vindictiveness, and hopeless muddling compromise. Their financial ineptitude and bellicose jingoism were largely responsible for Athens' final defeat in the Peloponnesian War, and reached a nadir of arbitrary irresponsibility during the first half of the fourth century. It is, incidentally, one of the most curious paradoxes on record that ancient Athens, the city-state identified in the modern mind with democracy in its pristine form, should have left no specific manifesto of democratic political theory: even odder that almost every philosopher or political theorist of the period whose work has come down to us is violently anti-democratic in tone.[1] Plato, Aristotle, Thucydides, Xenophon, the so-called 'Old Oligarch' (ill-named: he comes over as more of an Angry Young Tory), all have pronouncedly right-wing, anti-liberal views. In their political vocabulary, good, rich, and well-born are synonyms; so are bad, poor, and worthless. The first group

[1] Professor Havelock, in that provocative and stimulating work *The Liberal Temper in Greek Politics,* has argued for a truly democratic tradition, associated with Sophists such as Antiphon, in the mainstream of Greek (or more specifically Athenian) politics during the fifth century. This, he argues, was afterwards eclipsed—and deliberately suppressed—by the adherents of 'closed' systems such as Plato and Aristotle. There may be something in this, but hardly as much as Professor Havelock would like us to think. Conspiracy-and-suppression theories are always fairly suspect; and the plain truth must be that even if such a tradition existed, it lacked the support which would have got it implemented, even during the fifth century; and had it been implemented, it would have foundered, sooner rather than later, on those rigid class-divisions.

constitute The Few (*oi oligoi*, hence oligarchy), while the second are The Many (*oi polloi*). As a political-cum-moral system this at least has the merit of classic simplicity. The entrenched and rigid snobbishness of Greek intellectuals is an alarming but highly significant phenomenon.

Few people stop to ask themselves why Aristophanes, who so regularly attacks men like Cleon, Hyperbolus and Cleophon for their public conduct, should show such marked consideration for Nicias by comparison, though Nicias laid himself just as wide open, and on precisely similar grounds; or indeed, why he so regularly gets a laugh out of Euripides' mother selling vegetables in the market. The answer, clearly, is class-prejudice, and of a rather complex sort. Nicias was taboo as a conservative gentleman, while Euripides' mother had let the side down by engaging in so banausic a pursuit as market-gardening.

Aristotle remarked that 'in such democracies each person lives as he likes; or in the words of Euripides, "according to his fancy". This is a bad thing.' He did not need to have read the Old Oligarch before formulating this proposition; it is a fundamental tenet of the closed-society mind, whether in the fourth century B C or the twentieth century A D, whether to the right or left of the political spectrum, whether in Russia, Portugal, Greece or Czechoslovakia, whether in Cromwell's England, Mao's China, or the Paraguay of the Jesuits.

It is often argued that, in Athens, the upsurge of the closed-society mind was directly due to the catastrophes produced by the Peloponnesian War, in particular by the failure of the Sicilian Expedition. These things, to be sure, accelerated the process; they led to democratic hysteria and irresponsibility, which in turn sharpened the knives of the right-wing *ultras*. (Anyone who wants to get a good idea what the atmosphere in Athens was like during this period, just before the *coup* of the Four Hundred, should read Aristophanes' *Lysistrata*. Behind the fusillade of sexual jokes—themselves a kind of reaction to the general tension—there emerges a mood of paranoiac anxiety and suspicion, with the Chorus seeing conspiracy under every bush.) What the idealists refuse to admit is that the whole concept of the *polis* contained much less freedom and democracy in the modern sense than their admiring picture of it presumes; that Pericles, *mutatis mutandis*, said just what Aristotle did when he damned those who contracted out of politics—the *apragmones*, who did nothing for the commonweal, the *idiotai*, who were mere private individuals, the semantic implication being that this status labelled them as what we today would term idiots. The Athenian city-state believed in anything but the individual doing his own thing; he was there to serve the *polis* for every day of his life, as the worker-bee the hive, as an Israeli *sabra* the kibbutz, as a collectivized Russian peasant some hypothetical five-year plan. Paradoxically, theoretical advocates of the closed society like Plato and Aristotle became far more vociferous at the precise point when the tyrannous control of the *polis* over its members was slipping. Starry-eyed advocates of genuine individualism should stop making up fantasies about Periclean Athens and turn their attention to the great urban complexes of the Hellenistic kingdoms, which provide them with all they could possibly want, from the affluent society to fake-pastoral poetry, from solipsistic minority creeds devoted to the existential cult of the individual to exotic food-fads and in-group astrology.

But the notion of fifth-century Athens as the source of all democratic virtues is built into the myth at foundation level; so the virtues must be found somewhere. By that now familiar process known as doublethink, classical apologists extol Pericles' radical imperialism, boldly label it 'democracy', and silence any lingering critical doubts with the sheer weight of their moral self-assurance. The success of this technique, however, depends on two main factors, both of which have come under heavy fire during the present century: the first is the notion of a 'Greek miracle' which, like Athena, emerged suddenly full-grown, and not even from Zeus' head, but *ex nihilo*; and the second is the bedazzled admiration which countless generations of scholars, humanists and schoolmasters (not always the same thing, though all imbued with a built-in streak of authoritarianism) have felt for Pericles himself. On the first count, it is now a cliché that the dazzling chiaroscuro of Greece's Golden Age long blinded her admirers to its true origins, but that, equally, for the past half century 'hints of earlier and other creation' have been forcing themselves upon the scholar's awareness.

The Cyclopean masonry embedded on the Acropolis was linked with Mycenae and Schliemann's revolutionary discoveries. Jane Harrison and J. C. Lawson probed into the 'beastlye devices of the heathen' and emerged with some highly un-Apollonian findings, since refined, expanded and diversified by Professor Dodds. Sir Arthur Evans revealed a rich and alien civilization at Cnossos. Scholars in other fields, Egyptologists or Hittitologists, began to push back the frontiers of history and to produce unsuspected connexions with the hitherto sacrosanct Hellenic world. Homer abruptly ceased to be a fairy-tale, Herodotus was no longer the Father of Lies, while Chimaeras and winged griffins betrayed not a vigorous imagination but Oriental influence. The sophisticated Roman attitude to Greek mythology, maintained without change at least since the Renaissance, was no longer tenable. Much of what had been myth was now, slowly and painfully, brought into the compass of pre- or proto-history; and the change of perspectives which this involved—the process is still going on—had an immense and largely unsuspected impact on traditional attitudes to the 'Greek miracle'. Greek history could no longer be said to begin with the First Olympiad, any more than the world (according to Archbishop Ussher's famous calculation) sprang complete from the hand of God, without benefit of evolution, in 4004 B C.[1]

And what about the fatal lure exerted by Pericles himself? One obvious point is that after half a century of political

[1] In one sense, of course, Ussher turned out to be quite right; if for 'the world' we substitute 'civilization', casting a glance at the Fertile Crescent and the great river-valley cultures of Egypt and Mesopotamia, few would argue with his evaluation in general terms. And before the superior rationalist dismisses his quaint and foolish fancies with brisk self-assurance, he might pause to reflect on two things. The Greeks themselves were more than a little vague about the dividing-line between myth and history (see below, pp. 132 ff.); and the nineteenth-century

totalitarianism (for which a preliminary half century of political do-goodery obligingly paved the way) it is impossible for any thinking liberal to idealize Thucydides' hero without some very pertinent caveats. Since the Second World War, some (though by no means all) scholars in England and Germany have stripped a good deal of the charisma from that lofty-minded figure. A plausible, if perhaps over-reactionary, case could be made out for Pericles having been not simply a ruthless imperialist (which has its attractive side for some people) but also a priggish, humourless, over-rational, cultishly intellectual, self-opinionated megalomaniac, blind to individual emotions, and hell-bent on moulding Athens—at incalculable cost—to his personal vision of the ideal city-state. In the circumstances any tendency towards hero-worship could perhaps do with a little cool scrutiny, especially since one of the stock excuses for Periclean Athens' bully-boy activities in the Aegean—the expansionism, the bloody-minded treatment of the subject-allies, the precipitation of the Peloponnesian War—is her high-minded pursuit of art.

The sensible lay reader may think this is a bad joke. Not a bit of it. Let me quote chapter and verse from that distinguished and eminently respectable historian Dr Victor Ehrenberg, who has in his time known what it feels like to be on the run from a totalitarian regime. On the outbreak of the Peloponnesian War he has this to say in *From Solon to Socrates*:

> It is hardly justifiable simply to see in Athens 'the aggressor'. Her dynamism and expansive imperialism had the justification, *at least as long as Pericles directed Athenian policy* [my italics], that it was not an end in itself but went together with the aims of social progress and cultural supremacy. Against the conservative forces represented by Sparta, Athens was the champion of new and even revolutionary ideas.

Periclean myth—popularized, if not invented, by Grote, and sedulously propagated ever since, though not perhaps for identical reasons, by English schoolmasters and Greek politicians—is just as far-fetched, in its own way, as anything Ussher ever dreamed up.

Justifications of *Lebensraum* through superior *Kultur* are all too familiar from recent history; but to find them enunciated by a liberal and highly distinguished academic from Prague (whether in the context of the Thirties or today) is, to say the least of it, disconcerting. The claims of the ideal, as Gregers Werle found, can lead one into some very odd *galères*.

We should remember, too, that Pericles' contemporaries were not nearly so enthusiastic about him—a useful touchstone, and one that can be profitably applied to that other much-mythified figure from the Greek world, Alexander III of Macedon. Not all of the surviving obloquy can be written off out of hand as mere political muckraking from the opposition: the picture it builds up is too consistent, too plausible. His enemies mocked his physical peculiarities—the long 'squill-head' which resembled that of Akhnaten (could they, medically speaking, have had megalomaniac symptoms in common?) and which he always concealed, in portraits, with a helmet—and lambasted his icy self-esteem; they nicknamed him 'the Olympian', a sobriquet which exactly suited his aloof and superior detachment, his penchant for manipulating individuals in terms of abstract theory. Almost all the anecdotes told about him are faintly distasteful, even when—perhaps especially when—designed to flatter. On his deathbed he declared that no Athenian had ever put on mourning because of him: a claim so grotesquely false that one wonders whether his mind was wandering when he made it. The young men who died in Egypt and Cyprus and Thrace, the countless thousands who fell victim to the Great Plague and the horrors of the Archidamian War—did he feel no responsibility for them? Was his mind so invincibly proof against mundane reality?

The whiff of sheer loathing that still reaches one across the centuries from a comic playwright such as Hermippus is both disconcerting and significant: at times he seems on the verge of stuttering incoherence from the pressure of his anger. Disapproval of Athenian policy when it came under the influence of his radical group extended, moreover, far beyond mere local opposition. Pindar, for example, never wrote a poem favourable to Athens after about 460, and it is no accident that this was when Pericles and his friends began to make their determined bid for power. We know what his goal was: it is embodied in the Funeral Oration (and indeed all the evidence we possess points in the same direction). His entire career—not to mention the words Thucydides puts in his mouth, which are more often carefully excerpted than read in their mind-chilling entirety—reveals him as a high-minded moral bully who believed himself called upon to establish Athens, regardless of internal or external opposition, as the political, cultural and commercial leader of all Greece.

Yet behind all this lay something far more real, if seldom mentioned: something of which Pericles himself was well aware. This was the spectre of famine, the struggle for economic independence. Even when Athens was a great imperial thalassocracy, she still had to import nine-tenths of her wheat and almost all her timber from abroad, in markets which she could neither trust nor control. This fact explains much of Pericles' aggressive foreign policy: he needed to bring some major source of timber and grain *within the empire*. In a sense it is easier to sympathize with Periclean Athens when we realize that much of her imperialism sprang from dire practical need rather than from simple free-wheeling hubris. If only Pericles had admitted something of this—but no, his line was that Athens had a moral right to her position of supremacy: the end justified the means. His entire public career was devoted to furthering Athens' greatness; yet every step he took made his city's ultimate downfall more inevitable. Like all rational planners, he had ideas which looked admirable in the abstract; but—again like all rational planners—he had, and gave rein to, a sharp contempt for emotional prejudice. Thus time and again he found his cerebral concepts failing disastrously when put to the test.

When, after the outbreak of war with Sparta, he brought the countryfolk of Attica into the city, when he refused to let Athenian hoplites measure their strength against Spartans in the field, he was concentrating, to the exclusion of all else, on his scorched-earth-cum-naval-raiding policy. He seems not to have considered for one moment (or, at very best, to have considered and dismissed) the psychological effect of burning farms, enforced idleness, or the tacit admission of military inferiority—any more than he foresaw the disease and hysteria which were almost bound to develop among those crowded refugees. He went his way regardless, indifferent to opposition or protest, conceptually armoured against his own factual and psychological ignorance; he *knew*, and that was that. At any time, in theory, the *demos* could have thrown him out of office; but he had so brainwashed the electorate with a mixture of imposing rhetoric and cheap imports that this step was never taken until the war had revealed the shoddiness of his policy in terms which not even the meanest Athenian citizen could mistake, and even then—so little could anyone conceive an alternative to him—he was voted back on to the Board of Generals a year later, half dead of the plague and with all his ideals in ruins.

By now Pericles' special appeal should be fairly obvious. No active, idealistic intellectual with a didactic job, a veiled contempt for people as individuals, and a generalized passion for putting the world to rights could possibly resist him. Zealous radicals in particular would be less than human did they not identify subconsciously with this high-minded, authoritarian figure, tirelessly reorganizing the ungrateful masses for their own good, an early exponent of the planned society who (rather like the Aunt in Tennyson's *Princess*) was all for preaching 'an universal culture to the crowd'—especially if it made the crowd content with its lot, and was accompanied by trade imports, at preferential rates, from the long-suffering subject-allies. Yet he offers plenty to the right no less than the left: Victorian empire-builders could not resist him, either. Even your modern right-wing Hellenist (see below, pp. 47 ff.) while paying lip-service to his 'democracy', can take comfort in the assurance that such radical nonsense was really a blind, designed to placate the *canaille*—the public works programme, of course, fulfilled a similar function—while an effective dictatorship or administrative junta (something, perhaps, along the lines of a Cabinet Committee) got on with the serious business of government.

The teachers and preachers, in fact, whatever their political persuasion, find Pericles' air of social-cum-moral uplift surreptitiously bracing. In a famous phrase he once described Athens as 'the school of Hellas', a bland example of that paternalistic conceit which, provided it emanates from fifth-century Athens, even the most intelligent critic seems ready to swallow, and without any apparent sign of nausea. Since Pericles identified himself even more closely with Athens than the late Charles de Gaulle did with France, it is a fair bet that he had himself cast for the role of schoolmaster. What it will be interesting to see is how far this image gets further tarnished by association with the present (1971) political regime in Greece. No one, I think, has yet pointed out that if Mr Papadopoulos and his colleagues are modelling themselves on any one character from Hellenic history (apart, perhaps, from Peisistratus) it is, clearly, the Olympian: moral regeneration, protreptic nagging, high-minded patriotic rhetoric, public works schemes—they don't miss a turn.

Indeed, one of the issues on which the present regime has been most criticized (and with most justification)—that of stage and press censorship—had a first-class precedent during the Periclean regime, which reminds us that any government in the world will exercise some form of suppression in this field if it feels itself sufficiently threatened. (The fireproof, as was well remarked, have no particular qualms about children playing with matches.) In 440 two of Athens' allies, Samos and Byzantium, revolted, and an expeditionary force was sent out to reduce them. (Among the generals was the playwright Sophocles, who had produced his *Antigone* two years before; as a jackbooted imperialist he proved something of a flop, however, since he spent most of the campaign on the neighbouring island of Chios, chasing pretty boys. Where this leaves him on the moral snakes-and-ladders board is something of a problem. Pericles thought little of his military talent, and rather less of his sex-life.) This punitive act of reprisal brought down such a barrage of abuse on Pericles' head that he imposed a stage censorship for two years. Every man has his limits; and after one comic poet had referred to Pericles' Milesian mistress Aspasia as 'his bitch-Hera born of sodomy', the Olympian may have felt he had had enough.[1]

But then free speech—*parrhesia*, the Greeks called it—though much vaunted as an Athenian amenity, was at best an intermittent privilege during the last decades of the fifth century, especially in the more sensitive areas of religion and social standards, let alone of political life. Cleon hauled Aristophanes into court on a libel charge. The entire period was characterized by a series of witch-hunting trials against religious, ethical, and scientific unorthodoxy, culminating (just after the turn of the century) in the condemnation and execution of Socrates. It will not have escaped the notice of any reasonably unprejudiced observer that the Colonels' various pronouncements on the need for conformity in matters of Church and State are dead in line with this central reactionary movement: history, in Greece more than most places, tends to repeat itself.

At the same time, of course—a more popular line with orthodox liberals—this is where Mr Papadopoulos and his fellow-pundits land on the opposite side of the intellectual fence from Pericles and his friends. When Anaxagoras was exiled—and indeed narrowly escaped with his life—for asserting that the sun was a lump of matter rather larger than the Peloponnese, the odds are that his prosecutor was a patriotic, pious, old-fashioned member of the officer class. We have come quite a long way since then; but if the Professor of Astronomy at Athens University no longer feels constrained to talk out of the corner of his mouth when speaking disrespectfully about the equator, it is men like Galileo and Kepler he has to thank for it, not the Patriarchs and General Staff officers who are concerned to up-

[1] Another reason for Aspasia's unpopularity at the time of the Samian Revolt was because it was widely believed (whether with reason or not) that, as a Milesian herself, she had urged Miletus' case to Pericles during the political quarrel between that city and Samos which was the direct occasion of the revolt.

hold public morals and (now as then) are not above infiltrating the most outrageous propaganda into the educational syllabus, *pro bono publico*, in order to achieve their desired end.[1]

But here we come up against that endemic danger which any Age of Enlightenment contains: old traditions, superstitions and social sanctions are tossed out on the scrap-heap, but nothing of comparable psychological value is put in their place. (Attempts to fill the gap, such as the ill-fated Feast of Pure Reason [*sic*] during the French Revolution, are nearly always a ludicrous flop; rationalists seem to lack imagination when it comes to ceremony.) If Pericles really wanted Athens united behind him in a mood of patriotic confidence, the last way to achieve such an end was by undermining traditional religious and ethical assumptions, as he and his intellectual circle consistently did—a practice which doubtless made them feel comfortably superior to the common herd. Only a tiny minority, in any civilization, can live by reason alone (both Communists and Catholics have always seen this very clearly) or are emotionally equipped to deal with the naked truth.

Truth, unfortunately, however desirable a commodity in the abstract, seldom turns out to endorse the accepted *status quo* (one good reason why most conservative juntas indulge in wholesale censorship; radical ones do the same thing, but for rather different reasons). Thus its pursuit, laudable *per se*, almost always turns out a socially and culturally disruptive process. Hallowed beliefs and comfortable illusions go down before it like ninepins. Men eat the apple of the Tree of Knowledge and find themselves spiritually naked. A lump of molten metal the size of the Peloponnese is hardly compatible with the myth of Helios and Phaethon; nor, one imagines, would a mountaineer's report on

[1] The obsessional fear of Communism in Greece (which, one may add, is only too well justified) can produce some very curious *bêtises* from the sedulous *fonctionnaires* in the Ministry of Education. One persistent rumour which I have never been able to confirm one way or the other is that left-handedness—after a brief modernist spell of legitimacy—is now banned again: partly (one presumes) on the old quasi-magical grounds (left = *sinister*, etc.), but partly, it is alleged, to avoid even a symbolic taint of left-wing politics.

conditions at the summit of Mount Olympus have been received with wild public enthusiasm outside a very limited circle. When traditional religion begins to hive off into philosophy at one end of the scale, and meteorology at the other, society may look out for squalls; and more often than not it will be the thinker and the weatherman who become the first storm-casualties. All civilizations function within a protective girder-like structure of archetypal myth, superstition, metaphor, magic: outmoded but emotionally charged attempts to come to grips with the circumambient forces of nature. Remove this framework, and anarchy, chaos and despair are liable to ensue. Members of any given society know this in their bones: hence the rough and often hysterical treatment they almost always hand out to their intellectual pioneers—especially since the latter are seldom endowed with tact, make their pronouncements in a shatteringly blunt form, and suffer from that common intellectual delusion, the belief that people will gladly be educated in unpalatable matters if the upshot is for their own good.

The Athenians depended as much as any other group upon those complex emotional props which bind a society together—more, perhaps, since their intellectual break-through from archaism to fully rational thought-processes was accomplished within two or three generations, too fast for the emotions to keep pace with it, so that inductive reason was left (as it were) with a residual underpinning of highly primitive emotions and beliefs. Thus they enjoyed a large number of comforting superstitions, which tend to crop up, disconcertingly, in the most improbable places. They had the semblance of overall pattern and order in the city-state, but found this very much at odds with the old tribal loyalties of blood and kinship (this dilemma is a regular theme of Attic tragedy, as was realized by Hegel, among others; the *Antigone* exemplifies the clan-*polis* conflict in its purest form). They believed, with nostalgic fervour, in the superiority of the heavy-armed yeomen-hoplites who fought at Marathon. They wanted to believe in the old gods. As prop after comforting prop was knocked out from under the collective psyche of the

Athenian man in the street, he not surprisingly rounded on those whom he believed—and with some justice—to be responsible for his predicament. Intellectual scepticism has many virtues; but comforting and sustaining ordinary people is not prominent among them. Hence the late fifth-century drive against blasphemy and heresy, the purging of dangerous philosophical ideas.

The most notorious example of this was the trial and death of Socrates in 399 B C. Till recently it was common to regard Socrates as an almost Christ-like figure (but was not Christ, too, the most disruptive of social iconoclasts?) and the charges against him mere malicious nonsense. Today it is quite another matter; opinion is steadily veering round to the view that, on their own terms, the Athenian jurymen had good reason for bringing in a verdict of 'Guilty'. So respectable a scholar as François Chamoux, in *The Civilization of Greece*, gives Socrates very short shrift indeed. It is all too easy to see why he incurred the anger of his fellow-citizens. However dutiful he might officially show himself towards the State and its gods, by encouraging young men to question the structure of their society Socrates *was*, in a sense, corrupting them—just as his relentless ethical prodding inevitably turned their minds to what might, very fairly, be described as strange new gods. None of his careful disclaimers could control that central idea.

Furthermore it could be argued that he *was*, ultimately, responsible for the political ruthlessness and moral ambiguity which later cropped up in several of his prize pupils, such as Critias and Alcibiades. Aristophanes has often been taken to task—wrongly, I feel—for what is described as his 'travesty' of Socrates in *The Clouds*, the implication being that, contemporaries though they were, the comic playwright had no more sense than to lampoon Socrates as though he were a Sophist like Gorgias. To which it might be replied that the Socratic *method* had more in common with those of the Sophists than its defenders are commonly disposed to admit; and that *The Clouds* is not a philosophical critique, but domestic satire of a peculiarly shrewd variety, its object being to pinpoint precisely those *social* consequences of the Socratic dialectic which most worried ordinary Athenian citizens—the disruption of family ties, the use of logic to circumvent truth rather than pursue it, and, as Chamoux observed, 'the endless raising of doubts and the habitual lack of any positive conclusion'. It goes without saying that Socrates never intended any such results; but he does seem to have had a curious blind spot as regards the *accidental* repercussions of his teachings, placing great reliance on the purity of his own intentions—not always an adequate criterion for judging one's acts within their social context.

The undoubted virtue and probity of Socrates' personal life was no adequate compensation for the charged and potentially destructive concepts which he peddled with such assiduity. What the public saw was a man who challenged the entire fabric of their society, an irritating logic-chopper who filled boys' heads with inflammatory rubbish, preferred Spartan institutions to the home-grown variety (an oddly aristocratic trait in an ex-stonemason; but then Socrates, like certain Oxford and Cambridge dons, seems to have had a weakness for well-connected youths, especially if their blue blood also ran to good looks), encouraged sentimental homosexuality of the idealized non-functional sort, and, worst of all, produced dangerous political extremists. We all recognize this character: he is the stereotype of what Americans are fond of describing as a 'subversive'. The totalitarian planning which came into vogue with Plato, the idea of an intellectual power-elite, was partly a conscious reaction against the excesses and disasters of post-Periclean democracy; but it also represented an attempt to counter the dangers of free-wheeling philosophical speculation and progressivism. In some ways there was no more profoundly anti-Socratic thinker than Plato.

Whatever the Greek miracle was, then, it can hardly be identified with the cultural by-products of fifth-century Athenian imperialism. By the end of Pericles' legendary era, a reasonably close-knit and cohesive social structure was rapidly vanishing into the melting-pot. Sceptical (not to say anti-religious) speculation had undermined the foundations of society without putting anything more solid in their place. Imperialistic ambition had sapped Athens' moral fibre, involved her in a long and idiotic war, and brought her (at least for a while) to military and economic ruin. Pericles' essay in 'imperial democracy', that oxymoronic contradiction in terms, had led to civic anarchy, extremism both of the Right and of the Left, two semi-fascist *coups d'état*, and at least one full-blown reign of terror. The real message of Euripides' late play *The Bacchae* (which, incidentally, he wrote in Macedonia) was that reason alone is not only not enough, but can be an active menace. By the end of the fifth century this lesson had been learnt the hard way. The *polis* was doomed, the age of the individual dawning; nothing better exemplifies this transformation than the contrast between Aristophanes' late and early plays. *The Acharnians* belongs to the old world, the *Plutus* to the new; so different are they in tone and treatment that we may be grateful for the latter play's unchallengeable ascription, since otherwise some ingenious German scholar would inevitably produce a thesis arguing that it was not by Aristophanes at all.

And what, I can hear the reader protesting at this point, about Athens' artistic and intellectual legacy? Surely creative achievement is valid irrespective of the circumstances which produced it? Indeed yes; but the odd thing is, when one gets down to it, how little of the intellectual break-through was achieved in Athens or by Athenians. The real revolution in thought had taken place a century or more earlier, far away on the seaboard of the eastern Aegean. If the Greeks have a claim to immortality it is, first and foremost, through their discovery of rational, scientific thought. It was the Ionians who, as Professor Finley observed, first asked 'the critical questions about the earth and the stars and metals and matter'; who pioneered a method of systematic inquiry into the facts of physical existence, and applied rational human criteria to the determination of their meaning. 'Man is a rational being' Finley noted. 'If he asks rational questions, he can, by the unaided efforts of his intellect, discover rational answers. *But first he must discover that about himself.*'

This discovery, it can be argued, is the Greeks' true 'miracle'. It would be hard to conceive of a more momentous advance, or one which operated in more numerous fields of human inquiry, from history to biology, from physics to ethics. Egyptians and Babylonians might have accumulated astronomical or mathematical data, but always for *ad hoc* purposes, most often tied up with their gods. It was the Ionians who floated *historia*, scientific inquiry, free of the mythic or religious framework in which it had hitherto been encumbered. Their thinkers, Thales, Anaximander and the rest of them, observed everything around them, from the cosmos to the smallest rock-pool with its teeming minuscule life; and where they observed, they speculated. Their omnivorous curiosity took in the sky and the heavens and the gods, first causes and evolutionary development, medicine, biology, physics, history. The world was truly their oyster. (Xenophanes, for instance, noted the fossil imprints of fishes and seaweed in the Syracuse quarries, and from them deduced a cyclical theory of geological history, with recurrent floods as the destructive factor.) They were the pioneers, not only of natural science, but also, as Professor Huxley points out, of the 'first systematic geography' and also of 'critical, secular history'.

Such a people and such a phenomenon are worth the closest scrutiny. Is it possible to isolate the factors which made this 'miracle' possible? To begin with, the Ionian seaboard was cosmopolitan in a way the Greek mainland could never hope to be: every major trade-route—from Egypt, Russia, Central Europe, and the East beyond the great Anatolian plateau—met and crossed somewhere between Rhodes and the Dardanelles. Along these routes there passed not only merchandise, but also ideas and beliefs. Xenophanes' satire on Olympian anthropomorphism was strongly influenced by Persian religious tenets. A region which accepted countless languages and customs as part of its daily scene was not likely to take a stuffily ethnocentric attitude to life: that narrow *polis* parochialism which later characterized Athens and most of the mainland powers had no place here. When every other person you met was a foreigner, it became hard to build up a tradition of xenophobia.

This intelligent and flexible curiosity is reflected in a historian like Herodotus, who came from Halicarnassus, the modern Bodrum. Herodotus is making an 'inquiry' (*historia*) about human beings. Hence his attempts to synthesize so many branches of knowledge, his unprejudiced willingness to recognize that anything to do with human institutions can have relevance to a specific theme such as the Graeco-Persian Wars. History in our conventional sense forms only one element in the *Histories*. The rest is a wide-ranging amalgam of geography, natural science, economics, agronomy, philology, anthropology, theology and, not least, medicine. Herodotus' research is far more modern than we would expect, more broadly based on collateral disciplines (at times he writes for all the world like a twentieth-century comparative ethnographer), less dogmatic, less strictly political-military-constitutional. But when we compare him with his great successor, Thucydides the Athenian, we see that, though no more than thirty years separated them, the two men belonged to wholly different worlds.

It was the cosmopolitan against the parochial, the international versus the national outlook, wide ethnic tolerance opposed to the narrow patriotism of the *polis*. Each had its virtues; but the *polis* was essentially a short-term phenomenon, and its adherents always ran the risk of expanding their partial view of life into a universal cultural or political system which it could ill support. Thucydides is insular and parochial where Herodotus is wide-ranging, opinionated where he is broad-minded. Thucydides' horizon is bounded by the concept of the city-state, with its local jealousies and microcosmic ambitions: perhaps this explains why he is so cynically shrewd about the perennial elements of man's political psyche, but on the wider issues tends to seek refuge in vast impersonal abstract laws. Personalities do not interest Thucydides any more than do ethnographical digressions. Where Herodotus will offer you a choice of opinions, and quote the evidence for them, Thucydides prefers to cite no authorities at all, and pronounce judgment *ex cathedra*. Herodotus' mind was shaped by the Presocratic philosophers, that of Thucydides by the Sophists, from whom he learnt his thorny, antithetical style, his diagnostic attitude to history.

It is no accident that while the Ionians were laying the foundations of modern European science, philosophy and literature, Athens' most distinguished cultural figure was Solon—who, characteristically enough, made his mark as a social and political reformer, and wrote mnemonic poetry commemorating his reforms: dull if unexceptionable iambics and elegiacs on the removal of boundary-stones, the cancellation of debts. In one sense Solon was an index of all that followed. The whole evolution of fifth-century Athenian literature—Thucydides, the tragedians, Aristophanes—is centred upon an ineluctably political core. It is, in fact, *polis* literature. Reading it, we can glimpse the dialectic struggle of a city that grew up too fast, in which man's archaic tribal duties to the gods struggled for priority with his duties towards his fellow-citizens, and himself. It celebrates the slow, painful struggle to escape from tribal dogma into a new world, a world of abstractions and civic law in which the clan vendetta (let alone human sacrifice) had no place. With Solon we catch this process at a very early stage, largely untouched by the bright illuminations of Ionian thought, reaching towards a new political philosophy virtually *ex nihilo*. It is a fascinating experience; almost as fascinating as the spectacle of the Presocratics struggling to achieve mastery over language, coming to terms with linear thought, advancing from the concrete image to the abstract concept. The two processes, in fact, are intimately related; they went on throughout recorded Greek history, and some of the dialectical conflicts they posed have not been resolved yet. It is, put broadly, the perennial struggle of reason against nature, the social group against the clan, the rule of law against the rule of kinship, scientific thought against superstition.

We may not be so sure as were our progressivist great-grandfathers that this process is wholly beneficial, or that all manifestations of the natural, irrational function—from lyric poetry to religious mysticism, from the erotic instinct to the magic of metaphor—are simply outmoded instruments of perception or romanticized variations on a straight biological urge—the *élan vital*, Shaw's sadly antiseptic Life Force (it took a poet to see that force driving the flower through the green fuse). The reservations we have about reason are those such as can only be maintained when the beast of unreason has been fought for centuries and, if not tamed, at least made tolerably familiar. In classical Greece the process was only beginning, and fraught, therefore, with a kind of nightmarish yet exhilarating urgency. Yet has the present age any real grounds for feeling that the battle is won—let alone that it should never have been fought at all (as many non-combatants would now maintain)? We in this twentieth century have learnt, by bitter experience, that a climate of liberal, rational opinion is not something which can be taken for granted as part of Western Europe's intellectual heritage. It is an ideal to be constantly fought for, with unremitting vigilance: a precious acquisition, all too easily lost. Who in 1900 could have predicted all the vicious and tawdry machinery of intellectual totalitarianism—systematic brain-washing, slanted propaganda, the down-grading of concepts such as truth and freedom to mere counters in the political power-game, the contemptuous dismissal of all honest intellectual endeavour, from the Ionians' day onward, as 'bourgeois objectivity'—that latter-day reversion to the mindless collectivism of the tribal dance?

Yet, as history should have taught us, such things are neither new nor exceptional (both Alexander and Augustus, for instance, knew a good deal more about propaganda and brain-washing than any Victorian politician). Truth for truth's sake is not a natural objective of the human mind, which by and large much prefers myth to history, group comfort to unpalatable and asymmetrical fact. As Professor George Huxley rightly says, the 'ferment of Ionian society' provided special conditions, 'the right climate for free ratiocination'. But this climate could not and did not last; fifth-century Athens (as should by now be tolerably clear) was very far from all-tolerant, and still in fact caught up between the tensile counter-claims of new mind and old psyche, tribe and *polis*. The Athenians' persecution of Anaxagoras and Socrates might have been inconceivable in the Miletus of Thales and Anaximander; but even Milesian tolerance must have had its limits. When the Ephesians exiled Heraclitus' friend, the law-giver Hermodorus, they did so with the words: 'Let no one be best amongst us; or if one must be best, let him be elsewhere and with other men.' Exceptional ability always provokes envy, conformism is the greatest virtue, and steady sniping at established tradition among the most heinous social crimes. Indeed, it is some cause for astonishment that the Ionian thinkers were allowed to flourish as they did. No one, surely, can have escaped a twinge of uneasiness in Colophon when Xenophanes suggested that Thracian gods had red hair and Ethiopian gods flat noses.

All intellectual advance demands an obstinate indifference to tradition, custom, and accepted belief; and so long as man remains a social animal, such indifference will continue to inspire fear and anger and retribution. Socrates, Galileo, Marx, Freud, Christ himself—could any of these, by any stretch of the imagination, be regarded as *popular* among their more respected contemporaries? What gives fifth-century Athens its peculiar fascination for us is not that it pioneered the breakthrough of reason (that job, as we have seen, had already been done by the Ionians) but rather the extraordinary dialectical tension it built up between the claims of tradition and advancement, of tribal and political *mores*, of reason and unreason. This tension provides the mainspring of all Attic drama; it is detectable in the constitutional reforms of Solon and Cleisthenes; it crops up, with a plethora of archaic survivals, in Athenian homicide law; and the worst thing, in a sense, that can be said about Pericles and his intellectual friends is that they suffered from the common progressive delusion of supposing that the primitive and irrational could simply be legislated out of existence. Looked at in this way, the Parthenon may be regarded as Pericles' tribute to pure unalloyed reason: hence the highly emotional reactions, pro or con, which it so often produces.

If man, as Protagoras said, is to be the measure of all things—the giddy presumption of this claim is not always appreciated as much as one would hope—then how (the Athenians must have asked themselves) are we to deal with our unfortunate legacy of blood-guilt, mythic and arbitrary gods, totem, taboo and superstition, all this archetypal hand-luggage we have embarrassingly brought with us into our brave new age of civic reason? This is the precise point at which whole-hogging rationalists like Pericles went so appallingly wrong. It is all very well to pursue the Apollonian sweetness and light of a planned social collective; but archaic horrors cannot be got rid of simply by taking thought. Just how ineffectual the movement was can be grasped at once by a glance at Athenian laws relating to murder, which were deep-rooted in tribalism, vendetta, and ritual blood-guilt, and even as late as the fourth century still bristled with archaic survivals.

There were no less than six ways of bringing a killer to justice in ancient Athens, and five available courts in which to do it, including one, the Prytaneion, which could give judgments against animals or inanimate objects. Vengeance could only be exacted against a killer on behalf of the murdered man, normally by his next of kin; and if he forgave his murderer before dying (there is no known example, but the principle stands) then no one could take action against the guilty person. Despite this multiplicity of courts, the State could not initiate a prosecution. Traces of the vendetta, of ritual defilement, peep out everywhere. It might be argued, without stretching the point too far, that one object Aeschylus had in mind when writing his *Oresteia* was to remove the self-perpetuating vendetta from private hands and turn it over to a civic court of justice. In the *Eumenides* (and indeed in the *Prometheus*) the problem of what to do with the arbitrary, vengeful, bloody-minded deities of tribal primitivism is all-absorbing, and the solutions highly significant. Blood-guilt, symbolized by the obscene pursuing Furies, is to be exorcized by way of the statute-book. Athena herself will intervene to modernize Athenian justice and cast a democratic vote in favour of acquittal. The archaic, arbitrary, vengeful Zeus of the *Prometheus* will mature into something uncommonly like a Periclean statesman.

The moral presumption of this programme is only matched by its stupidity. In their efforts to acclimatize the Olympian pantheon to Athens' new and somewhat idiosyncratic brand of limited social democracy, Aeschylus and Pericles between them came very close to killing Zeus stone dead as an active religious concept; by the end of the century the former tribal father-figure was well on his way to becoming an abstract idea, and what the philosophers left over the meteorologists picked up. Far more dangerous, certainly in psychological terms, was their naive attempt to neutralize dark irrational daemons such as the Furies, together with the whole bloody, ghost-haunted legacy of Athens' pre-rational past. The attempt not only failed; it had effects which could not be undone. To put it bluntly, a man who kills his mother is going to be haunted by guilt whatever a court of twelve good men and true tells him; when it comes to cleansing the bosom of *that* sort of perilous stuff ritual purification has it all along the line. What is more, to envisage the Furies as an *external* phenomenon at least gave the sufferer some measure of psychological protection; but when clever rationalists laughed such a notion out of court (literally as well as metaphorically) these pursuing horrors did not give up so easily. They sat demurely while a civic committee put fancy costumes on them, changed their name (that old crypto-magical standby so dear to all rationalists) and offered them a niche under the Acropolis. Then, the moment it was dark, they winged their way back to the place from which it had taken aeons to remove them—the inner recesses of the human mind—and there they have remained ever since, defying all efforts to remove them. In a broader sense, they went underground, along with various other chthonian creepy-crawlies, and began to pop up again, in disturbing places, as the Peloponnesian War dragged on.

The Parthenon is the most perfect expression of a partial (and necessarily incomplete) attitude to life, a soaring rejection of the past on which it stood, the Acropolis that reached back in an unbroken cultural sequence to the Mycenaean era and beyond. It is a triumph of civic planning, a palace-like home for a larger than life-size but quintessentially human (indeed, municipalized) goddess, a testament to imperial pride and ambition, a repository for wealth, a statement of secular faith in which the numinous had, and has, no part whatsoever. It housed Athena, blown up in chryselephantine splendour (and, one fears, somewhat ostentatious vulgarity) but with all those gold and ivory plates carefully detachable for the record. If we admit this, then we can cheerfully grant it the rest: its mathematical symmetry, the perfect harmony of its proportions, nothing too much, the Golden Mean, even the aesthetically satisfying *entasis* of its columns. The Parthenon is a tribute to mathematics: a morally neutral science, one of the few disciplines that *can* function by pure reason, which is why the Athenians were so passionately addicted to it, and showed such brilliance in the field of mathematical theory. But what nurtured mathematics was perilous for a humane discipline such as history. The Athenian passion for seeing life as the imperfect projection of some transcendental Idea enabled them to treat history much as Humpty Dumpty treated words. They seldom saw the dangerous gap between fact and generalization. Clever rationalists can always find plausible explanations for shabby conduct; and were there not the Sophists on hand, teaching young men how to make the worse cause appear the better?

It took the romantic liberal rationalists of the Age of Enlightenment and after to replace Pericles on the pedestal whence he had long been ousted by Caesar and Augustus and Alexander, figures better calculated to appeal to the ambitious *virtù* of any Renaissance prince. But once the myth had been resuscitated, it proved capable of surviving almost anything, even heavy infusions of Teutonic emotionalism. It is what bedazzled Hellenists too often cling to today, finding the dream more acceptable than the gritty and sometimes disconcerting facts (it is no accident that, till very recently, none of the key major inscriptions relating to Athenian government in the period 450–30 BC had been made easily available in translation). Scholars, like the rest of humankind, cannot bear very much reality. The most famous English Hellenist of this century never set foot on Greek soil (but then, Arthur Waley never visited China, either). That great authority on Greek education and culture, Werner Jaeger, could never bring himself to go up and look at the Acropolis when he was in Athens, for fear that the reality would not match up to his dream of it. Yet such terrors are, in the last resort, without any convincing foundation. Fifth-century Athenian achievement was real enough, in all conscience: Sophocles and Pheidias and Aristophanes can rest on their work with pride, knowing that it proved, in Thucydides' famous words, a 'possession for ever'. Fear of disappointment only creeps in with grotesquely overblown expectations, the pure oxygen of romantic fantasy. We should be able to judge such memorials without losing our sense of proportion: to deify these makers and thinkers is no compliment, and indeed something of a contradiction in terms. One could as easily worship the Parthenon, an act that might have daunted even Robespierre.

Perhaps the most depressing aspect of the myth today (now, with cheap travel and mass communications, even more widespread, superficial and stereotyped than ever: one can only hope it may soon perish of sheer inanition) is the kind of people, by and large, who still subscribe to it. Anyone who has travelled on a Hellenic cruise, or attended any kind of classical congress, or even watched groups of high-school teachers being shepherded round the Athenian Agora, cannot help feeling that many of these mild, worthy, middleclass people (often patently innocent to the point of other-worldliness) would feel very much at sea if suddenly transported to Periclean Athens as it really was. 'Bald heads, forgetful of their sins—' Yeats' famous lines are, alas, even more apposite today than when he wrote them, the gap between dream and reality has widened into a Grand Canyon of the mind, so that at a time when classical scholars are becoming tougher, more realistic, more willing to dispense with the romantic shibboleths of the past, myth-addicts still cling fiercely to their Edith Hamilton paperbacks, and refuse to listen. (Perhaps this is truer of the middle-aged than of the young, who made *The Greeks and the Irrational* into something like a best-seller, and, being largely free of that brainwashing process, an old-fashioned English classical education, come to the subject with far less built-in emotional prejudice.) Such people are professional myth-addicts; and a visit to Greece can often test the myth severely. It is no accident that so many of them isolate themselves as far as possible from the country's living speech and society, preferring instead to tread a well-beaten summer tourist-track from one set of ruins to the next, or browse round insulated museums, with the culture-stoned and somnambulistic air of two-legged ruminants after fresh pasture.

This brings me back, by way of epilogue, to my novelist friend on the Acropolis. While we were still sitting in silent (and mildly befuddled) contemplation of the Eleusis cement-works —with an occasional furtive glance back over one shoulder to make sure Reason was still with us—what must have been the first cut-price conducted academic tour of the year came into view: Yeatsian bald heads, bulging alpaca jackets, baggy trousers, bifocals, gingham dresses and shapeless cardigans, sensible shoes, flat busts, and endless copies of the *Guide Bleu.* Camera shutters clicked neurotically, like death-watch beetles up a blind alley. My companion stared, and shook his head. At this moment (with truly Homeric appositeness) there came a splendid clap of thunder, and the sky exploded with rain. My friend, who looks rather like Zeus the Cloud-Gatherer anyway (though not even he would describe those flowing locks of his as hyacinthine) beamed hugely, as though he had produced this effect himself. We watched the torch-bearers of culture scatter unhandily for cover: what had become of those eternal blue skies? 'Well,' Zeus said, judiciously, 'it's a beginning.' There seemed no possible answer to this Delphic pronouncement. We sat and laughed, with true Olympian malice, sodden, suddenly happy, while rain hissed down on broken marble and pitted column, the grey enduring relics of an imperial dream.

Clio Reviewed

A SURVEY OF PROGRESS AND REACTION IN GREEK HISTORIOGRAPHY

1 *THE CONSERVATIVE ROMANTICS*

IT IS NOW nearly sixty years since J. B. Bury published his one-volume *History of Greece*. The decades which followed have seen profound modifications, of more than one kind, to the picture which Bury drew. To begin with, the sheer bulk of new evidence has meant that prehistoric Greece, in particular, is now better known to us than a scholar such as Grote could ever have dared to hope. When Bury wrote, Schliemann had only recently excavated Mycenae, and Sir Arthur Evans had not yet unearthed the fabulous Palace of Cnossos. No one had so much as heard of Linear B, let alone set a cat among the linguistic pigeons by deciphering it as a species of proto-Greek. The work achieved since the turn of the century by archaeologist, epigraphist, and linguist (to name but a few of those responsible) has revolutionized the ancient historian's perspective. In particular, it has encouraged him (though resistance, as we shall see, remains both stubborn and wide-spread) to take a somewhat less parochial view of his chosen preserve. If he is forced, through lack of other evidence,[1] to view the dawn of Greek history in a Pan-Mediterranean context which includes, among other outsiders, Egypt, Assyria, and the Hittites, there is at least a chance that the habit may stick when he moves on to the fifth century. If he is also brought to the conclusion that Greek science owed more than he cares to admit to Babylonia, or that there is a great deal to be said, *pace* Aeschylus if not Herodotus, for Persian institutions, so much the better. As has already been suggested, one of the biggest

[1] Though shortage of evidence can have its dangers too; the correlation of Homeric epic with Geometric pottery is a classic case in point.

handicaps from which ancient Greece has ever suffered is the myth attached to the Greek miracle.

Perhaps even more important than the accumulation of new evidence is the changing overall attitude to the study of ancient history as such. This change, it hardly needs saying, is intimately connected with the world-shaking events of the last half-century. Our judgments, choice of subjects or evidence, and assessments of such writers as Thucydides or Polybius, are all conditioned by our own rapidly changing ethics and morals. It so happens that the troubled era through which we are living today approximates more closely to conditions in Greece and Rome than did the period of relative stability enjoyed by our great-grandfathers; and this, predictably, has given a fresh dynamic impetus to historical research. For us, such things as Corcyraean *stasis*, city-state fifth-column activities, the political propaganda of a Caesar or an Alexander, and the enslavement of ancient satellites and minorities, are living realities. Torture and witch-hunting, far from having been abolished by the advance of science, are flourishing as never before. We have witnessed the collapse of several empires, including our own, and the near-total disappearance of the hieratic class-based society; thus we are far less tolerant of cultured imperialism (however paternalistic) and view upper-class rhetoric with deep suspicion. We do not mind saying, loudly, that many idols which our Victorian predecessors were disposed to worship with uncritical enthusiasm seem to us shabby, hypocritical, or tainted with gross political immorality. Marx and Freud, at however many removes, have left us their legacy of economic analysis and subconscious motivation, just as logical positivism, and the memory of several highly offensive totalitarian regimes, have undermined our enthusiasm not merely for Plato's philosophy, but also for his politics.[1]

[1] Those who consider that the city-state long outlived its usefulness (though not its popularity among nostalgic political theorists) prefer, by and large, to deal with periods of moral anarchy and cosmopolitan individualism. The enormous increase, during recent years, of research on Hellenistic Alexandria and on Byzantium is no

There are, obviously, many dangers latent in these developments: some of them were pinpointed by Professor Arnaldo Momigliano (one of the widest-read and most enlightened of living ancient historians) in his Inaugural Lecture as Professor of Ancient History at University College London some years ago. He pointed out, among other things, that reaction had gone too far and too fast: that the proper statistics for undertaking detailed socio-economic studies of Greek history were not yet available (a point since taken up in greater detail by Professor Finley and others), that Marxism, psycho-analysis, and the 'neo-Augustinianism' of Professor Toynbee all tended to produce unilateral approaches to the 'eminently many-sided history of Greece', and that, of recent years, evidence had been distorted, not only for partisan purposes (a perennial hazard) but from sheer lack of common sense. All this is undoubtedly true, and to have it pointed out is a salutary corrective; but it can hardly justify a desperate attempt either to pretend that the last fifty years have not happened, or else that a morally neutral stance is the only legitimate one for an ancient historian. Both phenomena are typical of that romantic, class-conscious conservatism which seems to have been built into ancient historiography since Thucydides' day; and the second tends to conceal an active, if unadmitted, sympathy with the more extreme manifestations of right-wing totalitarianism.[1] It is, perhaps, worth scrutinizing this trend with some care (especially since it would seem to have, by and large, escaped notice by students of historiographical form), and for this purpose I propose to examine several well-known and widely-read studies which have appeared since the war, and to study, *inter alia*, the degree of progress or reaction which they reveal.

accident. Perhaps the most typical works dealing with the ancient world produced during the last few decades have been Rostovtseff's *Social and Economic History of the Hellenistic World* and Professor Sir Karl Popper's *The Open Society and its Enemies*.

[1] I prefer, with occasional exceptions, to avoid the words 'fascist' and 'fascism', which by now have almost totally lost their specific meaning, and are little more than an all-purpose pejorative noise employed by anyone not actually right-of-centre.

An obvious starting-point, both on account of its all-inclusive nature and bearing in mind the wide audience (students especially) which it is intended to serve, will be Professor N. G. L. Hammond's *History of Greece*, first published just over a decade ago, and since purged of some of its wilder flights of fancy in a second edition. Paradoxically, despite his up-to-date knowledge—including close familiarity with the language and topography of modern Greece in peace and war—Professor Hammond remains a kind of High Tory Hellenist, and his work a good deal more reactionary in tone than the third edition of Bury.[1] The first thing which is bound to strike the reader is Hammond's scale of values, as demonstrated quantitatively in the space which he allots to various topics; the second is the overall planning by chapters. To take the latter point first: Hammond, like Bury and his predecessors, tucks away such matters as art, religion, philosophy and literature in rather perfunctory chapters on their own (one sub-section is comprehensively entitled 'History, geography, medicine and comedy') —a habit which still exercises its lure on the historian of antiquity, despite persistent criticism over many years (see below, p. 70). If there is one thing which all students of history should have learnt during this century, it is that any civilization must be studied in its totality, as a nexus of interrelating phenomena. Philosophy and medicine and sculpture are not activities which take place in a cultural void; social studies form part of every historian's essential equipment. Here, as in so many other ways, Herodotus justifies his proud title as the Father of History in an unexpectedly modern way. It has taken us over two millennia to catch up with the wise old Ionian's methods; yet Professor Hammond—despite a glowing tribute to his professional

[1] Perhaps not so paradoxical after all; freedom-fighting in Greece (with unimportant exceptions) has always been a speciality of upper-class if not aristocratic foreigners—Byron typified the pattern rather than set it—with a weakness for romantic royalism and a heavy dose of the 'Greek miracle' to sustain them. It is no coincidence that Professor Hammond's opposite number during his career as a guerilla leader during the last war was the Hon. C. M. Woodhouse, now a Conservative M P of fairly pronounced views and the author of a book entitled *The Philhellenes*.

predecessor in Halicarnassus—never seems quite to have appreciated what Herodotus was about. Instead, he rhapsodizes over his 'limpidity and charm', and raps him over the knuckles, as an afterthought, for believing in oracles and not having an adequate grasp of military tactics.

This tendency to fault Herodotus for not going about his business like a nineteenth-century classicist (or, perhaps more to the point, like Thucydides, whose mesmeric effect on Greek historiography is not lightly to be set aside) can be extremely irksome. It is at least arguable that Herodotus, like Tacitus after him, was perfectly entitled to consider the minutiae of battle orders as irrelevant to his main thesis, and that it is not morally obligatory to be as avid a military historian as Thucydides or Professor Hammond. It is also clear enough that Herodotus' reputation for error, here as in other matters, has been somewhat overrated. He certainly had his faults, not least of which (*plus ça change*) was a tendency to be dazzled by his aristocratic informants. He may not have been so clever as Professor Hammond when it comes to analysing the battles of the Persian Wars (though I must put it on record that Hammond's interpretations of Marathon and Salamis seem to me wrong-headed in a way that almost verges on perverse genius). But he did possess the insight and originality of the true creative historian; whatever defects one may lay at his door, dullness, impersonality, and a fatal addiction to historian's cliché cannot be reckoned among them. With Professor Hammond plots are invariably hatched, tyrants extend their sway, and much play is made with those tired old metaphoric entities the body politic and the ship of state, which should have been abandoned years ago. It may all be part of Professor Hammond's nostalgia for *temps perdu*, but reminiscent aphorisms, if not carefully watched, are always liable to degenerate into mere duck-billed platitudes.

The influence of Thucydides is only one degree more marked on Professor Hammond than that of the stiff-upper-lip tradition in which he (like most English scholars) was brought up, and which attained an apotheosis during his most gallant wartime career. This *History of Greece*, as far as emphasis and arrangement go, follows the Thucydidean pattern in almost slavish detail. It contains 651 closely printed pages, excluding an index and several appendices. (There is, for some inscrutable reason best known to the author, no general bibliography—though at least he goes one better than Thucydides by briefly documenting his sources.) At the most generous estimate, not more than 85 of these pages in all are devoted to art, architecture, literature, medicine, science, philosophy, historiography, political thought, religion, music, mathematics, and the social sciences. All the rest is political, military or constitutional narrative. Socrates gets two paragraphs (of which one is devoted to his trial) and a few scattered references. Slavery is brushed off in two or three pages five-sixths of the way through. There is no adequate discussion of Delphi; and though Professor Hammond does his best with economic matters, he obviously agrees with the Greeks themselves in finding such things intrinsically banausic.

Where his narrative really catches fire is (not altogether surprisingly) in any account of military operations; lucky for him that warfare bulked so large in the affairs of the Greek states. Like most historians, he has his favourite characters, and they turn out more often than not to be generals. Alexander's achievements actually coax a faint if sullen glow from his otherwise cold and ashy prose. Epaminondas and Philip of Macedon also win enthusiastic approval from him. He has a marked weakness for playing-field ethics; one remembers, without surprise, that he spent a period as Headmaster of Clifton. Perhaps that is why (one can think of no other explanation for so astonishing a verdict except moral disapproval) he tags Themistocles with that fine old wartime label 'lack of moral fibre'; while the lame Spartan, Agesilaus, is damned with faint prose in a style much akin to that which the late Lord Attlee employed in his memoirs, when discussing some worthy celebrity whom he particularly disliked:

> In the long war which followed Agesilaus was the outstanding military commander on the Spartan side. He was very popular with citizens and mercenaries alike. He led his men in battle and was wounded at Coronea. He excelled in the arts of subterfuge, ambush, and rapid raids, and he had returned from his last campaign in Asia with 1,000 talents' worth of loot.

One gets the impression that Professor Hammond considers the 'arts of subterfuge' only one degree less reprehensible in a soldier than picking up personal baksheesh on active service; no wonder he has it in for Themistocles.

In many respects, let it be conceded, this book does supersede Bury, even in the latter's revised third edition. Professor Hammond is up to date on Linear B and the proper relationship between Cnossos and the mainland. He has acquainted himself with all the latest evidence in the archaeological and numismatic fields, even though the use he makes of this material may sometimes cause raised eyebrows among the specialists. His sections on colonization are illuminating (though now eclipsed by John Boardman's exemplary monograph *The Greeks Overseas*) and the reader is never for long allowed to forget those states, such as Thessaly or Epirus, which tend normally to be treated as peripheral to Greek history. He has some sensible, but hardly new, remarks to make about the interrelationship of tragedy and changing social ethics at Athens: but this chapter, aptly entitled 'The Cultural Crisis in the Peloponnesian War' he somehow contrives to seal off from the rest of his book, so that its influence on his general method remains negligible.

It is in his sections on prehistoric Greece that we can legitimately expect most from Professor Hammond; and it is precisely here that his covert romanticism breaks loose and has a field-day, kicking over the traces of conservative scholarship and at times verging on pure imaginative fantasy. Impervious though he is to so many modern trends, he has nevertheless allowed himself to be seduced by, of all things, the historico-mythological lure. Ever since 'Attarissyas, the man of Ahhiyava' was identified with Atreus, King of Achaea, our more romantically-minded scholars have been making efforts (often as rash as they are praiseworthy) to push back the frontier-line dividing history from legend (see below p. 135). In many cases this is well justified; but as Sir John Forsdyke demonstrated in that admirable monograph *Greece before Homer*, the task of extracting a hard core of fact—above all chronological fact—from Greek myths, like the attempt to reconcile traditional genealogies with putative historical figures, is a most chancy and perilous undertaking. Professor Hammond tackles it with breezy confidence, and also (as he himself admits) 'without the frequent qualifications and modifications which caution might enjoin', so that the unwary student will only guess that something is wrong somewhere (like an incompetent textual critic) when it offends his common sense or produces a patent absurdity.[1]

Behind Professor Hammond's biscuit-dry prose, then, there lurks a romantic, and behind the romantic a morally censorious reactionary: forewarned is forearmed. Characteristically, his penchant for dealing exclusively in immediate motives, whether military or political, is matched by a disinclination for appreciating the force of ideas as such in historical development. Indeed, he shows a most singular lack of curiosity as to *why* things happen at all (another typical feature of the traditionalist); sufficient for him that they do, and are documented. Nothing causes him surprise, or gives him pause for thought, not even the astonishing transformation of Sparta into the most thorough-going military caste-system the world has ever seen. This ability to take for granted what should provoke searching

[1] He may wonder, for instance, how the author knows that Minoan worshippers 'felt awe and devotion rather than superstitious fear', and just where the borderline between those two emotions may be held to lie. He may feel a certain unease at the admission of such characters as Pelops to the historical canon (no mention here of that ivory shoulder) though Perseus, Minos and Sisyphus are conceded to be 'enveloped in the mists of folklore'. He may—one hopes he will—boggle at the claim that Homeric heroes showed 'freedom from social or religious restraint'. But when he finds Theseus dated to 1250 BC, or the Phoenician alphabet to about 825, or reads that 'the father of old Priam, Laomedon, built the walls of Troy, and this refers to Troy VIIa, built c. 1300', he may feel inclined to accept Professor Hammond's informed *obiter dicta* as statements of fact. This would be inadvisable.

and (in the widest sense) critical thought is, in historical research as in other fields, one marked characteristic of romantic conservatism. Neither in the general nor in the narrower political sense of the term does Professor Hammond commonly display a radically inquiring mind. No one would guess, from the scanty space he devotes to Hesiod, that the crabbed Boeotian farmer-poet offers us priceless testimony, as rare as it is uninhibited, on the conditions and viewpoint of the common man during the latter end of the Greek Dark Ages. Generals, politicians, and other privileged figures bulk all too large in our sources. We cannot afford to neglect the voice of the underdog when, as with Hesiod or Archilochus (see below, pp. 153 ff.), it speaks out loud and clear.

Another useful test case for the romantic or rose-tinted attitude to Greek history is provided by Solon, a sixth-century Athenian politician who tends to collect rapturous moral tributes from the politically naive. In 594/3, or possibly 573/2, Solon was chosen *aesymnetes*, or arbitrator, by the embroiled factions at Athens in order to prevent civil war between the haves and have-nots; and the evidence we have for his activities, including a sizeable amount of his own political poetry, makes it clear that he was a very sharp operator indeed, who hoodwinked both parties while working out an elaborate justification of the social *status quo*. He afterwards claimed to have held his stout shield over both parties, to have ensured that the rich suffered no improper loss, that the poor did not rise above their proper station. Not only Professor Hammond, but also idealistic scholars such as Dr Ehrenberg and Professor Wade-Gery, tend to exaggerate his single-mindedness. They do not mention the interesting and by no means implausible story of Solon's three friends (all from well-connected and influential families) who are said to have made a killing through advance knowledge of his proposed financial reforms—thus providing the first known Bank Rate leak anecdote in history. Nor do they hint that his famous impartiality was something of a myth. True, on the face of it he steered a very straight course between peasants and landed aristocrats; and by refusing the land-redistribution claims of the first while clamping down on the more flagrant abuses of the second he managed to infuriate both sides, always a good sign of fearless indifference to anything save principle. Yet his reforms left the political and social power-structure untouched—and could hardly have been more beneficial to the rising middle class of landless aristocrats and successful merchants which constituted his own milieu. It could be argued that Solon was in fact severely practical, a good businessman who knew that insolvency and debt-bondage were bad for trade, and that Athens' only hope was to change from a purely agricultural to a commercial economy as fast as possible. But such a view, when applied to the great forerunner of Athenian democracy, lacks moral uplift, and is therefore ignored.

By now it should come as no surprise to find Professor Hammond taking what might be termed an Establishment view of Greek religion as well as idealizing Greek politics. He skirts round Pindar's discreet bowdlerization of divine myth; he is rather hard on Anacreon ('a frank individualist', he calls him, like a headmaster writing a report on a boy who lacked team spirit and vanished on Sundays to play golf) and obviously a little uneasy about Xenophanes' tendency to rock the official religious boat, though the philosopher's hints at immanent monotheism probably, in Professor Hammond's eyes, redeem that Voltairean gibe about the Ethiopian's gods being negroid, and those of the Thracians having red hair and blue eyes. Professor Hammond has a revealing tendency to call the Zeus of Sophocles 'God', and to refer to this deity as 'He' or 'Him', in upper-case; he also subscribes to the old quasi-Biblical theory that Zeus in Aeschylus develops morally into 'a supreme and benevolent deity' who 'carried mankind forward to a higher level of civilization and enlightenment'. *Credat Iudaeus Apella, non ego*. Nor, by now, should we be surprised by Professor Hammond's comparative indifference to the fate of such lesser breeds as Helots or Messenians. Time was when a brave young liberal like Gilbert Murray could become a Professor of Greek in his twenties; but those days are gone, and scholars have been moving imperceptibly to the right of centre ever since. When Sir William Tarn erected his elaborate defence of Alexander as a dedicated benefactor of mankind the writing was on the wall. Since then (with one or two signal exceptions) the really progressive classical historians have tended to be Marxists or fellow-travellers, while the rest (including Professor Hammond, and some *soi-disant* liberals who ought to know better) are lining up happily with the forces of reaction. To the best of my knowledge the last Professor of Greek appointed at Murray's tender age was Mr Enoch Powell: not, it might be thought, an entirely happy omen for the future.

But the summit of Professor Hammond's *arrière-gardisme* is only reached when he comes to discuss the morally ambiguous figure of Pericles. One might think it virtually impossible, in this present age, to still regard the Olympian as a gentle idealist betrayed by ignoble underlings and the machinations of low radicals; but Professor Hammond manages it. He even accepts, or seems to accept, all Thucydides' statements at their face-value: an even more remarkable feat. It is true that in his bedazzled worship of Pericles he is forced, at times, not to let his left hand know what his right is doing. Having described the great statesman's policies as 'consistent and shrewd'—notoriously, subsequent events proved they were not shrewd, whatever one may think about consistency—and having acquitted him of 'any preconceptions or prejudices, secular or religious', a remarkable tribute to any mere mortal, he then blows the gaff by admitting that Pericles 'insisted above all on the interests of his own city-state, and his insistence commended itself to the bulk of the people . . . he filled them with a sense of their great destiny, and he did much to realize that destiny'. But so, of course, did Hitler; and indeed, Professor Hammond is forced to confess that (in his own inimitable phraseology) 'the fair fame of [Athens'] democracy was smirched by acts of imperialist aggression'—though he protects his hero as far as possible by only letting rip against imperialism after Pericles is safely dead.

(This gambit has often proved a useful stand-by; for one interesting example of it see below, p. 80.) His account of the punitive expedition against Samos does not mention the fact that Sophocles served as *strategos* on it (though to little effect, it would seem); and Aristophanes' savage attack on it is only referred to a hundred or so pages later. Nor does it strike him as remarkable that the famous funeral apophthegm about the spring having gone out of the year referred to young men who had died in the execution of this shabby act of imperialist repression. Here is his summing-up on Pericles:

> His policy, like any policy, had its inherent defects; but, judged in the light of its results, it succeeded in securing an empire and in raising Athens to her zenith, although it failed to crush Sparta or unite the Greek world.

Those last few words are a notable understatement to describe the total moral and physical collapse which formed the price Athens had to pay for Pericles' political and cultural ambitions.

It is this kind of obtuseness—almost a blunting of moral sensibility—which is liable to puzzle and distress the intelligent young student, a figure notorious for viewing politics rather more exclusively in moral terms than do his elders. Nor, alas, is this work an isolated case. If the student has wit enough to turn up Professor Wade-Gery's *Essays in Greek History*, and can shoulder his way through the bristling quickset hedges of technical discussion, he will, however, find someone who speaks to him, on this particular issue, in a voice he can understand. 'Once the iron hand had been used,' Professor Wade-Gery writes, apropos Samos, 'the velvet glove was never again convincing; and Athens was to enter the Second Peloponnesian War weaker, in the moral elements of power, than she did the First.' And his summing-up of Thucydides forms an apt and heart-warming colophon to this discussion:

> The younger Thucydides was caught wholly by the glamour of Pericles: he thinks his Principate (gained over the elder Thucydides' body) most admirable: to him, the pity was that

> Pericles' ideas were inherited by Alcibiades, a man bound to ruin them by the fatal resentments which he created. He makes the Corinthians say of Athens the same things in effect which Pindar had said in Pythian VIII: yet what Pindar saw with disdain, Thucydides' Corinthians see with admiring envy. Pericles made him drunk with the idea of power, nor to the end of his life did Thucydides forget it.

It is that same glamour which, after more than two millennia, still has the power to bedazzle Professor Hammond's judgment. One cannot imagine him writing, as Bury did, an enthusiastic book called *The Idea of Progress*. Perhaps that is why, in so many ways, Bury's *History of Greece*, after half a century, still seems fresher, sounder, and, paradoxically enough, more modern.

It is curious how historical fashions can change with the times, not so much because of newly-learnt facts, but rather through a shift of moral climate in the historian's own society. The events of the last century exemplify this all too well: in particular, they have brought about a fundamental shift in the historian's attitude to the key concepts of power and reason. Those with a professional stake in this expanding department of Graeco-Roman antiquities are sometimes heard to observe, not without a tinge of self-satisfaction, that their subject has at last been 'put on a scientific footing'—by which, one presumes, they mean equipped with various ancillary techniques and purged of its grosser speculative generalizations. This is, by and large, quite true; any serious scholar nowadays confronted with dubious, fragmentary or inconsistent evidence (which most ancient historians would regard as a permanent occupational hazard) has a refined evaluative technique at his disposal which makes the Victorian giants, for all their vast erudition, look painfully slapdash amateurs by comparison. Yet this legacy was not, as its beneficiaries sometimes tend to assume, acquired exclusively, or even primarily, by the exercise of rational thought; it came about, rather, through various historical accidents and contingencies which transformed the climate of thought in which middle-class professional historians operate.

Towards the close of the nineteenth century it was still, for obvious if not sufficient causes, fashionable to acknowledge the intellectual supremacy of pure reason, the *pari passu* advance of rational *and moral* self-betterment. The brave new world would prove a playground for dedicated philosopher-kings; with Shaw and Wells and Russell and the Webbs to point the way, who could doubt that *homo faber* would soon emerge as *homo Fabianus*, the gentlemanly (and of course Gentile) heir to that ultra-English New Jerusalem dreamed up by Blake and William Morris? O brave new world that had such preachers in it, where security was such that Shaw could make cute little rationalist jokes about militarism and torture and dictatorships and religious persecution, because (the great under-pinning argument went) we have emerged from that fog of superstition and primitivism and mediaeval prejudice; we can reason anyone, sooner or later, into a reasonable frame of mind. The simultaneous development of comparative anthropology as a serious discipline, far from undermining such an attitude, merely served to encourage it: the comparison showed how real and tangible progress was. There was more than one opinion as to what should be done about the 'beastlye devices of the heathen', with missionaries pulling in one direction and Fabians (on the whole) in another; but that the devices were in fact both beastly and heathen—those two loaded epithets—no one doubted for a moment.

This shibboleth left its mark on most academic disciplines, and ancient historians of the period displayed certain well-marked characteristics which prove them no exception to the general rule. They believed, to begin with, that the truth was best arrived at by applying one's mind to a text rather than by scrambling over a battlefield; there were exceptions to this rule, but they tended to be eyed with a certain amount of well-bred suspicion. Topography was a sport better left to the amateur dilettante. Being reasonable men, moreover, they tended to assume that ancient writers—and, a *fortiori*, Greek or

Roman statesmen and generals—of whom they approved *were reasonable in the same way as themselves*. The results where such figures as Pericles, Alexander or Augustus were concerned can all too easily be imagined. They also, *per contra*, took it for granted (though they did not express the proposition quite in those terms) that sources which diverged to any marked degree from their own moral or rational standards were deeply suspect. Their faith in human reasonableness was ludicrously exaggerated, and their attitude to human uses of power so naive as to send a chill down one's spine; yet there is something enviable about such steadfast self-confidence, which a fashionable top-dressing of Tennysonian religious doubt never really contrived to disturb. It took the new Feast of Unreason to do that; the *Totentanz* which began with the First World War and has not yet ended, which ushered in the era of the technological barbarian, the killer with a doctorate, the hysteria of the Nuremberg rallies and the perverted logic of the Bukharin trials, the death camps of Buchenwald or Vorkuta, the hydrogen bomb and biological warfare, a world in which truth could be labelled 'bourgeois objectivity' and the mass media deliberately harnessed to programmes of brainwashing and lying propaganda. Liberals like Wells or Tarn looked on all this and despaired; the title of Wells' last book—*Mind at the End of its Tether*—summed the whole thing up to perfection.

Paradoxically, aspects of this nightmare run far closer to the world of antiquity than they do to nineteenth-century Europe or America; and thus we can understand, say, the psychology of Greek and Roman power-politics, the ultra-modern in-fighting and propaganda, better than our immediate forefathers could ever have hoped to do. They were clear-eyed and confident; the claims of the ideal had bitten into them, and there they had an instrument of perception denied to us. But their hubris was enormous, and in true Greek fashion brought about its retribution, its *Até*. They bowed down before Reason, and seemingly reasonable men massacred them with sub-machine guns. They celebrated the death of superstition and religion, only to be bemused by the witch-doctors of a new substitute religion called Communism. Today we can understand them better, and feel some sympathy for their dilemma, despite the oddly ambiguous legacy it has left us. It is easy to see, for example, why Herodotus got such a bad press from nineteenth-century scholars. His passion for oracles offended them: were they not the heirs of the Enlightenment? He was much given to interpreting events in terms of personal motivation; he was even naive enough, on occasion, to take myth seriously. This, of course, clashed with the fashionable trend in German historicism which saw history as 'dynamic necessity' or some equally fatuous abstraction. His anecdotal digressions were regarded as romantic and frivolous. Many a Victorian nanny drummed into young Master Tommy's head the hoary mediaeval proposition that fiction was lies, and both equally reprehensible: small wonder that when Master Tommy grew up to be Professor Thomas Didymus he stigmatized Herodotus as the Father of Lies. But what Victorian scholars resented most was Herodotus' civilized (and in our eyes ultra-modern) addiction to comparative ethnography. The proposition that social *mores* are purely relative, that history and geography form complementary aspects of one complex subject, never goes down very well with anyone for whom moral truth is not only absolute, but also indissolubly bound up with his own superior culture. The rationalists might despise the missionaries, but they shared more common cultural assumptions than either side would have cared to admit.

The sovereignty of pure inductive reasoning in ancient historiography produced results as grotesque as they were lamentable, which those who care for such things may peruse at their leisure in Myres' posthumous work *Homer and his Critics*. If a man regards ancient legend as a conglomeration of irrational fancy and childish fairy-tale; if he prefers to sit at his desk rather than tramp round the Troad, and to excogitate theories about epic rather than listen to oral bards in action, then it will be small wonder that he dismisses Troy as a minstrel's fancy and Odysseus as a solar myth. The joke about rationalists, of course, is how wildly irrational they are behind that elaborately logical façade; apriorism hides a multitude of sins, and every free-thinker carries a hare's-foot in his pocket while walking in the gutter rather than under a ladder. But such attitudes were dealt a shrewd blow by Schliemann, who, with crude empirical *simplisme*, took Homer as gospel truth, picked up a shovel, dug according to the book—and found Troy. It would be difficult to over-emphasize the psychological impact of Schliemann's discoveries on the academic world of his day; but the revolution which he heralded took a long time to make itself felt at all levels, and still has not captured every redoubt. Not all scholars who today laud Milman Parry's epoch-making research on oral techniques (while frequently misrepresenting his actual conclusions) were quite so enthusiastic when his fieldwork first appeared in print; and Homerologists might be a little less ready to make Odysseus sail off the map into the realm of faery if they had some practical experience of handling small craft up and down the Aegean.

Social and moral assumptions, then, begin at home; and historians, like translators, tend to work with one unconscious eye on the mirror. The past hundred years have seen what is probably the most far-reaching revolution in thought and social *mores* ever experienced by mankind. Over and above the shattering events of potential and actual destruction already alluded to, we have seen a scientific revolution which has transformed every aspect of our lives, from our eating habits to our musical appreciation, from birth through copulation to death in sober fact. On whichever side of the Iron Curtain we may happen to be located, Marx and Freud have left their indelible mark on us; we can never look at economics or the human psyche in quite the same way again—which includes, despite any disclaimers the historian may choose to make, ancient economics no less than modern, the Greek or the Roman psyche as well as his own and those of his contemporaries. The web of history is seamless: touch one, touch all.

This has had some very striking effects, as any student of

the subject will be aware. Since till comparatively recent times our predecessors shared most major assumptions of the classical tradition, those peculiar basic prejudices inherent in Greek and Roman writers tended to be assimilated without radical criticism. We have already (see above, p. 21–2) had occasion to note the predominantly right-wing, upper-class bias of most writers in antiquity. In particular, the ancient social attitude towards those engaged in commerce and trade was seldom questioned by nineteenth-century historians, themselves bred as gentlemen if not aristocrats, and accustomed to treating doctors as tradesmen. They were hardly inclined to balk at the scathing judgment passed by Demosthenes' nephew Demochares on Demetrius of Phaleron, who 'prided himself that there was much profitable trade in the city and that all enjoyed in abundance the necessaries of life'. This attitude Demochares stigmatized as 'taking pride in things that might be a source of pride to a tax-collector or an artisan'. The idealization of toil by Christianity and Socialism in turn—'Thou shalt earn thy bread by the sweat of thy brow' and 'workers of all nations unite'— has no counterpart in the ancient world. Professor Claude Mossé has argued persuasively that work was regarded as something degrading, 'a sentence to which no redeeming value was attached'. To be sure, some types of work were more degrading than others; a gentleman might, at a pinch, work on the land (provided it was his own, any kind of labour for hire being unthinkable) but not as an artisan, tradesman or *entrepreneur*. Behind it all lay the ideal of what the Greeks called *autarkeia* and the Romans *otium cum dignitate*, the rentier's dream of a self-sufficient competence (or parasitic idleness, according to your point of view).

One amusing, and highly significant, point about this thesis is the way in which scholars have consistently overstated it, from Victorian times until the present day: clearly it answers some deep psychological need which prevents too close a scrutiny of the evidence. Yet even the most casual survey at once makes it clear that the attitude to work in antiquity was by no means consistent, and shifted from place to place no less than between different periods. It is no accident that, so far as Greece is concerned, the main key quotations come from fourth-century authors such as Xenophon, Aristotle, Isocrates, and the Attic orators. Hesiod's father, like Solon after him, was a merchant; if the *Works and Days* does not idealize toil, at least it regards it as necessary and inevitable, a built-in feature of social life. In fact, the earlier we look back, the less prejudice one finds against trade or labour; no one seems to have thought any the worse of an Athenian aristocrat for going into business until the aristocracy had been infiltrated by the merchant class itself, and was under heavy pressure from ultra-democrats. In Italy, similarly, the further back one traces the pattern before Cicero's day (again, the *novus homo* from Arpinum is one of the theory's star witnesses) the more one begins to question his assumptions. Indeed, the ideal of the early Republic was a man like Cincinnatus, who lived simply, left the plough to command an army, and afterwards went back to his farm, without fuss or bother, and got on with the year's work. The contempt for work only arose, in fact, with the development of a large quasi-rentier class with sufficient income (derived from non-productive jobs like teaching, administration, or legal practice) and socio-cultural aspirations. Since this was, *mutatis mutandis*, precisely the slot into which most academic historians fitted, it is not hard to see why such a thesis appealed to them.

This bias has made any objective study of, say, the tyrants who sprang up in Greece during the seventh and sixth centuries BC extremely hazardous. The ancient literary evidence is mostly late or fragmentary; and since it proceeds from aristocratic writers like Theognis or Plato, it appears almost uniformly hostile—a fact not without its influence on modern writers. So recent an historian as Bury was not disposed to admit that an 'age of tyrants' existed at all. It was this dogmatic assertion that in 1922 led the late Professor P. N. Ure to write *The Origin of Tyranny*: a penetrating and (in every sense) revolutionary work which saw the tyrants as early capitalists in conflict with a failing aristocratic tradition, and aligned their ascendancy with an upsurge of commercial activity throughout the eastern Mediterranean. Through fanatic if understandable zeal, Ure considerably overstated his case, and his remarkable thesis was accordingly treated somewhat less seriously than it deserved. (Entrenched conservative prejudice probably played some part in the matter too; I shall return to this point in a moment.) Yet *The Origin of Tyranny* was a landmark in ancient economic history. In particular, Ure attacked the idea (propagated by ancient writers who made false analogies with the case of Dionysius of Syracuse) that the early tyrants were mere military despots. 'As a general rule,' he observed, 'the man who has secured a fortune at a single stroke does not care to improve it by years of patient and organized effort.' Comparing the Cypselids and Peisistratids, suggestively, with fourteenth-and fifteenth-century Italian merchant bankers such as the Medici in Florence, he put his finger unerringly on both their basic flaw and the cause of their unpopularity: 'There is one basis of political power that mankind has never tolerated,' he wrote, 'and that basis is mere riches.' With abundant corroborative evidence he drew a picture of a new wealthy bourgeoisie who used their money to force a way into the closed circle of political power hitherto controlled by blood and heredity. It is a not unfamiliar picture (one can see why Ure was rather suspect among many of his fellow-scholars); and subsequent research, while modifying it in some details, has developed it in others.

Ure himself observed that there was a pendulum-like swing in the degree of credulity which was given by modern historians to ancient evidence. Perhaps it might be more accurate to talk of an oscillation between traditional and progressive attitudes; the degree of credulity will then depend on how one looks at the evidence.[1] At any given point, too, there is bound to be a marked

[1]On the subject of tyrants, for instance, we may usefully compare the approach of Mr W.G.G. Forrest (*The Emergence of Greek Democracy*) with that of Professor Andrewes in *The Greek Tyrants*. The former uses Ure's basic methods, even if he rejects many of his conclusions; one knows where one is with him. Professor Andrewes is rather more dodgy. He cannot entirely avoid the economic background, and admits its comprehensive importance; but he is at pains to

contrast, not only between scholars of differing temperaments, but also between the pioneer research-worker and the compiler of general or popular texts. The Keynesian time-lag of intellectual absorption at different levels down the academic pyramid applies here more than in most places, and may serve to explain the Janus-like double face which the history of Greece—especially from the sixth to the fourth centuries B C—tends to present to the modern reader. Progressive scholars (see below, p. 76) may strip the gilt from the Periclean gingerbread and cut Alexander's charisma down to reasonable proportions; but these movements have hardly, as yet, made the faintest dent on material intended for general consumption.[1]

Open almost any school history, or a popular compilation with some such title as *The Greek Miracle* or *The Golden Age of Pericles*, or the average culture-conscious travel-guide, or (I much regret to say) the long-awaited general survey by Dr Victor Ehrenberg, who really ought to know better, and you can count on being bludgeoned into semi-consciousness by a string of time-hallowed laudatory clichés. Expository self-assurance is matched by a relentless enskyment of the subject. Adverse criticism (whether of political probity or creative achievement) seldom appears, and tends to err on the reactionary side when it does—for example the hoary old political myth, trotted out yet again in Dr Ehrenberg's *From Solon to Socrates*, that by the end of the fifth century 'democracy had degenerated into mob rule'. Too many classicists, as we have seen, though they pay lip-ser-

minimize it. (Here he stands in line with Dr Ehrenberg: see below, p. 72.) He emphasizes, so far as he can, the military element, and makes a good deal of the change from individual fighting to the hoplite formation; it is the hoplites, with their new sense of corporate loyalty and courage, whom he sees as the power behind the tyrants. This is true so far as it goes (and was long ago adumbrated by Nilsson in his article *Die Hoplitentaktik und das Staatswesen*) but even so the fact remains that the hoplite—who had to supply his own armour and equipment—appeared in the first place as a result of increased economic prosperity.

[1] The degree of time-lag may be judged from the fact that it is not all that long since an eminently sensible *Encyclopedia Britannica* article on Alexander by the late Edwyn Bevan was replaced by a stylized eulogy, in the most extreme Tarn manner, by Dr Agnes Savill—at a time when informed opinion had already made many of Tarn's views virtually untenable.

vice to a liberal ethic, remain fundamental authoritarians at heart, men who dearly love a benevolent despot provided he can offer their pupils moral uplift. (Peisistratus, duly described by Dr Ehrenberg as 'a great and wise ruler', is a nice case in point: how separate the dictator from the religious propagandist, or square either of them with the civic-minded economist who laid the foundations of Athens' future greatness as a cultural capital?) Unlike the idealized Socrates, whom they present (despite his antisocial, not to say morally disruptive, ethics) as a paragon of all the virtues, they prefer to frame familiar *obiter dicta* rather than worry themselves or their readers with awkward questions. Any dogma will do to beat a stigma.

It would be hard to guess from such writers' confident, didactic, smoothly marshalled paragraphs that much of the period they are discussing is worse-documented than any other in Greek history, bristling with interpretative cruxes and chronological ambiguities, a mine-riddled no-man's-land where specialists regularly blow themselves up on their own highly-charged theories, or slowly bleed to death on the barbed wire of hostile counter-argument and rebuttal. Redoubts bearing such grim labels as 'Pentakontaetia', 'Lycurgan reforms', 'Periclean Imperialism', 'Troezen Decree' or 'Cleisthenic Legislation' are regularly assaulted (though never captured for long) by bold commando units, which might well win more objectives if they spent less time lobbing hand-grenades at each other *en routé*. Epigraphists, archaeologists and numismatists snipe away with rare verve from mutually inaccessible fox-holes, and are much in demand as mercenaries: literary historians on both sides regularly employ them to support the most *outré* theories, while at the same time taking care to disclaim any professional knowledge of the techniques they employ[1].

It might be supposed, at first sight, that these two approaches to classical Greek historiography were divergent if not irrecon-

[1] Dr Ehrenberg claims *not* to be writing as an expert 'on works of literature, philosophy, science, or art'; one hardly knows which to admire more, his modesty or the canny way he forestalls criticism.

cilable, but close study of both soon reveals a number of significant common features. One finds the same cultural closed-shop mentality, the same apparent indifference to modern critical methods, or indeed to any non-classical discipline—symptoms indicative of a deep underlying conservatism. One also, more surprisingly, too often encounters a certain aesthetic rigidity, not to say obtuseness, which tends to disguise itself as sound scholarly contempt for merely emotional opinions. Exceptions exist, and are, *Deo gratias*, becoming increasingly common as time goes on; but it is still hard to find a first-class critical study of most major ancient authors, and those who go against the dead weight of classical traditionalism tend either to be apologetic, like Professor Dodds introducing *The Greeks and the Irrational*, or, when not actually Marxist, somewhat shrill and intemperate, as is Professor Havelock in *The Liberal Temper in Greek Politics*.

The historiographical programme which Dr Ehrenberg outlines during the course of his preface arouses the very highest hopes. He had, he tells us, two aims in writing *From Solon to Socrates*: 'The first was to show the unity of Greek history in every phase, a unity of political, economic, religious and cultural aspects...The other aim was, not simply to give a narrative, but to reveal the uncertainties of modern scholarship on many important questions.' No one could be anything but grateful for such a manifesto. At last, one felt, the tyrannous pattern of Thucydidean historiography was to be cast away, the mask of omniscience dropped, and all at a level designed to reach the student at school or university level, as simultaneous publication in a paperback edition made abundantly clear. But alas, having made this bold concession to progressivism, Dr Ehrenberg it would seem promptly got cold feet; at all events, his programme remains largely unfulfilled. The reader's doubts are aroused by a nervous caveat that 'political, military and social history must be the framework, indeed the centre, of any sort of general history'; intensified by a too-perfunctory roundup—inserted as the usual postscript—on sixth-century ideas;

and confirmed in detail by his final chapter, 'Know Thyself', a rag-bag into which is crammed everything that conventional historiography finds non-assimilable, from science to tragedy, from the Sophists to Socrates. Where, one well may ask (beyond the most timid of juxtapositions in such respectably cultural sideshows as an essay on 'The Age of Pericles') do we find that fundamental integration of evidence, that genuine return to a non-compartmentalized historical mainstream for which so many of us had hoped? This is not a mere matter of formal arrangement; it indicates a basic methodological attitude, and one very much at variance with Dr Ehrenberg's declared intentions.[1] This point is worth pursuing in some detail, since *From Solon to Socrates* embodies, in classic form, all the faults and virtues associated with what we may term 'conservative Hellenism'.

As far as method goes, indeed, this monograph has much in common with standard old-fashioned histories like those of Bury or Hammond than it does with the various innovating techniques developed by scholars such as Glotz, Hatzfeld, Webster or Finley, and by now, indeed fairly widely accepted as an instrument of *haute vulgarisation*: see, for example, the remarkable 'People and Places' series, or the volumes on 'Ancient Culture and Society' edited by Finley himself, where on external evidence such methods would appear to be editorially *de rigueur*—though not, as yet, applied on a really broad scale. Dr Ehrenberg's references to Glotz are conspicuous by their absence (an even more striking, but no less symptomatic, omission is Chester G. Starr's *The Origins of Greek Civilization*) and he is not above introducing a sketchy art-and-lit round-up with the words 'This seems the right moment to say a few words

[1] If he has read Delebecque's remarkable work on Euripides and the Peloponnesian War he gives no sign of it; he would probably dismiss such an approach as unsound, since his own concept of admissible evidence remains both narrow and conventional. He deals with Cornford's *Thucydides Mythistoricus* in a patronizing aside, and when he refers, slightingly, to N. O. Brown's 'socio-historical interpretation' of Sophocles, he follows the phrase with a bracketed exclamation point. In this particular case, as it happens, I would side with Ehrenberg against Brown; but what matters, surely, is the underlying prejudice which that little typographical comment reveals.

about matters outside the political field'. The Aristotelian pigeon-holing system adapted for classical historiography still seems to exercise a tyrannous influence over him; it would be interesting to know just where he supposes the boundaries of the political field to be drawn, the mysterious point at which art, science, politics, religion and all other conventional divisions of human culture suddenly separate out into non-interacting phenomena. The result of such an approach is just as one might predict: Dr Ehrenberg's narrative lacks vision, follows an all-too-well-beaten trail (with occasional daring little expeditions into the foothills) and, despite the masses of new and exciting material which it assimilates, contrives for long stretches at a time—as numerous students will testify—to be virtually unreadable.

This last quality (often, alas, counted as an anti-populist virtue among scholars) may have something to do with Dr Ehrenberg's second declared objective, that of laying proper emphasis on the lacunae and ambiguities in our evidence. Here he has been far more successful; yet the very degree of success achieved leaves a lurking dissatisfaction behind it. Uncertainty should function as a background to, and a check on, the formulation of original and (one hopes) incisive judgments; here, all too often, it produces a blandly qualified middle-of-the-road platitude. To confess ignorance is not the same thing as hedging one's bets. Between his earlier specialist works (often engagingly polemical) and the present survey, Dr Ehrenberg's ideas have somehow got over-cooked, until their prevalent flavour resembles nothing so much as that of the Parsee's cake in the *Just-So Stories*, which, the reader will recall, got baked and baked until it was done brown and smelt most sentimental. The sentimentality is, *au fond*, the starry-eyed sort which one associates with Lowes Dickinson, Werner Jaeger, Gilbert Murray, and (at a more popular level) Edith Hamilton. Though Dr Ehrenberg's formidable scholarship enables him to ride his Establishment horse on a pretty tight rein, many of the moral and political *obiter dicta* which he produces tend, inevitably, to be soft-centred.

Of Cleisthenes we read: 'Power was to him a means of creating the appropriate constitutional framework for a society on the verge of becoming democratic'. Did any politician, in any period of history—let alone an Alcmaeonid clan-leader of dubious principles and insatiable ambition—ever think remotely like this? No. Then how could a scholar with so much first-hand experience of ruthless power-politics come to write anything so naively idealistic? The answer, by now, should be clear enough. Far from relating his grim personal experiences to the ancient world (thus shedding light on them both) Dr Ehrenberg has plainly sealed the latter off from reality altogether. It is at such moments that the myth becomes, not merely preposterous, but an active menace to truth.

Dr Ehrenberg gives the impression of having—in Eliot's expressive phrase—had the experience but missed the meaning; sometimes one begins to wonder whether he has even had the experience. The middle-class gloss he gives to his favourite characters (predictably, he likes Cimon better than Themistocles) is only one symptom of this malaise; but then, when most ancent historians subscribe to essentially middle-class values, it is hard to escape the Marxist gibe that they all write bourgeois history, and in this respect Dr Ehrenberg does no worse than many of his colleagues. Another highly characteristic trait he reveals is an obvious distaste for economics. He will tackle the subject on occasion, but less often than the occasion demands (he excludes it, surprisingly, from his discussions of Solon's legislation and the expedition to Egypt), and one surmises that the subject tends to jar on his strong sense of political and moral idealism. Here, of course, he stands in line with the Greeks themselves. When Isocrates observed that Megara, towards the Isthmus of Corinth, had become extremely rich despite the poverty of her land, he attributed this, not to an advantageous situation for trading, but to the thrift and *sophrosyne* of her citizens: one cannot help feeling that the anecdote illuminates a good deal of modern classical scholarship.

Dr Ehrenberg, so acute on the detailed sifting of evidence,

tends to fall back on high-minded cliché when discussing root causes: often, indeed, he does not discuss them at all. We are told, in fascinating detail, just how the Pindaric and Aeschylean concepts of Zeus differed, but not a word as to *why* they differed. Could this perhaps be because Dr Ehrenberg, and those many scholars who think like him, regard such basic questions as belonging to the province of mere speculation, and thus better abandoned to non-scholars? Or are they anxious to avoid any issues which might seriously challenge their idealized concept of the ancient world? Again and again we end some crucial discussion no wiser, in essence, than when we began it. Too often a really important phenomenon (for instance the progressive swing from tribal to civic *mores*) is touched on, with maddening elusiveness, in one or two quick throwaway sentences. But it is the platitudes which, cumulatively do most to deaden understanding; and these are characteristic too. Dr Ehrenberg is by no means the only classical scholar who seems (when reaching a verdict on some character from antiquity) to be writing a kind of moral reference for scrutiny in the high courts of heaven—where, as MacNeice, himself a classical scholar, pithily pointed out, 'their tail-feathers shine/With cow-spit and bull-spit and spirits of wine'. Solon's 'moderate conservatism' is matched by his absolute integrity, the clarity of his intellect, and the passionate fervour of his ethics': it is like Gulliver's reaction to the Roman Senate during his voyage to Laputa. Such overblown eulogizing, besides being at odds with much of our evidence, tends to defeat its own ends: the paragon it evokes strains credulity well past the limit. Honest respect does not necessarily imply genuflection. Worse, this habit of moral exaggeration is offset by a strong distaste for anything construable as an overstatement when historical judgments are in question: this is to have the worst of both worlds with a vengeance.

Still, with all its faults, *From Solon to Socrates* does undoubtedly fill a serious gap for the English-speaking reader, and possesses virtues which (unfairly, perhaps) one would find more praiseworthy in a less distinguished historian. Dr Ehrenberg's mastery of ancient sources and modern scholarship is beyond cavil: almost nothing seems to have slipped past that vigilant eagle eye. Scarcely a page, moreover, fails to provide some illuminating comment (often parenthetical) on Greek life and letters, the fruit of a lifetime's study and reflection. Long before Montesquieu, for instance, the author of the Hippocratic treatise *On Airs, Waters and Places* perceived the effect that climate and environment could have on history; Dr Ehrenberg not only picks this up, but applies it, with interesting results, to his analysis of the Milesian philosophers. Often, and characteristically, he relegates his best ideas to a casual footnote: 'In 1919,' he admits, 'I wrote a student's essay on Aeschylus in which I spoke of Eteocles as a man tragically caught up in the process of transition from one age to another.' This essay sounds a good deal more exciting and worthwhile than some of the carefully inoffensive generalizations which have succeeded it. Almost all the finest passages in *From Solon to Socrates*—a point surely not without significance—are those which concern themselves with art, ideas, and literature rather than history in the old-fashioned sense, even though the latter dominates Dr Ehrenberg's text, and the former are only let in, as it were, on sufferance. In the last resort, I can't help feeling, Dr Ehrenberg is far happier viewing the Greek scene *sub specie aeternitatis* than plunging into the dirty temporal chaos of city-state power-politics.

Yet, in the last resort, this is simply not enough. Dr Ehrenberg does make one or two gingerly concessions to modern opinion; he even admits that 'it is possible to find some justification for democracy condemning Socrates'; but far too many vital issues are left hanging in mid-air, or blurred with mere grandiloquent generalizations. When we are told that what 'united the two attitudes personified in Sophocles and Pericles was the common belief in man's perfection, and in the final goal of human harmony', is it merely cynical to reply: 'Exemplified, no doubt, by the suppression of the Samian Revolt'? When we read that all characters in *The Phoenician Women*, with one exception, are 'self-centred, with no concern for the state', we expect a comment on this highly significant fact; instead, we are told that the play is 'a problem for the historian of literature and only in a very general sense significant for the general historian'. Perhaps, after all, one prime virtue of this book is its irritant quality, the way it continually provokes discussion and disagreement. If *From Solon to Socrates* fails to fire the imagination, at least it should provide a reliable conspectus of material for the next generation of students in ancient history; and by refusing to answer so many questions it may, with luck, drive them to seek answers of their own. Better still, it may, with luck, drive one of their mentors to attempt the job himself. The field is still wide open.

2 *THUCYDIDES AND THE LURE OF EMPIRE*

For at least a century (some might say since the Renaissance) a kind of charismatic aura has hung over Athenian history between 508 and 403 B C. As one more than usually frank scholar remarked, a few years ago: 'Most of us ancient historians have a sympathy for Athens and her Empire; no matter how impartial we try to be, our whole training as classicists, and possibly our political bent as well, incline us that way.' Even Grote, with his ferociously radical views, was glamour-struck to some extent by the Periclean mystique; and we should not forget that late-Victorian scholars such as Freeman, who by the very nature of things had a certain stake in imperialism themselves, never lost an opportunity of denigrating the 'Grotesque school of history'. But from about 1930 onwards the whole empire-building ethic, for obvious reasons, became progressively more suspect amongst thinking people; and this moral change was bound to be reflected in the attitudes taken up by ancient historians. It is no accident that Mme Jacqueline de Romilly's *Thucydides and Athenian Imperialism* was conceived and written during the 1939-45 war; such a work, as Professor Aymard remarked in his review of the original French edition, '*ne pouvait pas davantage faire abstraction d'autres expériences impérialistes*.'

During the past two decades, indeed, a small but highly articulate minority group has been systematically attacking Athens' reputation for moral and cultural supremacy. Armed with the records of the Athenian tribute-lists, and indifferent to the high-flown phraseology of Pericles' Funeral Oration, they have set out to show that from start to finish the Athenian Empire was promoted by pride, ambition, and self-aggrandizement, justified by a naked might-is-right ethic, and largely tied up with economic necessities and ambitions. Mr Russell Meiggs' devastating analysis in *Harvard Studies* of Athens' attitude to her subject-allies, Professor Vogt's violently hostile judgment on Pericles, Professor Strasburger's suggestion that Thucydides must have had his tongue in his cheek when summing up the Periclean virtues—all these, and many more essays like them, depend on a roughly identical moral climate of opinion, with clear-cut, uncompromising attitudes to such phenomena as slavery, atrocities, imperial domination, economic blackmail, or anything savouring of dictatorship, however benevolent and aspiring the dictator himself may be.

Such scholars, of course, have an invaluable witness in Thucydides, whose grimly pessimistic view of the human condition corroborates their own findings all too well. For Thucydides there are no moral absolutes—or at any rate, none which concern him as a historian. Again and again he takes it as axiomatic that all human behaviour is dictated by self-interest. His own personal sympathies are with Athens; it is as a citizen of the *polis*, in exile or out of it, that he makes his judgments. Yet the basis for such judgments has nothing to do with right or wrong, and little with the common decencies. Most often the sole criterion is whether the results of such-and-such an action or decision are beneficial to Athens: the city-state has its own all-demanding morality. In the great Mytilene debate Diodotus, urging leniency, employs precisely the same arguments as Cleon, who proposed a general slaughter of the population; both alike claim that their ideas, if implemented, will bring Athens more revenue, and help her to keep the subject allies under control. It has been argued that Thucydides, here and elsewhere, is not expressing his own views but those of the various political leaders involved in the events he describes; this could just be true, but the whole atmosphere and style of the *History* militates against it. In one of his lesser-known essays Zimmern put the case admirably:

> Thucydides can see only too clearly, and explain only too poignantly, the effect of war upon states and societies; but he cannot see, or never lets us know that he sees, its effect upon individual men, women and children. He tells us how the wild Thracians broke into a school in the peaceful Boeotian village of Mycalessus; but he tells it as an illustration of the dangers attendant upon the employment of mercenaries. He tells us about the selling of the women and children of Melos and Scione into slavery; but he tells it, in his Machiavellian manner, to illustrate the stupidity of the Jingoes...

Like Talleyrand, Thucydides is far less worried by crimes than by blunders.

It is in this sense, as Mme de Romilly so clearly sees, that we must read his account of the Peloponnesian War. It is the story of an imperialistic venture: a venture, furthermore, which failed, and by its very nature was bound to fail. 'Moreover,' she comments significantly, 'nothing seems to lie beyond this failure, except the hope to begin all over again, as Athens later tried to do, and, if possible, to do better in the future. Nowhere does he suggest that other solutions are possible'. Self-interest and brute force are the natural condition of society; yet Thucydides seems to say, Athens at the peak of her greatness practised a moderation which transcended this concept, and her imperial ambitions were a praiseworthy striving towards greater glory. His harshest criticism is reserved for that later, more degenerate imperialism, in which no motives remain but fear, necessity, greed, and the desperate determination to retain power. But of course (and Thucydides must have known this as well as we do) the essential nature of imperialism remains unchanged, whatever steps its exponents may take to render it more acceptable. Slavery is not affected by one man, or even a thousand men, being kind to their slaves; neither the Parthenon nor the plays of Sophocles modify, however much they may mitigate, the political system which, directly or indirectly, brought them into being.

This, broadly speaking, is the central thesis of *Thucydides and Athenian Imperialism*, and Mme de Romilly develops it in great detail. She rightly emphasizes Thucydides' passion for abstracting the principle underlying any historical event, his tendency to see all history in terms of political or psychological laws, his isolation of the 'one unchanging principle' behind Athenian imperialism which 'progressively led Athens, in the most logical manner possible, to think and act in ways that were equally deplorable'. Those who embrace imperialism cannot stop in mid-passage; they must continue to conquer. The more conquests, the more enemies; the more enemies, the less security; the less security, the greater the oppression. It is a fear-inspired vicious circle. But Thucydides—unlike Isocrates, and in contrast to some of his own modern critics—never made the mistake of arguing that other nations had committed far worse crimes; on the contrary, he went back to first principles and declared that crimes of this sort were inherent in the general nature of imperialism. Apropos the Melian Dialogue, Mme de Romilly says of him:

> In their greater preoccupation with action, his Athenians show the enterprises of the strong not so much as being lawful but as being successful and habitual. He is concerned only with the way men behave, and his Athenians do not need the encouragement of a general philosophical system: they make no attempt to discover whether their action is lawful or not; it must be lawful, since everybody acts as they do. They are thus more realistic than the philosophers, at the same time as the ideas which they put forward are less revolutionary.

In other words, Thucydides' instinct to formulate general laws is no guarantee that the conclusions he reaches will be either adequate or valid; and the reason for this may be sought partly in his limited concept of human nature, and partly in his obvious personal veneration for Pericles.

It is this last factor, oddly enough, which exposes him most to criticism, because of the logically tenuous basis on which it rests. Professor Strasburger is not the first scholar to have noticed that the Funeral Speech is placed in a context which makes it a macabre mockery; and that even without that context, there is a cold, smug, priggish quality about certain passages which no amount of high idealism can wholly camouflage. Today we are, perhaps, more impervious to the rhetoric of empire than our grandfathers were; the climate has changed, and where they were stirred by the clarion-note of civilized achievement, we can only feel our blood chill at that icy indifference to individual human lives, that unshakable moral self-esteem, that dogmatic and mandarin-like complacency in the face of death and disaster. Yet Thucydides draws him as a statesman without equal, the First Citizen who ruled Athens' titular democracy with wisdom and foresight, and whose death was largely responsible for the disasters that followed. Once again, the material success and well-being of the *polis*—coupled in this case, one suspects, with strong personal admiration—seems to be the sole criterion determining the historian's verdict.

It would be surprising if this trend in Athenian historiography had not provoked a spirited response from the pro-Periclean traditionalists. But here an odd situation arose, which has never had quite the attention it deserves. The dating of events during the Pentakontaetia, the half-century which elapsed between the Persian and the Peloponnesian Wars, is extremely hazardous. Many crucial dates depend on epigraphical evidence: the Panathenaic Decree, Athenian regulations for various subject-allies, Cleinias' decree to enforce stricter tribute-collection, Clearchus' decree imposing uniform coinage, weights, and measures throughout the empire. Now by a generally accepted epigraphical law, no inscription embodying the 'three-bar sigma' can be dated later than 445 B C. This means that all the decrees and regulations mentioned above, which demonstrate Athenian imperialism in remarkably uncompromising terms, are pegged in the early period of Pericles' administration—rightly so, as I would maintain. But the need to defend Pericles is rather more pressing than it was, and some of this epigraphical evidence makes the task a hard one. So far only one scholar has had the idea—a logical if desperate one—of down-dating the whole lot into the 420s, after Pericles' death; his arguments, though extraordinarily ingenious, have not been generally accepted.

Far more persuasive is the theory advanced by an Oxford scholar, Mr G. E. M. de Ste Croix (it has already crept into at least one text-book as though proven) which sets out to destroy the validity of Thucydides' evidence concerning Athens' tyrannous domination and enslavement of the subject-allies. According to this theory, the picture of hate-filled vassals always trembling on the brink of revolt is conditioned by Thucydides' personal circumstances; he was rich, a large property-owner who moved in oligarchic circles and had no great love for true Athenian democracy (or indeed for democracy of any sort, so that the material he collected in subject cities came from an equally suspect source). On the contrary, Mr de Ste Croix asserts, the democracies were all for Athenian rule, which brought them considerable benefits; and Thucydides himself reveals the degree of their loyalty to the supposedly hated mistress of the Aegean.

But this theory will not stand up to close inspection. It is true that the democratic party in any city tended to be pro-Athenian, because that was where its natural support lay; this did not imply that the city valued its autonomy the less, or welcomed the presence of Athenian overseers and garrisons. The common (as opposed to the intellectual) mind tends to dislike planned benefits when they disturb cherished emotional beliefs. Seen in the light of reason, the imposition of Athenian coinage throughout the empire was an economic blessing, while the tribute was a small price to pay for Athenian protection. But to the unreasoning, stubborn allies, all these things spelt slavery; and the long melancholy series of revolts punctuating fifth-century Athenian history shows how much they were willing to forego for the chance of freedom. As Mme de Romilly says, 'Why should so many speeches mention autonomy as an ideal, at all periods, if it had been really outdone by political opposition, so as to have but a second place in the people's thought?'

A third way of getting around awkward or unpalatable facts, of course, is simply to ignore them, or dutifully mention them once, and then never refer to them again. This both Mme de Romilly and the late Sir Frank Adcock, in that otherwise brilliant little monograph *Thucydides and his History*, tend to do in the crucial field of economics, which as a branch of learning has probably done more to modify our views on ancient history than any other new discipline. When Sir Frank tells us that Athens 'had little to gain from any large-scale enterprise in Sicily', one can only wonder what he means by 'gain'. Fifth-century Athens was forced to import at least three-fifths of her grain (probably the percentage was much higher) and almost all her timber, so vital for the building of transports and triremes; both the Sicilian Expedition and its equally disastrous precursor to Egypt, forty years earlier, were designed to bring a major source of grain *within the Empire* (I have discussed this point more fully in my study of the Sicilian Expedition, *Armada from Athens*). This also explains Athens' endless forays in the timber-bearing regions of Thrace, Macedonia, and Chalcidice. Until such sources could be secured, Athens, though the greatest sea-power in the Aegean, would always be dependent for her two most necessary imports on the whim of some barbarian chieftain.

Mme de Romilly mentions these things, but does not seem to attach much importance to them. Having made the very promising observation that Thucydides 'does not discuss the reasons which, with the whole sea before them, make the fleets setting out from Piraeus sail in one direction rather than another', she goes on to say that the economic motive has been over-emphasized by modern writers, and that 'for a fifth-century Athenian, the rule over the sea is a sufficient end in itself'. This simply will not do. It is quite true that Thucydides—well aware though he is of economic considerations—always tends to look for the abstract concept behind them, so that he describes an expedition in terms of love of action or the need for power, but we are not obliged to follow his example. A chronic shortage of raw materials will affect people in any age, whatever their notions of history. As Grundy saw long ago, it is virtually impossible to explain the odd campaign topography of the Peloponnesian War except on economic grounds.

It is hard, bearing all this in mind, to understand how Sir Frank can speak of the Peloponnesian War as one 'in which so far as right and wrong prescribe the actions of states, Athens was in the right', except from the most immediate and superficial point of view. Quite deliberately, and over a period of years, Athens had set out to capture every available market in the Mediterranean, and, ultimately, to force the Peloponnesian *bloc* into a position of economic and political subservience. The Persian Wars gave her the opportunity—which Themistocles lost no time in taking—to capture the Ionian carrying-trade through the Bosporus to the Black Sea and south Russia; the development of the Delian League enabled her to build a large fleet and explore Western waters as far as the head of the Adriatic. She ousted Corinth from her profitable trade with Sicily; her alliance with Corcyra, on the sailing-route to Magna Graecia, showed all too clearly what the next step in this war of coercion would be. As a demonstration of Athenian power, an object-lesson in economic blackmail, Pericles got an embargo placed on all trade with the little state of Megara, close to the Isthmus of Corinth: the Megarians were soon reduced to near-starvation. These are some of the facts behind the fifth-century 'Athenian miracle', and there is no point in disregarding them. Thucydides did; but Thucydides had his own idiosyncratic concept of history, and would not, I suspect, be grateful for the excuses Sir Frank makes on his behalf—as when, discussing his failure to mention the raising of the tribute, he explains that 'it was not a time when he could study the epigraphical material'.

But such minor cavils apart, Sir Frank's monograph is percipient, wise, and eminently readable—which, alas, is more than can be said for *Thucydides and Athenian Imperialism*, despite a quite exemplary translation. Mme de Romilly has linked up her study of Athenian imperialism as such with a piecemeal assault on the fearful Hydra of Thucydidean composition, so that each section contains historical conclusions all mixed up with an analysis of how, and at what period, Thucydides may be presumed to have written some particular part of his work, such as Pericles' crucial speech after the unsuccessful expedition to Epidaurus. This latter problem is one that has exercised all Thucydidean scholars—often to the exclusion of practically everything else—for several decades, and both Sir Frank and Mme de Romilly agree that no final agreement is ever likely to be reached. Seldom, indeed, have so many scholars advanced so many conflicting views on one topic. But today the main division is between those who think Thucydides did no more than take notes or make rough drafts during the course of the war, waiting till the defeat of 404 before he put the *History* into its final form; and those who believe that he wrote it piecemeal as events dictated, dying while text and revision were still incomplete. Mme de Romilly is an adherent of the first school, and Sir Frank of the second; both on technical and on common-sensical grounds it must be conceded that Sir Frank makes out by far the better case.

He takes a number of crucial passages and argues, most convincingly, that each of them was written soon after the events it describes. Thucydides himself tells us that he began to write the history of the war from its outset, and there is no reason to suppose that he changed his methods later. Collecting information and writing it up year by year would account for the extraordinary freshness to be found in the narrative of events; besides, as Sir Frank says, it is unlikely that he would 'leave to an unknown future the achievement of what he had set himself to do'. In these pages the historian emerges as a human, if not wholly likable figure, soured by the plague of which he had been a victim, exiled for a mistake which he could scarcely have helped (though it was expensive enough: Amphipolis was the key port of Macedonia, controlling the Pangaeus mines as well as the northern timber-route) but grimly, and with fanatical obsession, continuing to gather the evidence for his *magnum opus* until (perhaps while sailing home from Thrace with his revised manuscript) he died, leaving an uncompleted torso to be 'the possession for ever' of which he boasted, and a perennial temptation to historians with more ingenuity than discretion.

Scholars seldom over-enthuse about each other's public lectures. Dog may not eat dog, but indiscriminate tail-wagging is also frowned on. Yet from the moment of their delivery, in March 1968, it was clear that Mr A. G. Woodhead's Martin Classical Lectures, now published as *Thucydides on the Nature of Power*, had created a quite exceptional impact. The precise nature of this impact was not so clear. Specialists not normally given to hyperbole talked of spellbound audiences and hypothetically dropped pins. There was a storm of conservative praise—a significant pointer—balanced by a lesser, though even more virulent, counterblast of radical disapproval. Mr Woodhead had, it was plain, gone to the emotional heart of the matter, and found it—as Thucydides foresaw—perennially relevant. Now, over two years later, we have the text of the lectures, more or less as they were delivered (though augmented with notes, references, and the occasional significant *arrière-pensée*); and even in cold print it is not hard to see what all the fuss was about.

To begin with, Mr Woodhead comes over as a superb rhetorician; not, perhaps, the first attribute one might expect to find in the sober editor of *Supplementum Epigraphicum Graecum*, but highly suggestive when related to his chosen subject. He is a pastmaster of persuasive oratory, who would have been quite at home in the Agora—or in Aristophanes' play *The Clouds*. He argues his case with antithetical panache and dramatically apposite *exempla*. (At the climax of his final lecture, for instance, he takes his American audience to Appomattox Court House, where he evokes the confrontation between Grant and Lee, and an opportunely tolling bell sets him meditating on John Donne and the universal relevance of history.) He is at great pains, moreover, to dissociate the concept of power from what he regards as intrusive and inapplicable moral considerations; and it is this, finally, which clinches the strong sense of *déjà vu* aroused by his whole approach. Mr Woodhead, to put it bluntly, is a kind of latter-day Sophist, a Gorgias of our time: Thucydides' models have rubbed off, with uncommon fidelity, on his modern interpreter. This at once suggests that we should scrutinize his political, social and moral propositions with something more than normal caution.

The warning is all the more necessary because at first reading —and even more, *a fortiori*, at first hearing—Mr Woodhead has the intoxicating, if suspect, irresistibility of a Verrall preface. He writes like a polyglot angel, and his sheer breadth of reading is highly impressive. Quite apart from the relevant classical sources, he makes formidable play with Hobbes, Burke, von Clausewitz, Hooker, Machiavelli, Dryden, Wordsworth and Defoe. To avoid any imputation of old-fashioned stuffiness, he also quotes J. M. Barrie, Jules Feiffer, Theodore H. White, and the *Journal of Abnormal and Social Psychology*. The only reason, one suspects, that he does not refer to Edward Lutwak's *Coup d'Etat* —a work very much in line with his central thesis—is that it appeared too late for him to make use of it. His historical parallels range from seventeenth-century Holland to contemporary Vietnam, from Augustus to Barry Goldwater. His declared approach to history is what we might expect from such catholicity: 'We suffer with the fifth-century Greeks, and we rejoice with them, because their sufferings and their joys are in essence our own, and as such are therefore of supreme importance to us.' Or, as he elsewhere puts it, one's first instinct when confronted with a study of the past will be to ask: 'What is there in it for *me*?'

So far, so good: in itself such a programme is unexceptionable. At the same time it, like Mr Woodhead's definition of power, is slightly unreal, and for very much the same reason. In both cases the apparent condition of neutrality can only be maintained by non-involvement, indeed by non-action. The moment power is actually used, rather than being regarded as a concept *in vacuo*, it becomes a moral act. The moment any individual, Mr Woodhead included, starts asking what there is in it for *him*, which fifth-century attitudes and individuals best illuminate *his* world, history becomes, if only at one level, an adjunct to political (or social, or psychological, or spiritual) autobiography. Ostensibly, Mr Woodhead is writing about Thucydides' attitude to power in various contexts—those of the *demos*, the élite, the individual, the military machine (Sparta), the Great Power (Persia), and public opinion. In the process, however, he reveals, as was bound to happen, a remarkable amount of his own *credo* concerning this thorny topic.

While at times both his candour and his commonsense are beyond all praise—soft-centred cant or emotionalism get very short shrift in these pages—he also (like Mr Enoch Powell, whom in many ways he resembles) displays a kind of genius for building ruthlessly logical hypotheses on wrong-headed (or at best highly debatable) underlying assumptions. He treats as axiomatic, for example, Hobbes' famous dictum on power in *Leviathan*, which, since he sets such store by it, is worth quoting at length:

> In the first place, I put for a general inclination of all mankind a perpetual and restless desire of Power after power, that ceaseth only in Death. And the cause of this is not always that a man hopes for a more intensive delight, than he has already attained to; or that he cannot be content with a moderate power; but because he cannot assure the power and means to live well, which he hath at present, without the acquisition of more.

In other words, power is not merely a commodity everyone wants, but something that can only maintain itself by expansion. To these related concepts Mr Woodhead returns again and again, either through quotations (for instance Defoe's 'Nature hath left this tincture in the blood/That all men would be tyrants if they could') or else in *propria persona*. They form the cornerstone of his thesis. Yet it is at least arguable that both are complete fallacies, the product of wishful thinking by a minority-group of power-hungry intellectual fantasists. Every reader must know many people, some of them even connected with public affairs, who possess not the faintest itch for power, tyrannical or otherwise. Furthermore, the old-fashioned concept of inevitable expansion (a popular stand-by with Hitler, among others) is looking pretty shop-soiled these days, too.

Mr Woodhead's second main contention throughout, as already indicated, is that not merely the concept but also (with certain rather hedging caveats) the *application* of power should be treated as something natural, inevitable, and *morally neutral*: at one point, indeed, he argues that 'the bases of public conduct are without moral connotation'. Again, it is the fundamental argument which arouses most suspicion. That power is neutral and its exercise inescapable has long been known, and Mr Woodhead argues the proposition with a cool professsionalism worthy of Critias (whose name, significantly, is never mentioned, though his totalitarian ghost peers at us from almost every page). But the moral neutrality of power in action is quite another matter: it can only be sustained, as Mr Woodhead makes abundantly clear during his exposition, by playing verbal and conceptual hopscotch with every basic principle of justice and common human decency in the world.

For him—as for Thucydides, as for Demosthenes—'all arguments revolve, when the cards are on the table, around the requirements of expediency and advantage.... Justice involved your *time* [honour], *ophelia* [self-interest], and *deos* [apprehension]; that was a fact of life, and there was no need to dress it up in camouflage'. When we find the conflict on Corcyra being described as a 'natural process', or hear about Plato, in the *Gorgias*, 'taking the Melian Dialogue to an extreme'—which presumably means enunciating the brutal principles behind it more bluntly than suits Mr Woodhead's book—we see pretty clearly into which neck of the political woods we have strayed. This impression is confirmed in detail when a reasoned apologia for the oligarchic revolution of 411 is closely followed by an equally plausible panegyric on hereditary aristocratic rule. What is more, Mr Woodhead makes it clear that, in his view, anyone who dissociates himself from this Machiavellian attitude is a mere hypocrite. Like so many self-styled realists, he can be oddly simplistic, not to say obtuse, about the mainsprings of human motivation. Sometimes it is not wholly clear whether he is advancing his own views or those he professes to find in Thucydides; but since both can be subsumed, broadly speaking, under the heading of intellectual elitism, this makes very little difference to the main issue.

It is true that Mr Woodhead anticipates opposition to his views, but he is oddly mistaken about the form such opposition is liable to take. He assumes that 'we' want Thucydides (and, by implication, his interpreter) to be committed against power as such because 'we' regard it as 'intrinsically immoral'. Surely this is a slip of the pen? But no; a page later he feels called upon to assure us that 'the possession of power, and the employment of the authority derived from it, were not questioned by the Greeks *as they are by us*' [my italics]. It may be otiose to assure the reader that this is not the case; but Mr Woodhead himself clearly needs enlightenment on the matter. No one in his right mind objects to power *as such* (one might as well object to a car having an engine); but its perversion to destructive or immoral ends is quite another matter, and its exercise generally has been the subject of debate and control since the first emergence of ordered government. It all turns, in fact, round that moral purpose which Mr Woodhead is doing his level best to dismiss as irrelevant.

Despite his assertiveness, however, the illogicality of his position seems to have nagged at him from time to time. He is for ever throwing nervous sops to the liberals: hence the absence of any reference to a real hard-liner like Critias. He admits, in an unguarded moment, that morality *does* affect the way in which power is exercised, whether to 'honourable' or 'dishonourable' ends (this, presumably, is for the benefit of old-fashioned aristocrats who, while regarding the rest of the population as *canaille*, still persist in living by their own private code). He sees, too, that if his basic position is sound, it cannot need justifying; amidst the brilliant logic-chopping one detects, from time to time, a faint but unmistakable twinge of guilt. However, he complains, popular opinion tends to be 'more emotional and sentimental, diverted from a strict reckoning of policy on the basis of expediency by the intervention of what people consider to be humane and moral factors'. Connoisseurs of totalitarian self-justificatory techniques (from either end of the political spectrum) will find themselves on familiar and well-trodden ground here. The possibility that such factors might not only be real, but might also outweigh all considerations of *Machtpolitik* for any society that wished to preserve itself from barbarism and the law of the (possibly affluent) jungle, simply does not enter into Mr Woodhead's scheme of things, any more than it entered into that propounded by Thucydides. One begins to see why he has, in the past, written articles vindicating two such apparently disparate characters as Cleon and Peisander. What they have in common is a penchant for ruthless political terrorism, in Peisander's case allied with right-wing revolutionary activities.

On the basis of all this it would be easy—too easy—to dismiss *Thucydides on the Nature of Power* out of hand as half-baked and at times pernicious intellectual totalitarianism. Some of the evidence that could be cited to support such a charge is superficial enough; but some, again, is not. A hawkish attitude to the atomic balance of power, and an obvious admiration for Senator Barry Goldwater, though they will not win Mr Woodhead cheers from party-line liberals, are hardly evidence for moral wrong-headedness. The most serious consequence of his anti-moralist stance is that he seldom cares to distinguish between degrees of moral guilt. At times, too, his attitude to power is such that one wonders if he really understands, after all, what power *means*, or has ever witnessed its more unpleasant consequences at first-hand. One line in Auden's poem *Spain*, 'the conscious acceptance of guilt in the necessary murder', led George Orwell to remark, tartly, that 'it could only be written by a person to whom murder is at most a *word*'. One feels much the same about Mr Woodhead, not least when he makes his impassioned apologia for Antiphon, a page or two after blandly detailing the propaganda, double-think and executions, and the use of 'front men' (including Sophocles, though Mr Woodhead omits to say so) that were needed to make the 411 revolution even a temporary success:

> If our own political predilections cannot allow us to approve of what he stood for, we must acknowledge his right to stand for it, and we cannot but applaud the virtues of principle, thought and action which he brought to the championship of his right.

Three cheers for Hitler, Stalin, De Gobineau, the Inquisition, Julius Streicher, the organizers of the Bukharin trials, and the present governments of Greece and Czechoslovakia. Ripeness is all.

Yet in the last resort, even when we come upon such a passage as this, Mr Woodhead ends by compelling our admiration for his sheer stubborn determination to achieve historical honesty, however unfashionable or unpalatable the resultant picture may be. (How far he succeeds in this aim is quite another matter; it might also be argued, with some plausibility, that his conscious mind is not always one hundred per cent in control of his unconscious motivation.) If, in academic innocence, he has not fully appreciated the dangers of playing with fire, at least, like G. Mucius Scaevola, having once thrust his hand into the flames he keeps it there to the bitter end. What is more, he can claim a respectable intellectual ancestry for his views: the tradition that runs from Thucydides and the Sophists through Machiavelli and Hobbes to Nietzsche is not one lightly to be dismissed—though in the mid-twentieth century it is appallingly explosive material unless handled with extreme care. None of these thinkers, it is safe to say, and Thucydides least of all, ever took a neutral attitude to power, as Mr Woodhead would have us believe. Where he is far more convincing, and sheds much light on fifth-century *mores* as a whole, is in his analysis of Thucydides' attitude to popular government. He sees (as indeed Hobbes saw before him) that Thucydides, like Antiphon and the oligarchs generally, worked from an essentially aristocratic code of values.

The positive side of this code (as variously exemplified by, say, Homer, Theognis or Pindar) is clear enough: elitism has its virtues, and today it is as well that we should, now and then, be reminded of them. Mr Woodhead rightly emphasizes that Thucydides accepted 'a code of morals in which keeping one's word, being generous, and acting according to the virtues of justice are higher in the scale than life, wealth', etc. On the other hand he also makes it pretty clear, in another context, that 'justice' was all too often equated with 'expedience'—a view he appears to endorse. Still, Athenian right-wingers, from the Old Oligarch to Critias, were (whatever we think of their attitudes) intelligent, sincere and dedicated men: we do them an injustice if we suppose less, and this book drives the point home in a way that cannot be forgotten. Also, many of Thucydides' strictures against popular radical government—its excesses, factionalism and lack of judgment or proper training: Plato's 'government based on ignorance'—are all too well founded; and Mr Woodhead does not let us forget that either. The relevance of these points to the contemporary scene should be obvious enough.

Yet a point comes (and in fact came during the fifth century) when the aristocratic concept of government, the monopolistic nexus of blood, capital, breeding and virtue, must inevitably break down. Tribal dogma has no logical place in the *polis*. '*Kratos* [power]', says Mr Woodhead, summarizing Thucydides, 'must be exercised with *sophrosyne* [moderation, restraint] on the basis of *gnome* [sound judgment].' It is all rather like the gentlemen-radicals of the late nineteenth century, living on centuries of accumulated moral capital, and ineradicably paternalistic as a result. The reason why dynamic power should be exercised with *sophrosyne* is revealed elsewhere by Thucydides: he observes that thus 'the victims of it are less liable to create disturbances and commit atrocities'. We all know this approach: it is the well-tried dictum about being kind to your slaves. But unfortunately a time comes when being kind to your slaves will no longer serve: the only solution is to abolish slavery. In other words, a moral principle must be established, and an end made of tinkering with the *status quo*. This is a crucial distinction, which advocates of elitism and reform from within seldom grasp; a good many aristocratic or oligarchic governments have foundered on it. It is also, paradoxically, one of the great dangers besetting an 'open society' of the sort advocated by Sir Karl Popper: in the last resort, 'piecemeal social engineering' is no substitute for a firm moral stand, which needs to be implicit beneath all the empirical maintenance-work.

Mr Woodhead is at his best when he leaves general considerations and modern parallels (not always aptly chosen: there is all the difference in the world between an Englishman paying income-tax and an Athenian subject-ally paying the *phoros*) and deals with special fifth-century topics. His analysis of Sparta's and Persia's respective roles in Greek history is superb. He correctly isolates the 'fatal elements of indecision and inflexibility in the Spartan character', and has a memorable summing-up of Persia as 'a monolith with cracks known and exploited, but still great enough to be awe-inspiring'. On the other hand, he seems to have been absurdly (but revealingly) over-dazzled by the factitious and fly-blown charisma of Alcibiades, whom he brackets with Churchill and Garibaldi (I can't help feeling that in the latter context D'Annunzio might have provided a more apt parallel). Byron once remarked, with justice, that it was hard to recall what battles Alcibiades won; until well after the Sicilian Expedition his career had little to show for it but flashy political intrigue, military incompetence, and spiteful betrayal (unless one counts those chariot victories at the Olympic Games, which after all, were simply paid for, not achieved in person).

Perhaps, though, this hero-worship of Alcibiades gives us a

clue to Mr Woodhead's own attractive if baffling personality. He is not, after all, an oligarchic *éminence grise*, but something at once less sinister and more endearing: a passionate right-wing romantic, whose panache (unlike Cyrano's) is hidden beneath a modest cloak of unassuming—but highly formidable—scholarship, and who, in another age, would have charged with Prince Rupert at Edgehill, or have stood sword in hand beside Rudolf (Rassendyll) to uphold the royal honour of Ruritania. It is one of the sad problems besetting our own times that there seems, to-day, no honourable place for a man of this temper—and too many questionable lost causes (or successful rackets) to tempt his allegiance. Nature abhors a vacuum of any sort; the phenomenon demands closer study than it seems to have had hitherto.

Athens and Jerusalem

I

THE ART of history, as Professor M. I. Finley reminded us some years ago, is neither a natural nor an instinctive function of the human mind; but when we turn to the philosophy of history—that conveniently elastic term—it is quite another matter. Though man may require a certain rational impetus in order to study his past, he has never lacked the urge to excogitate ingenious *a priori* explanations for the world he has inherited. These explanations take many and wonderful forms, ranging from elaborate cosmologies to notions of challenge-and-response, from cyclic myths to economic statistics. But one feature most of them seem to share is a kind of creeping monadism. A philosopher of history, in fact, somewhat resembles a patent-medicine huckster bawling his wares in the market-place. He not only is convinced that he has found the elixir of life, the key that will fit all historical locks; he also spends a good deal of his energy assuring all comers that his rivals across the way are either knaves or fools. Cross the road, of course, and you will hear the same story repeated with a change of names.

Owing to various accidents of modern thought (not least among which have been the spread of semantics and developments in post-Positivist philosophy) critical attention is today focussed very strongly on the underlying principles of historical method. This is not to say that the critics agree amongst themselves, much less that the picture they present necessarily bears any real relation to what is going on amongst the historians. Mr Patrick Gardiner, the learned editor of that useful anthology, *Theories of History*, offers us (to take a handy example) what might be termed the rationalist party line. In the bad old days, says Mr Gardiner, speculative philosophies of history flourished *pari passu* with elaborate metaphysical theory. But since then a violent and welcome reaction has set in. The Last Post has been played over the metaphysicians (though some of them—one feels tempted to interject at this point—have insisted, embarrassingly, on sitting up and arguing the toss in their coffins on the way to the cemetery) and apriorism of any sort has been jeered out of court by historian and philosopher alike. The practising historians have striven to refine a technique which will eliminate observer-error and achieve true objectivity, while their critics have claimed, pessimistically and with some justice, that objectivity is (in this field at least) an unobtainable chimera. Analogies from the natural sciences, biology, and philosophy have been employed by every interested party, with chaotic results. In the dust of battle Clio herself has rather been lost sight of; and it hardly takes a cynical historicist to point out that Mr Gardiner's picture of the brave new rationalist dawn is so exaggerated as to be faintly comic. If ever there was an age in which disinterested reason was at a discount among philosophers of history, this is it. The old slogans are with us still, and have taken unto themselves a whole swathe of new ones as well.

Oh those splendidly presumptuous giants of economic or metaphysical speculation (often, one fears, indistinguishable) who never doubted that laws of a sort governed the human universe, and trusted that human history was moving towards an ultimately predictable future: Vico and Kant and Condorcet, Herder and Hegel, Comte and J.S.Mill, Marx and Plekhanov, Spengler and Toynbee—the last two, I can't help feeling, whales left stranded on our gritty modern beach as the large, self-assured, speculative tide of nineteenth-century metaphysics ebbed gradually out. Here are the mighty-voiced hucksters indeed, bellowing abstractions about Progress and Class and Universal Laws and Dialectical Materialism and the Science of History and heaven knows what else. So much for the death of apriorism. It has often been argued—and Mr Gardiner's anthology bears witness to the truth of the claim—that historical facts (not to mention practising historians) obstinately refuse to accommodate themselves to the theoretical principles laid down for them by philosophers. Professor Hempel's famous paper on 'The Function of General Laws in History' required so much subsequent qualification and tinkering that its principles degenerated into mere vague abstractions. Most serious historians have always veered by instinct in the direction of empirical thought, wisely preferring inductive to deductive methods, and recognizing that the human propensity for seeing and making patterns is one that they can well do without as a profession.

It is worth pointing out, however, since confusion would appear to exist on the matter, that empiricism and rationalism (let alone atheism) are not by definition identical. Since one of the most hotly debated methodological problems today centres on the historian himself—how far is he inevitably biassed? how much must we allow for his own historico-social context?—it is instructive to use Mr Gardiner, *qua* editor, as a test case with which to introduce the main subject of this discussion. As a good scholar he takes care to include views of every shade and persuasion—with one glaring and predictable omission. Apart from Dr Toynbee, who is in any case a religious law unto himself, theological historicists are conspicuous by their absence. Nothing from the *Civitas Dei* or Bishop Bossuet or Father Martin D'Arcy or Professors Christopher Dawson and Jacques Maritain: Mr Gardiner's position—a by no means isolated one—seems to be that of a rationalist, non-believing philosopher who *takes it as axiomatic* that religion is nonsense, and therefore simply did not find such troglodytic writers relevant to his subject. It hardly needs pointing out that such an attitude is no whit less aprioristic than anything in the works of the writers omitted: a view which gains confirmation from Mr Gardiner's remarks concerning those 'patterns or models which the philosopher . . . feels should represent the structure of any historical explanation worthy of the name'. In other words, there have got to be general historical laws in order to let the moral scientists keep a finger in the historical pie; but at the same time God is a dirty word which can conveniently be forgotten.

But God, like Nature, cannot be quite so easily disposed of. A quarter of a century, perhaps even a decade ago, few thinking people would seriously have proposed that historians should allow in their investigations for the workings of Divine Providence. Theological historicism, it was assumed, had died with the eighteenth-century encyclopedists, and now had no more than antiquarian interest. God, like some awkward algebraical factor, was omitted altogether from the calculations of most modern historians. They did not (with some few exceptions) explicitly declare themselves rationalists: they did not need to. Their position was apparent enough from what they wrote: they simply shelved the problem as though it did not exist. Their business was with the tangible activities of human beings; they dealt in written testimony and artifact. The impalpable, they implied, was beyond their jurisdiction (though this did not stop them using their own brand of moral yardstick); and the persistent superstitions of an uneducated general public could be conveniently dismissed with knowledgeable references to the Keynesian time-lag which operated in the dissemination of informed opinions.

Today, however, the picture presents a considerably altered appearance, and there are paradoxical features about it which would have delighted Chesterton. For some time now the liberal concept of historical method (and indeed liberalism generally as an intellectual and moral *credo*) has been subjected to increasingly heavy criticism. The grounds of attack are diverse, and some of them carry considerable weight. Liberalism is blamed for its arbitrary emphasis on secular postulates, for 'denying the indelible mystery and ambiguities of human experience'. Modern philosophers (and many scientists) deride the notion that complete objectivity of intellectual judgment is an attainable end; and the doctrine of infinite human perfectibility has also been pretty roughly handled—not least by disillusioned ex-Communists. The oddly naive idea that material advancement and growth of moral stature would inevitably progress hand in hand finds few takers in this atomic age.

Ethical relativism and *ad hoc* social or political legislation are widely blamed for all or any of our present ills, from totalitarianism to the hippy cult, from atheism to *Angst*. Empirical philosophy, anthropocentric humanism, pseudo-scientific dogma and a wholesale rejection of absolute values—these are rapidly becoming, as it were, the triggers in the stockpile.

Such a profound and radical reaction against the whole tradition of the past two hundred years—a reaction which has been aptly labelled the 'Retreat from Reason'—must inevitably contain within it the seeds of an obscurantism at least as dangerous as anything it sets out to replace. With infinite pain and labour, progressing by slow degrees, learning from his errors, man has, over the centuries, built an instrument of thought to guide his inquiries, and to protect him (so far as is humanly possible) from the myriad fallacies and self-deceptions which are his natural inheritance. Inductive logic, methods of definition and verification, proper consideration of evidence, allowance for observer-error, the clarification of language as a communicative medium—these, and these alone, are the barriers which stand between us and the mindless abyss. There will always be new truths to be learnt, unsuspected errors to be rectified, old assumptions to be discredited and discarded. That continues as a central tenet of what may loosely be described of the scientific method; and indeed, the opponents of an over-restrictive (and over-dogmatic) rationalism have a most valuable function to perform in this field. The real danger of the 'Retreat from Reason' is its liability to endanger common understanding. As Mr Charles Frankel observed in *The Case for Modern Man*, 'the appeal to absolutes is intellectually stultifying and socially disruptive because it introduces considerations for which there is no common evidence'.

The attack has been mounted almost exclusively by Christian apologists of one sort or another—from historians and philosophers of history to theologians, mystics, and the wilder species of apocalyptic visionary, for whom history appears to have stopped short with Archbishop Ussher, if not actually at the

Book of Revelations. There are several good reasons for this. In the first place—a factor which should never be underestimated, whatever its ultimate significance—the current climate of popular feeling is decidedly favourable to such an approach. The whole point about Dr Toynbee's *A Study of History* is that it found a vast and enthusiastic audience, even though its premisses and conclusions had been torn to shreds by countless European and American historians. Man's ineradicable 'natural Platonism', his obsession with symbols, his hunger to discover an overall pattern in history, his terror of ultimate chaos —all these are frequently presented as a good and valid reason for erecting such all-embracing frameworks: a startling proposition against which even such formidable Christian scholars as Father D'Arcy and Professor Maritain are not wholly proof. Most professional historians, it is true, have dug themselves more and more deeply into positions of entrenched rationalism (sometimes, I suspect, simply by way of protest); but even they are beginning to feel the inadequacy of their premisses. Professor Barraclough, for instance, has this to say on the subject:

> If [history] is to contribute towards an intelligent, well-informed and critical judgment of the problems of modern society, radical revision is necessary. In the first place, we must combat the fragmentation which has overtaken history, and accustom ourselves, once again, to look at the past as a whole; for unless we have a positive ideal of universal history, our history will inevitably tend to be less than universal. Secondly, we must seek for history an end outside itself—as it had, for example, when it was viewed as a manifestation of the working of God's providence. That statement is not intended to imply a return to a theological view of history (which, whether desirable or not, I regard as impracticable today); but it does mean that its study should have a constructive purpose and a criterion of judgment, outside and beyond the historical process.

That goes a good deal farther than most of his professional colleagues would commit themselves; Mr Alan Bullock, who has strenuously resisted any attempt 'to annex history to a metaphysical system' is probably typical of the general academic attitude. But during the past decade or two the wider public has shown itself more and more sympathetic towards the Christian apologists (heterodox or orthodox according to whether one looks at them primarily as historians or theologians). When in 1948 this outflanking movement was endorsed by Professor Butterfield, with his famous and immensely popular Cambridge lectures on 'Christianity and History', the writing was plain on the wall for all who cared to see it.

II

Historical loose thinking on the part of Christian historians (and examples could be multiplied almost *ad infinitum*) does not mean that they have not got a good deal to say which less committed scholars will ignore at their peril. I will return to this point later. But it does raise a vital issue of first principles. The Christian, in his consideration of the past, cannot but view it *sub specie aeternitatis*. He must accept the doctrines of the Fall, of Redemption, of the Second Coming: the 'intersection of the timeless with time', and all that this implies. He must reconcile the conflicting claims of Providence and Free Will. Above all, perhaps, he must ask himself whether purely temporal history can, in Christian terms, have any ultimate meaning at all; whether his Kingdom is, quite literally, not of this world. Without judging the spiritual validity of these claims one way or the other (a point over which too many secular historians have shown themselves as dogmatic as any Jesuit) it still remains true that they erect an impassable barrier between those who hold them and those who do not.

The barrier consists, precisely, in the use of absolute or transcendental criteria as such. The essence of theological historicism involves an act of faith which entirely eludes normal verification, and thus produces that failure of communication which Mr Frankel describes. It may be that the Christian concept of history is, in fact, the true one; but if so, it has been reached, in the most literal sense, by guess and by God, by Divine Revelation and suspension of reason. Once this crucial point is clear, it should become apparent that attempts to integrate it with liberal or scientific historiography must founder *ab initio*: the two systems rest on mutually unacceptable axioms. This insuperable difficulty does not prevent ingenious scholars and churchmen from performing miracles of doublethink in an effort to bridge the gap. The result is a curious, prolonged quarrel, in which each contestant appears to be shouting at the top of his voice in a language which nobody understands but himself. On the surface, at least, the secular historians have an initial advantage, in that their main role is a critically destructive one, analogous to that of a political opposition. As each new transcendental or apocalyptic theory is put up, they shoot it down briskly with a concentrated salvo of anti-metaphysical logic; it is like an audience of tone-deaf mathematicians throwing rotten eggs at a romantic concert pianist.

Theological historicists, on the other hand, have displayed an understandable but disastrous weakness for trying to convince the ungodly by borrowing their own weapons of argument. This ill-advised attempt to marry absolutism with scientific method has, perhaps, done more than anything else to discredit the whole movement among serious students. Mr Gerald Heard's efforts to give a moral purpose to biology, Père Teilhard de Chardin's attempted reconciliation of Christianity with evolution (which, *inter alia*, predicts a cultural super-organism developing in a direct line from physical mutations), the eschatological futurism of Josef Pieper: such works may give comfort of a sort to the faithful, but they also provide a field-day for irreverent intellectuals. Where they fail conceptually is in the divided nature of their premisses: their authors might have remembered the impossibility (according to Holy Writ) of serving both God and Mammon—not to mention that of putting new wine into old bottles, or *vice versa*.

Once the advocate of theological historicism enters the secular arena, and endeavours to justify himself among the Gentiles, he multiplies difficulties for himself. To take one obvious example, empirical historians have constantly asserted that it is none of a historian's business to make predictions. Sir Karl Popper, to look no further, is for ever belabouring us with this proposition. Yet Popper's own case offers pause for thought: when we look into it more closely we see that emotionalism is not a monopoly of the theologians, and that (as in Thucydides' case) claims to strict objectivity often have a touch of dexterous thimble-rigging about them. There is such a daunting air of dispassionate scientific precision about works like *The Poverty of Historicism* or *The Open Society and its Enemies* that we would do well to remind ourselves when, and in what circumstances, they were actually written. Both appeared (*The Poverty of Historicism* in a learned periodical) towards the end of the last war; and one of them is inscribed 'in memory of the countless men and women of all creeds or nations or races who fell victims to the fascist and communist belief in Inexorable Laws of Historical Destiny'. Sir Karl, for all his scholarship, is a passionately angry man, committed to free liberalism, like his contemporary George Orwell, with the fierce devotion of a Jesuit evangelist. It is as though he were holding his own private Nuremberg Trials, arraigning political criminals in some High Court of Scientific Justice. The charge against Marx is an obvious one; Hegel is presented as the philosopher who inspired not only 'the Marxist extreme left wing' but also 'the conservative centre and the fascist extreme right'; while Plato with his ideals (*ideals* is the dirtiest word in Sir Karl's vocabulary: where, one wonders, does that leave his own? perhaps one should emend to *other people's* ideals) gets the shortest shrift of the lot: he is the ultimate ancestor of every shade of totalitarianism, a view for which a good case can be made out, and Sir Karl duly makes it.

In *The Poverty of Historicism* he extends his campaign to take in what may roughly be described as the historical pattern-makers. A scientist himself, he deals very briskly with the misapplication to history of methods more appropriate to physics. 'In many historicist and evolutionary writings,' he observes, 'it is often impossible to discover where metaphor ends and serious theory begins.' So much for our poor theologian—not to mention Comte and Mill. The exponents of a pseudo-biological 'life-cycle of civilizations' provoke even more scathing comments. Sir Karl first sets up the historicists' skittles for them (rather better, as he suggests with pardonable complacency, than they could do for themselves), and then proceeds to knock them all down, demonstrating in the process a cool expertise and undisguised relish. Once again one gets serious doubts about his scientific objectivity: could it be (alarming thought) that the whole battle is simply a head-on emotional clash between irreconcilable temperaments, each seeking to advance behind a shield of what purports to be objective scholarship? And when Sir Karl has, single-handed, purged the Augean Stables of Platonic, Hegelian and Marxist social theory, what, we may ask, is left at the end? Just as we might expect, our old friend political empiricism, disguised under the unlovely title of 'piecemeal social engineering'.

The curious thing is that I doubt whether anybody is one penn'orth the worse for Sir Karl's comprehensive anathema. Mankind can be divided into analysts and synthetists, myth-makers and myth-breakers; Sir Karl simply belongs to the latter camp. For those who believe, no explanation is necessary, and no rational argument convincing. For those who do not believe, no explanation is possible, and no argument needed. It is not only the cuckoo who shouts all day at nothing; and at this point one is tempted to ask oneself for just whose benefit Sir Karl may be writing. Not, surely, for the rational historians: none of them still takes historicism ('this antique and tottering philosophy') with any degree of seriousness. Not, I presume, for the historicists themselves, who are no more to be argued out of their beliefs than a Marxist or a Catholic convert, and who will remain unmoved by Sir Karl's shrewdest short-arm jabs:

> To present such a venerable idea as bold and revolutionary betrays, I think, an unconscious conservatism.... After all, it may be the historicists who are afraid of change. Is it perhaps a

> fear of change which makes them so incapable of reacting rationally to criticism, and which makes others so responsive to their teaching? It really looks as if historicists were trying to compensate themselves for the loss of an unchanging world by clinging to the belief that change can be foreseen because it is ruled by an unchanging law.

At this point it is not only Plato's ghost who asks 'What then?' Only after a long while does the odd realization steal over us that Sir Karl is really talking to *himself*, marshalling all his resources of logic and rational faith to find an identifiable scapegoat for the monstrous horrors Europe has endured during the last half-century. Both *The Open Society* and *The Poverty of Historicism*, thus considered, are tracts against determinist dogma, extended polemical arguments designed to prove that the whole world—all mankind, Sir Karl would say—is not essentially and irremediably damned. At which point the theologian might well murmur, with a smile of recognition, '*Mon semblable, mon frère!*'

The main argument, however, stands. Not only Popper and Sir Isaiah Berlin, but (from a rather different viewpoint) Christian scholars such as Professor C. S. Lewis, have brought up a wealth of evidence to show that *all* 'philosophies of history' are, broadly speaking, moonshine, resting on false abstractions, unjustifiable generalizations, and necessarily insufficient data. Even Professor Butterfield, in *History and Human Relationships*, has modified his position to the point where he can observe that 'the kind of ethical judgments which historians like Lord Acton have been anxious to achieve are possible only to God'. It is in this intelligent and highly critical (if also highly emotional) ambience that the committed theological historicist must attempt to justify, not only a complete philosophy of history, but a predictive eschatology as well: the former (according to Professor Maritain) 'inevitably requires prophetic data'. He has a hard row to hoe; and he can hardly complain if his opponents assert that he put most of the stones there himself.

There is, moreover, an observable tendency among Christian

philosophers of history—especially those who, like Father D'Arcy, attempt to present their thesis in terms acceptable outside the circle of the faithful—to drag in Revealed Truth when all else fails, as though it were a wild deuce in the historical pack. 'It would not do,' Father D'Arcy writes, 'for a student to answer every question in history by saying that it was the finger of God.... It is when we have reconstructed the whole of human life and found it not self-explanatory that we must turn to religion.' This is having it both ways with a vengeance. In the first place, the student who holds what may be termed the Redemptive view of history cannot but see the finger of God everywhere; while the student who does not must regard Divine Providence as a phenomenon beyond his range of competence. A half-way position seems untenable on every count. Secondly, to reconstruct the whole of human life (as Professor Maritain points out) is beyond human powers; and thus in effect the religious explanation will become a mere substitute for baffled logic. This method of solving residual problems which resist normal investigation will hardly commend itself to genuine seekers after truth, whatever their personal beliefs.

One logical answer is that of an extremist like Karl Barth, who rejects liberal theology *in toto*, and denies any connexion at all between secular and divine history—a conclusion which both adheres to New Testament eschatology in the strictest possible way, and, incidentally, leaves the uncommitted historian free to operate at large within the temporal sphere. But, as Father D'Arcy candidly admits, 'if Barth be right then any hope of finding a Christian philosophy of history must be abandoned': in the long and complicated discussion which follows, this remark lingers uncomfortably at the back of one's mind. Father D'Arcy argues with great skill and finesse, quoting Père Malevez's conception of the Church as 'the extension of Christ in time' and Abbot Butler's ingenious theory of 'provenient grace' in an effort to reconcile Christian self-abnegation with the conflicting tradition of Christian humanism. Nevertheless, in the last resort he is once more forced back on Faith; and the whole argument suggests that the wish has here, as elsewhere, been father to the thought. At least one reader was left with the impression that the chief talent of Christian historicists is the art of squaring the spiritually desirable with the logically impossible.

This dilemma can be studied in its most acute form by an examination of the problems which Providence, free will, and determination raise for the Christian historian, and to which both Father D'Arcy and Professor Maritain devote considerable space, the first in *The Sense of History: Secular and Sacred*, the second in his monograph *On the Philosophy of History*. Since they are precluded theologically from accepting any form of scientific or idealist determinism (a point on which, rather improbably, they see eye to eye with Popper) they can and do launch a devastating attack (as does he) on non-Christian or overtly determinist philosophers of history: Schopenhauer, Nietzsche, Auguste Comte, Spencer, Spengler and Marx are all examined and found wanting. Hegel in particular comes in for a concerted cross-fire. He takes Progress for granted; he identifies Providence with the dialectic process; he is guilty of an ambiguous quasi-pantheism; he postulates a bogus abstraction called the *Weltgeist*, and regards himself as a kind of philosopher-god (a position which, we may recall, Professor Trevor-Roper once suggested that Dr Toynbee laid claim to). Paradoxically, such criticism will probably appeal more to convinced rationalists than to religious-minded (but doctrinally uncommitted) students of history. Hegel, Professor Maritain writes, 'warped and spoiled the philosophy of history in a pernicious way, because of his effort to re-create history—as well as the whole cosmos—as the self-movement through which eternal Reason, that is to say God, actualizes Himself in time (and finally reveals Himself in Hegelian wisdom).' Obviously such a view must be untenable by any orthodox Christian; yet the immediate and uncompromising rejection of so suggestive a theory demonstrates, as nothing else could, the rigid limitations within which Maritain and Fr D'Arcy are forced to work.

Obviously, as Fr D'Arcy recognizes, the gap between Providence and determinism is a very narrow one. While rejecting the sweeping historical assumptions and whole-hogging enthusiasms of the pre-Voltairean theologians ('Providence does not let us into the divine secrets to the extent demanded by Bossuet', he remarks, with ironic candour) Fr D'Arcy nevertheless stoutly maintains that Christian Providence is not, in any sense, determinist. Providence, he asserts, 'works in and through the freedom of individual men and women, and its law is love'. This agrees well enough with Professor Maritain's assertion: 'The true conception is that the divine plan is immutable *once fixed* from all eternity. But it is only fixed from all eternity *with account taken of the free default of man*, which God sees in His eternal present.' Yet shortly afterwards Professor Maritain also writes that 'the absolutely ultimate end, the final end of history is beyond history'. Furthermore, Fr D'Arcy quotes with approbation Newman's claim that 'God can quicken, stimulate, supersede, modify or give fresh direction to the powers of nature or the laws of society'. Such a compromise would seem to produce an arbitrary and intermittent determinism that leaves the situation more confused than ever.

It is no accident, I feel, that Fr D'Arcy leans so heavily on Vico, who produced an ingenious theory which might briefly be described as Progress tempered by Providence. Yet in the last resort we may legitimately ask whether there is any ultimate *raison d'être* for such theorizing. It will not satisfy the sceptical, while to the converted it may well seem supererogatory. Both Fr D'Arcy and Professor Maritain start from major theological axioms, on which the whole foundation of their discourse rests. When the secular historian reads, in Fr D'Arcy's introduction, that 'appeal is made to doctrines, which are accepted on faith and lie, therefore, outside the domain of the historian,' he may well be tempted to shut the book and read no further, objecting (as Fr D'Arcy himself makes him do) 'that the Incarnation ... or the Redemption have no more to do with history than Original Sin with anthropology'. If he does so, however, he will be making a great mistake; for while Fr D'Arcy and Professor Maritain are unlikely to convert him to Christian historicism, they will teach him a good deal about his own errors, omissions, fallacies and unconscious dogmas.

Most important of all, perhaps, he will be forced to reconsider his position and principles as a historian. 'What is most important in history?' Mr Frankel asks. 'Is it ideas or faith, technology or great men, property systems or geography?' For all his large claims to open-mindedness and empirical method, the liberal historian too often either takes these questions for granted or deliberately by-passes them as irrelevant. Here Fr D'Arcy has some cogent remarks to make:

> Trained in the art of weighing evidence a historian can know how to avoid exaggeration and jumping to conclusions; he can apportion the degree of certainty belonging to each statement he and his fellows make. He is, however, seldom interested in giving a philosophical justification of historical knowledge; it is sufficient for him that other historians, critics and intelligent readers should be in agreement on what is the subject matter of history and what are the standards of judgment. Like the answer to a famous puzzle, *solvitur ambulando*.

This is a dangerous position. The assumption that history can be measured in exclusively secular terms is a dogma. The relativist rejection of evil, the belief that 'moral disagreements are merely matters of taste'—this, too, is a dogma. The concept of force or *Machtpolitik* as the final directive of social authority, the underlying notion that 'the satisfaction of human desires is the entire substance of morality and the purpose of all history'—these constitute perhaps the most arbitrary dogmas of all.

The complacency implicit in such an ambivalent attitude may be largely ascribed to the profoundly unscientific assumption that a liberal historian can ever achieve full objectivity of method. Human nature being what it is, objectivity has been far too often identified with the desired end; and thus an imposing empirical edifice is often built up on grossly prejudiced axiomatic foundations. Karl Mannheim saw this fallacy very clearly. His criticisms might perhaps have had a wider impact had he not wedded them to a wildly Platonic scheme in which an intellectual élite was to unite and correct the various astigmatic views of historians throughout the world. Would-be universalism is the curse of any philosopher of history; and it is, incidentally, a curse which (by reason of their *a priori* assumptions) alights from time to time on Fr D'Arcy and Professor Maritain. To assume, as the Christian must assume, an absolute scale of moral values makes for considerable difficulty in assessing a pre-Christian or non-Christian civilization. Not surprisingly, both writers are silent concerning the influential modern school which treats history in terms of socio-anthropological 'cultures'.

There is no denying, however, that both scholars, Fr D'Arcy in particular, give the sceptical empiricists a very good run for their money. Fr D'Arcy comments forcefully on the *ad hoc* nature of much modern thought, pointing out how theories of progress have tended under pressure of events to be replaced by theories of pessimism. (This criticism, though, tends to back-fire; it is just as applicable, one would have thought, to St Augustine as to Spengler.) He is every whit as caustic as Sir Karl Popper—though not, one suspects, for quite the same reasons—about the attempts to assimilate history to the physical or biological sciences, not to mention the relativist's assumption of continual change and development in history. Seldom, too, can the functional limitations of logical thought have been more forcefully presented: this section of Fr D'Arcy's thesis is a masterly achievement.

Where he may seem less successful is in his criticisms of the secular historian for ignoring, minimizing, or falsely evaluating the religious factor in any discussion or interpretation of the past. There is a very clear distinction (better recognized today, perhaps, than it was fifty years ago) between accepting the transcendental truth of a religious phenomenon, and allowing fully for its influence on human motives and actions. This distinction Fr D'Arcy does not always make clear. An agnostic scholar, even an atheist, is not debarred by his convictions either from understanding the religious temperament or from assessing historical events dictated by religious motives: indeed, the very neutrality which he professes may enable him to steer his way more clear-sightedly among the conflicting claims of rival creeds and schismatic factions. It is fantastic to suggest that such an historian would omit religious considerations (for example) from his exposition of Jewish history: the discussion of Hebrew monotheism in such a context does not necessarily involve an appeal to 'extraordinary or miraculous factors'. Here Fr D'Arcy seems to be tilting against a windmill which (with insignificant exceptions) ceased to turn some time ago.

There is not, and can never be, any final conclusion to the claims and counter-claims, the perennial, radical controversy between these irreconcilable doctrines of historical method. Ultimately, perhaps, the controversy itself, if only by compelling both sides to take fresh stock of their position from time to time, provides its own justification. In this respect Fr D'Arcy's study—scholarly, good-humoured, and within its imposed limits scrupulously fair—will probably achieve a more sympathetic hearing in the opposition camp than Professor Maritain's more intransigent monograph, which is illustrated with the most extraordinary metaphysical diagrams, and contains numerous aggressive *obiter dicta* calculated to scare off all but the most tolerant of sceptics ('The Devil hangs like a vampire on the side of history' is a fair and characteristic example). Yet there are passages in *The Sense of History* which, partly by the unexpectedness of their approach, partly through the dramatic immediacy of their language, seem to open up whole new perspectives before us:

> The multitudes of obscure individuals flit into history and out again; they grow into vast hordes in the East, building the Pyramids or crossing the Hellespont; they die in their thousands in the plague of Athens, in the mines of Syracuse or at Lake Trasimene

and Philippi; they storm the Bastille, gather outside the Palazzo Venetia or perish in concentration camps. Even those whose portrait is finely drawn and who peer out at us in the pages of a skilled historian are necessarily stylized and remain as reticent and mysterious as the Mona Lisa. Even our own composed judgments on those we know skip the mystery which every individual life enshrines. We like the silhouette more than the frightening reality, or we cling to the tangible image because it is more easy to manipulate. We treat others as things, take on the ready-made ideas of our time and submerge ourselves in their current.

At such moments as this we cannot but recognize how arbitrary and insubstantial are the systems we all of us create to redeem time past from its oceanic chaos and immeasurable multiplicity of incident. The lesson which Fr D'Arcy has to teach us is a lesson of humility—a virtue not over-conspicuous among empirical historians. Even the rationalist who scorns metaphysics may well pause to reflect on the limited nature of his *idées reçues*, the vast uncharted areas of truth and knowledge which still lie beyond the scope of his inquiries. In the last resort he would probably accept Fr D'Arcy's modest and restrained verdict:

> We have to accept our human condition, the historian's own dependence upon his time and culture, and it is better to side with Kant than with Croce, and admit that the past as lived is a kind of noumenal world, whose existence we must admit, but of which we can never have proper knowledge.

Though Fr D'Arcy often writes as though he had temporarily forgotten those words, and Professor Maritain would probably find them too concessive for his own brand of historical proselytism, they might well serve as any historian's motto. Further than that it is hard to go with certainty. An aphorism of Mr William Golding's sums up the problem succinctly, and may stand here as colophon to a debate (one facet only of this vast problem) which has no inevitable conclusion: 'What men believe is a function of what they are; and what they are is in part what has happened to them.' The question remains open.

III

How does the rationalist historian respond to this new (and presumably uncongenial) trend? The academic answer—and it is one which must compel a good deal of sympathy—is that no scholar worth his salt will be stampeded by emotional fashion into abandoning a position originally taken up and held on logical grounds. There is, one feels, much unspoken resentment against theological historicism in particular because it employs unfair weapons. While all other historicist tendencies, such as Spengler's, can be argued out of existence on the grounds that they resemble (as it says on driving licences) a 'track-laying vehicle steered by its tracks', there is always the uneasy feeling that Divine Providence belongs to that mysterious Group F which this category specifically excludes. One of the most notable things about a book such as Sir Karl Popper's *The Poverty of Historicism* is that in it he has not one word to say about the theological position, presumably dismissing it as beneath contempt and not worth discussion—an aprioristic assumption if ever there was one.

This is a sphere where reason no longer operates; and the difficulties are treated, in a commendably explicit fashion, by Professor Christopher Dawson, an admirable historian and the first occupant of Harvard's Chair of Roman Catholic Studies. In *The Dynamics of World History* he has this to say:

> It is very difficult, perhaps even impossible, to explain the Christian view of history to a non-Christian, since it is necessary to accept the Christian faith in order to understand the Christian view of history, and those who reject the idea of a divine revelation are necessarily obliged to reject the Christian view of history as well. And even those who are prepared to accept in theory the principle of divine revelation—of the manifestation of a human

> truth which surpasses human reason—may still find it hard to face the enormous paradoxes of Christianity.

Presented with such an ultimatum, any conscientious historian may perhaps be excused for protesting that this is simply a highfalutin way of having one's cake and eating it: not everyone can bring himself to cry *credo quia impossibile est.* Is there, then, no common ground on which scholars such as Professor Dawson and their secular critics can meet?

In fact the essays collected under the title *The Dynamics of World History* (most ably edited and annotated by Mr John J. Mulloy: one only wishes he had chosen a title less liable to make critics like Popper or Von Hayek spit with rage) overlap to a surprising degree with less committed preconceptions. It is true that Professor Dawson writes as a professed Catholic historian, *pro Deo et Ecclesia*, and can quote with approval the words of Joseph de Maistre, written shortly after the French Revolution:

> Providence never wavers and it is not in vain that it shakes the world. Everything proclaims that we are moving towards a great unity which, to use a religious expression, we must hail from afar. We have been grievously and justly broken, but if such eyes as mine are worthy to foresee the divine purpose, we have been broken only to be made one.

But he manages to square his religious views, in the most ingenious way, with a staunch advocacy of anthropology and sociology as ancillary techniques in historical method. To say that his position is syncretically achieved would be something of an understatement. He has taken the sociological theories of Comte, Le Play, and St Simon, given them an infusion of divine essence from St Augustine, and added a top dressing of Aristotle, Fustel de Coulanges, Burke, and (of all people) the German romantics, such as Herder. The whole bears a striking resemblance to the thought of that great Berber historian Ibn Khaldoun, who had the same preoccupation with Religion and the Tribe as world forces, and, as Professor Trevor-Roper put it,

> found the 'essence' of history in that social organization and social dynamism which underlies the 'accidents' of political change, and who sought to penetrate and analyse that essence...He was an intellectual conservative in the classical...tradition, a devout believer who sought a *via media* between the strict and the liberal interpretation of the Law. Though he applied rational criteria, he was not a rationalist. He might end with applied science, but he began with Revelation.

Mutatis mutandis, that is an exact description of Mr Dawson's position today; and it hints both at the many points of contact he has with other progressive (if non-Catholic) historians, and where he sharply breaks company with them. He never lets us forget—as it so often is forgotten—that the great world religions are not a kind of cultural by-product thrown off by major civilizations. He can put his finger with unerring accuracy on the spiritual lack which invalidates Marxism as an enduring emotional creed, and, incidentally, has some tartly apposite remarks to make about its founder: 'The fact is that Marx was himself a disgruntled bourgeois, and his doctrine of historic materialism is a hang-over from a debauch of bourgeois economics and bourgeois philosophy.'

Professor Dawson has a keener eye than most historians for the complex nature of a culture, in the technical sense of that much misused term, and makes illuminating remarks about the influence of environment on civilization: here his debt to Le Play is most noticeable. He is never less than a pleasure to read; his prose is close-knit, witty, elegant; his arguments clear and cogently presented. Why is it, then, that one's pleasure is infiltrated by a feeling of irritation, as though one were the victim of a half-successful confidence-trick? Perhaps the most subtly deceptive characteristic of Professor Dawson's method is its apparent foundation on modern scientific principles. Like Spengler, who observed that 'the history of a culture is the exact counterpart of the history of an individual being or of an animal or of a tree or of a flower', he is much given to analogies from the natural sciences. Words such as 'dynamism', 'organic structure', 'polarity', and other metaphorical borrowings from biology and physics crop up with some frequency. There is talk of the Id and the Super-ego in a religious connotation. We have learnt from Popper and Von Hayek just how fallacious some of these analogies are, and how misleading it can be to describe historical events in terminology more appropriate to the classification of a physical species. And yet, significantly, Professor Dawson's interest in science stops short at the metaphorical stage; in *The Dynamics of World History* there is no mention of such truly dynamic figures as Copernicus, Kepler, or Galileo, and no entry, in a copious index, under the heading 'science' itself. What Professor Dawson would appear to have done, through the guidance of some subtle if unconscious instinct, is to neutralize his most dangerous opponents by apparently assimilating them into his system. The old adage 'If you can't beat 'em, join 'em' comes to mind here; except that with some skill Professor Dawson has seen to it that *they* join *him*.

This becomes clearer still when we consider his approach to such figures as Marx, Gibbon, Wells, Spengler and Toynbee. The first three get off comparatively lightly. Professor Dawson is more sympathetic to Marx—saving the question of spirituality—than we might expect; but then he shares with him, as with D. H. Lawrence, a bourgeois detestation of the bourgeois and all his works. He appears even to believe in Sombart's 'bourgeois soul' (that alarming if bloodless entity) and equates the victory of bourgeois civilization with the triumph of industrial urbanism, another King Charles' Head of his but one against which he makes out a damning, if familiar, case. Gibbon he treats with positively diabolical skill, emphasizing his dependence on Catholic historiographical tradition (a piece of research which drew praise from that disinterested scholar Professor Momigliano), making discreet play with his early conversion, and concluding with these acute remarks:

> The apparent completeness of Gibbon's success points to the fundamental weakness of his treatment. His essentially negative explana-

> tion of Christianity leaves the post-classical world devoid of form and meaning ... [Tillemont] succeeds ... in the understanding of the past, while Gibbon only succeeds in explaining it away. To Gibbon the story of the Christian Empire and the civilization to which it gave birth is nothing but the history of an illusion. The world had conceived emptiness and brought forth wind ... There remained only the shadow of the great name of Rome, like the shadow of a great rock in an empty land.

Here, of course, Professor Dawson skirts the greatest and most daunting paradox of European culture: the fact that Christianity should have spread and developed—perhaps only survived—through the timely support of a civilization, and an intellectual tradition, to which it was, in essence, profoundly antipathetic. The split mind of the Christian humanist is an all too familiar phenomenon, and Professor Dawson is no more immune to its problems than the next man. The temptation to write off one's more vociferous opponents as hot-gospellers who somehow took the wrong turning becomes almost irresistible to a man in his position. The Wells who wrote *The Outline of History*, for example, he describes—anti-Catholic mania and all—as 'a frustrated evangelist who was always on the verge of producing an apocalypse or founding a new religion': in other words, as a theological historicist *manqué*. It is the most effective, and irritating, neutralization conceivable.

Spengler and Dr Toynbee he treats rather more harshly: they have taken up positions which, though not identical with his, are perhaps too close to permit of clear focussing. Many writers committed to a particular religious stand-point find it easier to swallow an exotic, or even an atheist, than the purveyor of a similar but rival creed, and Professor Dawson seems to be no exception. He clearly prefers a Muslim to a Puritan; what he thinks of Professor Butterfield we can only surmise, since he never refers to him. Like the priest in the Irish joke, he can take historical prostitutes (metaphorically speaking) in his stride, but seems to draw the line at Protestant historians. For all that, the anthropological half of his mind (can one ever avoid this split as a Christian historian?) is extremely acute: one can speak without inconsistency of these two halves, since their owner so often declares that the two aspects of human culture which they represent must, somehow, be combined, yet seldom achieves a satisfactory synthesis in the event. This gives a subtly schizoid quality to even his best work, but is no more than we might expect given the conditions in which he is forced to operate. 'What we need', he writes, 'is a scientific sociology which... must recognize at once the determination of natural conditions and the freedom of spiritual forces, and must show how the social process embraces both these factors in a vital union like that of the human organism.' Is such an ideal (allowing for the spurious analogy) possible even on its own terms? It seems doubtful, and Professor Dawson does not increase confidence in his programme by various characteristic (and perhaps inevitable) self-contradictions. On one page he condemns the dismissal of matter and the body as evil; on almost the next he is declaring that on the advent of Christianity 'religion was no longer an instinctive homage to the dark world of the Id': and then, to complicate matters further, sets up Western moral effort and discipline in favourable contrast to the 'cosmic libido' represented by Hinduism.

He is not above question-begging in the most ingenuous way; of metahistory (which stands in much the same relation to history as metaphysics does to physics) he expresses his approval —'provided always that it is good metahistory'. His flirtation with Spenglerian biology and environmental influence sets him skidding several times on the very edge of determinism: this, indeed, seems the most dangerous feature—from his own viewpoint—of his attempt to form a spiritual and geopolitical synthesis. Yet all this, surely, is no more than the inevitable upshot of any attempt to grapple, at a fundamental level, with the 'intersection of the timeless with time'. Easier for the theologian to ignore historiography altogether, and to treat the temporal entirely *sub specie aeternitatis*. Easier for the historian, *per contra*, to invoke a kind of secular benefit of clergy which exempts him, as a good rationalist, from the need to investigate (or even mention) non-verifiable phenomena: no accident that linguistic analysis became so popular among philosophers just when it did. We should not, then, be surprised to find that Professor Dawson's best work, historically speaking, was done on the pre-Christian era, for example in *The Age of the Gods*, when, to put it bluntly, he could dodge the main issue confronting any Christian historiographer. The Good Time might be coming, but had not yet arrived, and could thus, for the time being, remain unmentioned.

But such tactics merely stave off the inevitable. When it comes to the crunch, Professor Dawson, like any other Western intellectual, is heir not only to the Christian revelation, but also to the no less powerful legacy of Graeco-Roman rationalism. Despite such dubious fringe-areas of contact as early Stoicism, the two phenomena have been in acute conflict from the very beginning. To give up either was too heavy a price for most thinking people to pay; so theology took to circle-squaring, a habit it has never entirely shaken off. Despite all the ingenuity of St Thomas Aquinas, no true reconciliation or resolution has ever been achieved; perhaps it never can be. But both Christianity and the classical tradition—as a cultural and moral no less than an intellectual or spiritual experience—are indissolubly built into the European psyche, where they set up untold stresses and conflicts. Even if coexistence is the best we can hope for, the problem, being perennial, is perhaps worth another airing.

IV

The great rhetorical question posed by Tertullian—'What has Athens to do with Jerusalem, what the Academy with the Church?'—sums up, in succinct form, one of Christianity's thorniest historical dilemmas. It is ironical, to say the least of it, that the dissemination of Christ's *kerygma* beyond mere local ethnic and linguistic frontiers should have been made possible only by international Greek culture and the imperial administration of Rome, since Graeco-Roman culture (whatever

Christian humanists may say) was fundamentally opposed to the entire concept of Christianity as such. Thus the immediate successors to the Apostles found themselves in a highly ambivalent position. If they were to spread the Gospel message effectively, they would have no option (as St Paul for one saw very clearly) but to borrow wholesale from the philosophy, literature and rhetorical techniques of a pagan culture which they were committed to destroy. While morally condemning the classical heritage out of hand, they found its accumulated wisdom an indispensable cloak for their own cultural and philosophical nakedness. Besides, in order to make a real missionary break-through they had to beat the pagan free-thinkers on their own ground and with their own weapons.

Anyone who wants a brief, lucid, and refreshingly unheated account of this odd phenomenon should read the opening chapters of Professor Werner Jaeger's *Early Christianity and Greek Paideia*, which distils a lifetime's research into the 'condition of complete simplicity, costing not less than everything'. Professor Jaeger draws a neat preliminary picture of those elements in the Hellenistic, or Graeco-Roman world which proved apt material for Christian apologists. First and foremost comes the common language of the Mediterranean sea-routes, the Greek *koiné*. Then there are the literary models—the Epistle, the Acts, Didaché, Apocalypse and Sermon. Professor Jaeger is most illuminating on pre-Christian religious tracts, those curious documents which shade off into the fringe activities of semi-mystical philosophies such as early Epicureanism. He has some wise things to say on the influence of the Stoics, and sees the crucial importance of the Christians' decision to employ, for their own ends, the techniques and arguments perfected by the Sophists. Persecution merely served to put them yet deeper in their opponents' debt; being forced upon the defensive, they found themselves compelled to enter the field of apologetics—and where else could they find enlightenment on this subject but in the handbooks of pagan rhetoricians?

It does not require much imagination to see what subtly

deleterious effects this trafficking in hostile ideologies—always for the highest motives—might have upon those who embraced it. The ball, as it were, remained permanently in the Christian court; to begin with Christianity was faced with general indifference, which might occasionally flare up into active enmity, and what curiosity there was about this new sect tended to have a philosophical emphasis. As Professor Jaeger pleasantly remarks, the Septuagint 'might never have come into existence, were it not for the expectation of the Greeks in Alexandria to find in it the secret of what they respectfully called the philosophy of the barbarians'. As for the enmity, that had its roots in a tangled mixture of politics and superstition well analysed by Professor A. D. Nock in *Conversion*, where he attributes the popular anti-Christian attitude to

> . . . the idea that the welfare of the Roman State hung together with the due performance of the traditional Roman rites. . . ; the belief in Jonahs—I mean the belief that the misfortunes of the Empire might be due to this widespread apostasy; a general willingness to accept additional rites which made the Christian refusal seem cantankerous and unreasonable; and also a widespread readiness to believe the strange stories of sexual excesses and ritual murder and cannibalism which always attach themselves to a sect which is under the ban of social disapproval . . .

It is clear from this and similar arguments just how difficult the position of the early apologist was, and just how many oblique temptations assailed him. In order to achieve his declared aim—the world-wide establishment of the Kingdom—he was compelled to fight on enemy ground, with weapons borrowed from his adversary; he found himself clothing the simplicities of the Sermon on the Mount in the complex garments of Greek philosophy, while the rhetorical jawbone with which he smote the Philistines was one all too patently fashioned by the Philistines themselves.

No doubt these early Christians assured themselves (as Marxists were similarly to do a couple of millennia later) that the end justified the means; and indeed, the paradoxical piquancy of the whole phenomenon, in purely historical terms, is that no other conceivable means existed. But there was a heavy price to be paid, mostly in the sphere of intellectual honesty. A Christian apologist could not (and still cannot today) avoid the problem of how to reconcile the faith he professes with the Graeco-Roman civilization in which it was nurtured. He must take up one of several clearly defined attitudes on the subject; and this, all too often, he was (and is) singularly loath to do. The embarrassed squirming, under hostile scrutiny, of a modern Christian with a weakness for the classics is rather like that of the respectable public schoolboy forced to admit the existence, on Speech Day, of an outrageously exotic stepmother.

But the arguments exist, and have all collected a distinguished roll-call of supporters down the centuries. At one extreme there stand the independent spirits such as Tertullian, who are for jettisoning the classical heritage in its entirety. This radical proposition at least has the merit of ruthless logic behind it; but like so many ruthlessly logical propositions, it was very soon seen to be a practical impossibility. (Tertullian himself was by no means immune to the pagan *Zeitgeist* of his age; in his apologetic work, as Professor Nock demurely observes, 'the redemptive operation of Christ lay in deliverance from demons rather than in deliverance from sin'.) But if pagan culture is *not* to be rejected *in toto*, how can its manifestly pernicious ideology best be immunized? That was the question confronting the Early Fathers, and an agonizing one it proved. There were two main lines of thought on the matter, the eclectic and the allegorical: both must appear highly suspect to any uncommited observer.

The eclectic approach finds its most forthright exposition in Basil of Caesarea's famous oration on the study of Greek poetry and literature, and its educative value for young Christians—a work which, as Professor Jaeger says, 'always remained the supreme authority on the question of the value of classical studies for the church'. While rejecting the religious and moral content of ancient poetry, Basil is quite prepared to praise its form—a species of *faute de mieux* aestheticism which modern literary moralists must view with acute embarrassment. But for the committed Christian—one, that is, who sees all history hinged round the cardinal point of Christ's Redemption; who, as Father Hugo Rahner puts it in *Greek Myths and Christian Mystery*, 'knows by faith that there was once a man who is God'—Basil's compromise solution can seem both valid and significant. If all history before Christ was a foreshadowing of, and preparation for, the Redeemer's Coming; if all history since that Coming must be viewed *sub specie aeternitatis*; and if it is true (to quote Father Rahner again) that 'the heritage of the Greek spirit only attains immortality when it is secure within the shrine of the Logos whose words are recorded in the tongue of Hellas', then Basil of Caesarea is both justified and reasonable in his treatment of the classical heritage—too reasonable, perhaps, since he shrank from the final logic that committed various ancient writers (perhaps including Sappho) to the flames.

The whole edifice of *Greek Myths and Christian Mystery*, like many such works, stands or falls by its central belief; and this makes it a hard text to criticize unless one shares its initial premisses. When Fr Rahner describes Christian humanism as 'that wonderfully bold and widely ranging gesture of the Hellenic Christian, that gesture whereby he fetches everything home to Christ, the spring of water and the stars, his sea and his swift ships, Homer and Plato and the mystical numbers of the Pythagoreans', an antipathetic reader may well be forgiven for feeling that the whole process is uncomfortably reminiscent of that cranky brand of pseudo-scholarship which delights in creeping monadism and deep speculation concerning the Great Pyramid. Fr Rahner, quoting Harnack (of all people), shows a very proper contempt for 'this comparative mythology which endeavours to connect everything causally with everything else'; *his* thesis is that it all leads back to Christ, and since his mystico-allegorical theories are advanced, as it were, behind the protective banner of declared faith (he is one of those interesting Catholic scholars who stretch their net to include Jung) rational criticism is disarmed in advance, simply through lack of common premisses.

It might be argued that the chief interest of *Greek Myths and Christian Mystery* is symptomatic rather than critical: it forms a singularly pure example of the third major Christian technique for dealing with an all-too-recalcitrant classical inheritance—I mean the mystical allegory. To many early Christians it seemed self-evident that the works of ancient authors (Homer included) were manifestly impious if taken at their face value. Some were for a burning of the books; others, less rigid in their moral sectarianism, argued persuasively that the true meaning of Homer and the rest lay hidden beneath a veil of allegory. Pseudo-Heracleitus declared (as Professor Jaeger reminds us) that 'the allegorical method ushers in a new age in which readers with a refined moral taste and purified religious faith will be able to enjoy their Homer again without being deterred by Plato's scruples.' We should, perhaps, be grateful to the allegorizers for providing this convenient loophole, since otherwise Homer might well have gone the way of Sappho; and it is, one admits, hard to see how rabbinical tradition could have dealt with an erotic poem like the *Song of Songs* except by explaining it allegorically. But history was to prove that the allegory, like the Freudian dream, is a game at which almost anyone with a lively imagination can play. Fr Rahner plays the game very well indeed; but I can't help feeling that this wasn't his primary object, that he is claiming some sort of scholarly validity for the imaginative edifice he builds with such delicate and loving care. To inject moral significance into moly and mandragora, to gloss Odysseus' homecoming with overtones of the human soul's journey towards heaven, past endless sirens of temptation —all this is no doubt spiritually uplifting, but it tells us very little about Homer; and what Fr Rahner *does* say about Homer is the kind of take-it-or-leave-it statement that is not susceptible of proof, and which Catholics no less than sceptics may find somewhat irksome: 'Guided by the genius of poetry, this blind singer touched with trembling hands the primal forms of truth, and for us this makes him the forerunner of the Word that appeared to us clothed in the flesh of man.'

There is much about Fr Rahner's book that is good, sensible, and penetrating. His use of Jungian archetypal symbols in a Christian context is persuasive; so is his approach to the traditional idea of direct influence between the mystery cults and Christianity, where he prefers to see two largely independent phenomena which employed 'terms of fundamental human experience' while sharing 'a common cultural apparatus, a common system of social custom and convention, and a common stock of ideas and practices in civil and domestic life.' He is sensibly forthright about Christianity's direct tactical borrowing from pagan ritual:

> I think I have shown once again how ancient Christian worship, secure in the knowledge it derived from divine revelation and apostolic tradition, made use of whatever served its purpose in pagan thought, how it did so quite boldly and with a true Greek largeness of mind, and how it thus fashioned a garment for the mysteries of Christ.

Here, of course, we are back to Basil's thesis again. It might be argued (and in one passage Fr Rahner seems half to admit) that Christianity absorbed a good deal more of purely pagan thought than Christians, ancient or modern, have quite realized. One also feels that at fairly frequent intervals throughout *Greek Myth and Christian Mystery* Fr Rahner is, as they say, boxing clever. He is really *too* extreme in his rejection of any direct mystery-cult influence on the Church. His authorities throughout are somewhat partial: no Guthrie, no Dodds, and only two brief allusions to Frazer—he actually manages to get through a chapter on the Mystery of the Cross without bringing in Frazer's Hanged God, which may strike the reader as a trifle disingenuous. He is very anxious to prove that the sacrament of Baptism does not contain a magical derivative element. He has a detectable weakness (like the Church in his somewhat infelicitous translation of a vexed passage in Methodius) for turning 'psychics into pneumatics'—a Delphic phrase which would, one imagines, yield up its meaning more easily to a modern Greek than to an English reader.

Speaking of second-century Gnosticism, Professor Jaeger remarks that there must have been 'some need for this strange sort of religious ersatz'; and to judge from the history of allegory, it seems clear that a similar need lies behind this complex and at times frankly rather tiresome phenomenon. Few would argue with Fr Rahner's statement that 'since the West has turned away from the custodian of mystery it has died of the utter sterility of its pure intellectualism,' though his corollary—'Only those peoples will live on who have suffered themselves to be reborn out of the mysteries' motherly womb'—may perhaps find fewer takers, and some might argue that there was more than one candidate for the role of custodian. A professing Christian who still maintains a passionate devotion to the world of Greece and Rome does not really want to be told, apropos Odysseus and the Sirens, that 'this mast is the cross and the Christian conquers by freely consenting to be bound to it'; that, like Sir Thomas Browne's mystical Mathematicks, is an intellectual game each person can play for himself. We remember St Jerome, agonizing over his passion for Cicero; above all, perhaps, we remember the dynamic, tortured figure of St Augustine. Ultimately, perhaps, we will have to declare our allegiance; but how many of us must have murmured, down the ages, something akin to Auden's famous parody: 'Make me good, Lord—but not yet'? The dear city of Cecrops is not, and cannot be, the City of God. Perhaps Tertullian was right after all.

Myths and Symbols

'MYTH,' Thomas Mann once declared, 'is the foundation of life, it is the timeless pattern, the religious formula to which life shapes itself.' That statement alone is enough to show how radical a change our general attitude to myths and mythology has undergone during the past half century or so. To rational High Churchmen of the Age of Enlightenment or progressive anthropologists in the late Victorian era, such a statement would have been blankly incomprehensible. Even to imaginative inquirers such as Frazer, Lawson or Jane Harrison, the scholarly *de haut en bas* approach (here as in the field of radical politics) was still very much in fashion. The fumbling devices of primitivism were studied and found wanting. Myth represented an early, pre-logical mode of human thought, which, as Professor Grimal once remarked, 'saw the world as a stage for a dramatic conflict between capricious wills... To study myths, it was believed, was to review the errors and follies of man,' Few books better illustrate this self-assured mood of condescending superiority than that eighteenth-century oddity, Dr William King's *An Historical Account of the Heathen Gods and Heroes*.

King is a fascinating character from the age of Swift: a pugnacious High Tory, a book-grubbing dilettante, a rum and bibulous pamphleteer ('I remember', Pope remarked waspishly, 'Dr King would write verses in a tavern three hours after he could not speak') who got himself involved in the famous battle between Bentley and Boyle over the spurious *Epistles of Phalaris*. He wrote *An Historical Account of the Heathen Gods and Heroes* a year or two before his death in 1712, and was paid £50 for it. The poverty and illness which dogged him through this period could hardly be guessed at from his robustly self-assured style. His prose is quaint, and his use of initial capitals somewhat idiosyncratic: when describing Bacchus he tells us that 'several cruel Daemons, Satyrs, Sileni and Tityri, used to accompany him with Cymbals and huge Exclamations'. The workings of his mind betray that implacable prosaic logic which is the hallmark of the Augustans, together with a brisk contempt for all fanciful flim-flam: 'The story of this God [Glaucus]' he informs us severely, 'is very fanciful, and shows the Extravagance of the Poetic Invention'. But what surely will most tickle a modern reader is his absolute moral self-assurance, particularly over religious matters. He writes as a convinced Christian, who knows that all he describes it the merest heathen idolatry, and is never slow to trounce any deity—Zeus in particular,—for loose sexual conduct. There is no Tennysonian Honest Doubt in Dr King's mind; he *knows*. What is more, his attitude persisted for a surprisingly long time (partly, no doubt, through mythology being relegated to the schoolroom, where every kind of patronizing, authoritarian, or censorious mind found its natural habitat, and no adequate opposition to its *obiter dicta*). Nathaniel Hawthorne, for example, agonized over classical myth with all the exacerbated fervour of his New England conscience:

> These old legends, so brimming over with everything that is most abhorrent to our Christianized moral sense—some of them so hideous, others so melancholy and miserable .. was such material the stuff that children's playthings should be made of! How were they to be purified? How was the blessed sunshine to be thrown into them?

His ingenious suggestion (put in the mouth of a young friend) was that myths originated in the pure Golden Age before evil existed, and that children, in modern times, were the only representatives of that happy era.

Charles Kingsley, too, once declared that children were the sole survivors of the Golden Age, who could truly understand the significance of the Greek myths; and, in a very different sense from what he intended, that earnest clergyman was quite right. Children do grasp mythology with more intuitive acceptance and understanding than their over-rational elders; and they need it at a much earlier age than was, until comparatively recently, thought necessary. Yet it might be argued that the re-telling of myths for the young (and in particular the Greek myths, these being central to the whole European tradition) in itself constitutes a form of rather subtle censorship—a view supported by the fact that the phenomenon is a comparatively recent one, which only began during the nineteenth century. If we discount Fénelon's moral tract *Telemachus*, the first attempt to bridge this presumptive gap was made in 1808 by Charles Lamb, with *The Adventures of Ulysses*. This has been described (with pardonable hyperbole when one looks at the competition, such as *Sandford and Merton* or W.D. Cooper's *Blossoms of Morality*) as a 'refreshing oasis in the moral desert' of children's literature; but an isolated oasis it remained, for nearly fifty years. Macaulay's *Lays of Ancient Rome* appeared in 1842; but child-mythography proper really dates from 1853, with Hawthorne's *Tanglewood Tales*, followed three years later by Kingsley's *The Heroes*. These two works satisfied the market, by and large, till after the turn of the century; then Andrew Lang's *Tales of Troy and Greece* appeared in 1907, and A. J. Church's *The Children's Iliad* in 1908. Since then the industry has expanded steadily, but without throwing up any really memorable work.

This is not altogether surprising when one considers the tradition within which its practitioners were called upon to operate. To begin with, myths were looked down on as mere quaint tales for savages or children; and secondly, what a savage in his ignorance might enjoy was liable to be strong meat for a middle-class, well brought up, and at least nominally Christian child of Victorian parents, so that considerable censorship, not to say emasculation, was also *de rigueur*. In addition to their ignorance concerning the nature of myth, such writers also had only the haziest idea, (how, given their preconceptions, could it be otherwise?) of how a child's mind worked. They vaguely assumed their young readers to be either quarter-witted miniature adults or innocent prelapsarian angels. The first tradition stemmed from Puritanism and the second from the Gothic Revival;

both treated the child on adult terms rather than its own. Hawthorne, for instance, was under the odd delusion that children would be puzzled or incredulous when confronted by a biological impossibility like a Centaur: accordingly he produced the following explanation for them—in the middle of his story:

> I have sometimes suspected that Master Chiron was not really very different from other people, but that, being a kind-hearted and merry old fellow, he was in the habit of making believe that he was a horse, and scrambling about the schoolroom on all fours, and letting the little boys ride upon his back. And so, when his scholars had grown up, and grown old, and were trotting their grandchildren on their knees, they told them about the sports of their schooldays; and these young folks took the idea that their grandfathers had been taught their letters by a Centaur, half man and half horse. Little children, not quite understanding what is said to them, often get such absurd ideas into their head, you know.

Two points may be observed about this monstrously patronizing explanation. In the first place, it destroys the emotional impact of the Chiron myth by rationalizing superiority, and thus, in a sense, negates its entire function. Secondly, Hawthorne is really *talking to himself*. It is he, the Victorian adult, who has to explain Centaurs away to his own satisfaction; any child will accept them without turning a hair.

The so-called 'morally disconcerting nature' of many Greek myths as the original sources told them was, similarly, something that bothered adults rather than children. Today, as one psychologically-minded wag has put it, the Jung are not so Freudened as they used to be; but in point of fact (as a glance at early editions of the Brothers Grimm makes quite clear) they never were. A child has a veritably Aristotelian appetite for purgation through pity and terror, and suffers positively if deprived of it; he needs someone or something to make his flesh creep. Also, below a certain age the young possess a kind of built-in protection against more adult taboos, especially in the complex field of sex, allusions to which simply pass over their heads altogether unless guilt-ridden grown-ups insist, compulsively, on rubbing their noses in the dirt *pro bono publico.* This is what psychologists refer to as the 'latency period'. 'You must not fancy, children,' Kingsley wrote (as if the thought would ever have occurred to them spontaneously!) 'that because these old Greeks were heathens, therefore God did not care for them'; and went on to suggest—shades of Frazer!—that the sons of Hellas were lapsed monotheists. So, stage by stage, the raw mythic content of the old legends was diluted: the magic was lost, the story prettified and toned down, and the whole caponed package served up in costive Wardour Street English with a patronizing moral bromide tucked away somewhere between the lines.

Today, of course, moralizing has (at least on the surface) gone out of fashion; but the urge to protect our tender young from life's grimly basic realities—without regard for whether they want or indeed need such protection: no one consults *them* on the matter—has, if anything, increased. Modern advances in this field of studies, however, strongly suggests that it may be the children who will have the last laugh. We all have been told (believing it literally is another matter) that unless we become as little children we shall not enter the Kingdom of Heaven; it now looks as though without this essential precondition we are unlikely to enter the kingdom of myth either. Irrational, arbitrary gods, bloody horrors, howling illogicalities, all the things over which adults gag or falter—children can take them in their stride. Children are essentially intuitive rather than rational, thinking in imagistic rather than linear terms, and for over a century now have had to put up with adults who attempted to smother their natural intuition with doses of sweet reason and sentimentalized innocence, turn and turn about. The result—and the reaction—can be seen in a work such as Mr William Golding's *Lord of the Flies.* If children reject myth as boring, dull, old-fashioned, or irrelevant to their own lives, it will be entirely because of faulty adult presentation; and if the myths are forgotten or cast aside, our children will be poorer in spirit for the loss. Prometheus and Dionysus, Perseus and Heracles, the great myths of wandering and discovery, the epics of siege and battle, the slaying of monstrous beasts, dragon or Minotaur—these are much more than fairy tales (a *genre*, incidentally, which the Greeks simply did not recognize); they are archetypal patterns of man's essential humanity.

The Greeks themselves, great rational thinkers though they were, did not suffer noticeably (not, at least, before the Hellenistic age of scholars and libraries) from a compulsion to euhemerize or aetiologize their mythic inheritance. Even after Herodotus and Thucydides, they still had only the haziest notions of the difference between myth and history. Thucydides himself, though he rejected fabulous legends, was not above calculating the size of the Achaean army at Troy from the Homeric Catalogue of Ships. Cities and families alike forged mythical genealogies for themselves—thus consciously blurring the distinction still further—with all the ingenuity of a modern parvenu aspiring to a respectable entry in Debrett. Records such as the Lindian Chronicle or the Parian Marble include in supposedly historical records such names as Cadmus, Minos, Cecrops, Orestes and Heracles. Relics multiplied with equal disregard for truth; the bows and arrows of Pandarus were as ubiquitous in historical times as, later, were fragments of the True Cross or Queen Elizabeth's bed. If different accounts of the same myth did not tally, a fresh myth was concocted to explain the discrepancy. An early logographer named Acusilaus, as Sir John Forsdyke reminds us in *Greece before Homer*, 'professed to have found his genealogical information on inscribed bronze tablets which his father dug up somewhere in his garden'. Later authors were more sophisticated in their deceptions. The history of the Trojan War attributed to Dares contains romantic portraits of those involved: 'Helen was as handsome as her fair-haired brothers, simple-minded, charming, with very fine legs, a mole between her eyebrows, and a tiny mouth.' (Cinecittà producers, please note.) When we reflect that Ctesias connected Darius' Behistun sculptures—made only a hundred years before

—with the shadowy Semiramis, or that Herodotus, the Olympic register, and the Parian Marble give three completely discrepant dates for the historical Pheidon of Argos, it becomes, in Sir John's words, 'manifestly futile to look for chronological reality in computations based on prehistoric legend'. In general, too, the attempt to extract history from myth, like oil from a pressful of olives, though it has yielded good results here and there, has left the main corpus—and significance—of the myths untouched. The real gain has been at a deeper and less purely temporal level.

Gone, now, are the days of mere carping rationalism, the superior sneer at primitive attempts to evaluate the universe in anthropomorphic terms; psychologists and anthropologists alike—Jung above all—have demonstrated how deeply the human mind is bedded in a mythical matrix, coeval with the childhood of the race. Today we know that myths, like the poor, are always with us; that they form a vital and constant ingredient of our psyche, an indispensable instrument for observing and controlling phenomena, for imposing some kind of human order on natural chaos. Many things which we formerly assumed to possess objective reality—including, ironically enough, the notion of human rationalism and progressive perfectibility—turn out to be, after all, essentially mythic in nature. Politics, no less than sex and religion, breeds its own archetypes, if not its own Gestalt. One rather odd consequence of this revolution is that no one any longer quite knows how a myth is to be defined; or rather, everyone thinks he knows, and each definition tends to disagree with the next one. One classic example of this was provided by the *Larousse Mythologie Générale*, first published in 1935, and brought out in an English translation some years after the war (1959). There seems to have been no previous understanding between the editor, M. Félix Guirand, and his various contributors—or indeed between either of these parties and Mr Robert Graves, who contributed a characteristically idiosyncratic introduction to the English-language edition—about just what a myth *is*. To make confusion worse confounded, several contributors (not to mention Mr Graves himself) seemed to define the elusive thing differently at different moments. M. G.-H. Luquet, for example, claimed in the section on Prehistoric Myth (which was, in point of fact, largely to do with sympathetic magic and cults of the dead) that 'myth . . . implies a belief in supernatural forces'; later, when dealing with Oceania, he declared:

> An examination of the pantheon, in our opinion, does not properly speaking constitute mythology, which according to etymology is the study of myths. A myth is not just any sort of legend, not even a legend in which superhuman personages take part, but an explanatory legend, meant to give the cause or origin of such and such a fact of actual experience.

One might perhaps elaborate this a little and say that myth is any central fact of human experience which is given dramatic, universal, and personalized form by way of explanation or enlightenment. But this salutary approach did not, by and large, recommend itself to M. Luquet's fellow-experts, who tended to catalogue gods and goddesses at great length without any direct references to their mythic activities at all.

It is beginning to look, indeed, as though the pendulum of anti-rational reaction may have swung too far the other way. All knowledge—self-knowledge in particular—is bought at a price. We eat the apple, we look at the world and our neighbour with new eyes; and then, before we quite know what has happened, we are on the long road that leads from Eden to the psychiatrist's couch, a flaming sword barring our return, misty Jungian archetypes looming ahead of us. To be or not to be, we mutter existentially, but the slings and arrows we suffer in the mind are those generated by what M. Paul Diel calls *une psychologie quasi stratosphérique*, and if we take arms against anything, it is a bewildering sea of symbols. In one way and another, the symbolic interpretation of myth is beginning to get something worse than out of hand. As a method it possesses enormous potential; but it has also, from the very beginning, contained the seeds of its own ultimate destruction. For one thing, the whole symbolic approach is fundamentally anti-historical. Symbols, in particular those dealing with the human psyche, operate almost by definition in a context of supposedly timeless conditions and characteristics. If myths have the same validity for us as they did for our remote ancestors, it follows (we are told) that they must be studied—like so much else these days—*sub specie aeternitatis*. It is true that the reason for a myth's perennial and enduring nature is, precisely, its archetypal, non-historic essence, its basic congruence with the deep universal springs of human experience. Yet because of this trend the equally promising—and equally necessary—approach offered by myth-as-history is being progressively abandoned.

I am beginning to suspect, perhaps unfairly, that the reason for this may well be that myth-as-history's best-known, if not most expert, adherent is beginning to give the theory a bad name among serious scholars. Robert Graves, as we know, inclines to the school of thought which sees myth as a 'dramatic shorthand record of such matters as invasions, migrations, dynastic changes, admission of foreign cults, and social reforms. . . . One constant rule of mythology is that whatever happens among the gods above reflects events on earth.' Homeric scholars at least will give a cautious assent to this last proposition; but it smacks far too much of cerebral *ex post facto* improvisation, and in practice, as any reader of *The Greek Myths* will testify, tends to go too far and too fast: Mr Graves might find it a little hard to fit the Oedipus myth or the castration of Uranus into such a pattern without leaving a lot of unanswered questions hanging in the air. Mr Graves tends, I can't help feeling, to confuse attributes with definitions: this also applies to his suggestion that 'mythology is the study of whatever religious or heroic legends are so foreign to a student's experience that he cannot believe them to be true'. Is incredibility, in fact, the criterion of definition? Then what is to become of Mr Graves' 'dramatic shorthand record'? Or is this just another case of what he once described as his weakness for baiting the scholars with moonshine and green cheese? Not that one needs to worry all that much; these things tend to go in fashions, and it may not be all that long before Max Müller and his followers are rehabilitated, so that figures such as Odysseus or Heracles once more pursue their tortuous symbolic path through the zodiac as walking solar calendars. But do we in fact have to declare ourselves for one end or the other of the egg? Are not *both* elements, the ritual-symbolic and the historical, inextricably bound up in every myth, and in fact expressed by the same symbolism?

'It is the object of the myth, as of science, to explain the world, to make its phenomena intelligible.' This definition of Professor Grimal's hits the nail squarely on the head. It is a pity that the old-fashioned approach to mythology has been so radically rejected: despite its tendentious air of superiority it did latch on to one all-important fact—that myth represented a mode of perception, a way of looking at things which characterized a certain stage in man's development, a tool for formulating ordered patterns in time and space. But this process was never restricted to the timeless phenomena of psyche or cosmos; it also dealt constantly with the Heracleitan flux created by experience. It took a jumbled kaleidoscope of things-done and things-seen-or-heard, and hammered them into a meaningful sequence called the past. All myths, whatever other function they may have, exist in and contribute to this sequence; they cannot wholly escape the historical process.

But the balance between these opposed elements is hard to maintain without toppling over on one side or the other. All mythologists tend to be *parti pris* : just as excessive preoccupation with the eternal aspects of myth will produce poetic fiction in disguise, so over-emphasis on historical actuality will lead to the theory known as Euhemerism, which regards *all* myth as nothing but distorted or dramatized history. 'Thus,' says Professor Grimal, 'the Hydra of Lerna was interpreted as a swamp fed by eternal springs [a highly plausible theory, as those familiar with the site can testify], and when Heracles cut off the heads of the monster, he had, according to this theory, diverted the streams supplying water to the marsh.' Now many students of myth who would die rather than write Mr Graves a blank academic cheque would nevertheless argue that this theory has much truth in it. That early mode of perception which operates through juxtapositions of image and symbol rather than by a consequential train of logic—poetry thus always precedes prose, just as metaphor precedes simile—may well have recorded events in such a manner. And the recording of events, let us make no mistake about it, was a prime object in myth-making. Romantic modern scholars, nurtured on the post-Wordsworthian concept of creative originality, are prone to forget that conscious and deliberate fiction (except at the simplest level of popular entertainment) is a luxury which only the advanced society can support.

The fallacy of Euhemerism, of course—and indeed of most theories in this field—is to assume its own universal applicability. Furthermore, both Euhemerists and symbolists tend to be bedevilled by their own intellectual sophistication, and to project it on to the society they are studying. From the moment when any civilization reaches the stage of rational, conscious thought, it will swiftly lose its natural ability—and inclination—to interpret phenomena in mythical terms. Such mythopoeic faculties as it retains will tend to be restricted to poets, whose numinous quality resides in their (strictly anachronistic) familiarity with magic and metaphor. Very soon its scholars and thinkers will find themselves in the same self-conscious relationship to their mythological inheritance as we do today—that is, on the outside looking in. Given such a situation, it is hard to avoid back-tracking one's own sophisticated assumptions, and crediting *homo mythocentricus* with deliberate, logical motives in shaping his concept of the world.

The trouble with symbols, of course, is that we can, Humpty Dumpty-like, interpret them to mean almost anything we please. One becomes acutely aware of this while reading a study such as M. Diel's *Le Symbolisme dans la Mythologie grecque* : for him the mythic hero is '*le représentant de la poussée évolutive, la personnification de l'élan spiritualisant*'. Daedalus symbolizes '*l'intellect perverti, la pensée affectivement aveuglée*; Bellerophon's winged steed represents '*l'imagination créatrice et son élévation réelle*'; while Chaos in the *Theogony*, as we might expect, '*n'est pas une réalité, il n'est qu'une dénomination symbolique.*' The shirt of Nessus becomes a mere image of abstract lust, symbolically adhering to Heracles' flesh. Again and again, at the risk of sounding banal (M. Diel's most fearful witch-word, and I can see why) one feels like saying: 'Well, yes, I can see how you might take it that way: I don't happen to agree; but in any case both our reactions are purely personal and subjective.' Such *aperçues*, in fact, however attractive, can scarcely form the basis of a serious thesis, since they fall by definition beyond the reach of logical argument. M. Diel offers considerable rewards to the persevering (he also has some pleasantly sharp things to say about his Freudian and Jungian predecessors in the field) but the cumulative effect of his book is like being plunged into an ever-thickening fog. Nothing is what it seems at its face value. Concrete facts, persons and events blur, melt, are reduced to mere generalized abstractions. M. Diel heads one section, on the Argonauts, '*La Combat contre la Banalisation*'; like so many French intellectuals, he appears to find mere facts a trifle vulgar, and cannot rest until he has fed them into his symbolical mincer and made systematic hash of them.

It is interesting, and revealing, to compare M. Diel's interpretations with those put forward by Mr Jack Lindsay in *The Clashing Rocks*: where they overlap they might be discussing quite different episodes. If M. Diel has a bee in his bonnet about *banalisation*, or reduction to the commonplace, Mr Lindsay suffers from the equally disconcerting tendency to see shamans under every burning bush. For M. Diel the Symplegades '*sont figuratifs de la double menace qui plane sur toute l'entreprise: débauche et tyrannie*'; Mr Lindsay, on the other hand, sees them as the entry to the other-world, the gateway of initiation, deriving their imagery in the first instance from the spasmic movement of the vulva in childbirth—a pleasantly eclectic mixture of Freud and Van Gennep's *Rites de Passage*. When such widely divergent views can coexist without apparent incompatibility, it soon becomes clear (if it was not so from the beginning) that the whole business of symbolic interpretation—whatever the intrinsic value of symbolism—means no more than backing one's emotional fancy.

Mr Lindsay's central thesis—which owes an acknowledged debt to the work of Jane Harrison and Francis Cornford—is roughly as follows. Shamanism was characteristic of the old pre-Olympian religion in Greece. The losing battle which this religion fought against the Olympians underlies much Greek mythology, and in particular can be regarded as a formative element of early Greek drama, which crystallized the conflict in personal and symbolic terms. Mr Lindsay's theme is by no means without its attractions, but he can hardly be said to present it to its best advantage. His methods of argument are even more *outré* than those employed by Mr Robert Graves in *The White Goddess* (what *is* it about the symbolic interpretation of myth and early religion that so discourages decent sober scholarship?) and he has a similar tendency to play hopscotch with dubious etymologies. Minoan and Mycenaean religion, which might well have torpedoed his case, he sidesteps altogether. His main line is to stick the all-purpose label of 'shamanism' on any magical, prerational or marvellous element in the myths. Thus Ajax and Caeneus become shamanistic magical warriors, and Heracles, with his Labours, a shamanistic 'defier' of the Olympians. Mr Lindsay is almost as hot on defiance as M. Diel is on *banalisation*. (I shall return to this point in a moment.) The device of *stichomythia*, we are told, originated with the 'mantic riddle-contest,' and even Socrates' airborne activities in *The Clouds* become a parody of the shaman's ascent to heaven.

Mr Lindsay may acknowledge Cornford's influence, but I can't help suspecting that Professor Dodds has had a hand in the matter too. For two decades now that yeasty work *The*

Greeks and the Irrational has been doing its work, and today the dough is beginning to rise with a vengeance. It looks as though shamanism is getting to be the latest OK fashion among mythical symbol-hunters, and indeed Mr Lindsay's book bears a striking resemblance to another, slightly more recent study, Mr E. A. S. Butterworth's *Some Traces of the Pre-Olympian World in Greek Literature and Myth* (Berlin 1966). Mr Butterworth, too, finds shamans everywhere in the pre-Olympian world: to Mr Lindsay's list he adds Agamemnon, whose death—we might have known it—was a ritual sacrifice: nothing so dull and commonplace as a historical matter of adultery, usurpation, and murder for revenge. (To read some of the more whole-hogging ritualists one might be forgiven for supposing that life in the ancient world was just one unending riddle-and-symbol liturgy from the cradle to the grave.) The Homeric poems, for Mr Butterworth, are full of tell-tale hints about sacrificed kings, which the poet—despite his marked patrilinear prejudice—could not entirely eliminate from the traditional text. Though Mr Lindsay also posits a mythic structure for the *Iliad* and the *Odyssey* (Helen appears as a fertility-goddess, Odysseus as a tribal bear, and Penelope as a wild duck) this particular angle, so reminiscent of Frazer and Hocart, appears to have escaped his notice.

We do, as it happens, know quite a bit about various shamans, mostly from Herodotus. But they all belong to the late archaic period of colonization and expansion, when Greeks penetrated the Black Sea and planted outposts in the Crimea. Scythians were much addicted to shamanism; it does not seem to have flourished indigenously on Greek soil. That it was a widespread phenomenon during the Bronze Age is pure speculation, and highly improbable at that. The Linear B tablets not only give no hint of a matrilinear (much less a shamanistic) society, but positively indicate that the Olympic pantheon may have been established much earlier than was once supposed. Absence of evidence, however, never deters Mr Lindsay; indeed, he can often turn it to good account. 'Almost all shamanistic elements', he writes, 'have been carefully excluded from the *Iliad*'—thus transforming an unfavourable *argumentum ex silentio* into a sinister conspiracy of suppression.

The trouble with theories and arguments such as these is that they cannot be subjected to any of the usual testing criteria: they create their own symbolic and associative logic as they go along. The situation is often worse confused by the fact that their authors tend to dress them up in the trappings of conventional scholarship (Mr Lindsay's documentation looks most impressive until one begins to examine it in detail). It is, therefore, extremely hard to disprove many of the assertions made: one is thrown back on the appeal to sheer implausibility. As a mode of criticism this perhaps carries more weight than has generally been allowed. One major by-product of the symbolic approach to myth, from whatever angle, is, surely, apparent blindness to ordinary common-or-garden human behaviour. When ritual and symbol come in through the front door, historical—and indeed psychological—common sense all too often flies out of the window. Just what motives drive poets or scholars to create these timeless never-never-lands of symbol and myth would make an interesting study in itself. For the present, however, it may be more profitable to examine one particular myth that is firmly rooted in human and tribal experience, thus leaving the symbol-game at something of a discount.

For Mr Lindsay the whole of Greek drama is crammed with defiant-shaman heroes; but not all of them, alas, can be presented so convincingly as Prometheus, a figure who appeals no less surely to Mr Lindsay's radical sympathies than he does to those of Professor Havelock in *The Liberal Temper in Greek Politics*. Indeed, Mr Lindsay's theme of defiance (leaving the shamanism aside) has much in common with Professor Havelock's most striking argument, which he likewise hangs on the Prometheus myth, and which gives his book pretensions to a universal theory. This hypothesis has considerable relevance for the present age, and if true could throw a flood of light on ancient politics and thought alike. It is by no means a new notion, but it has never hitherto been applied in quite this way. What Professor Havelock posits, in fact, is a perennial, innate, radical opposition, extending into all fields of thought and activity, between two types of mind which may be roughly described as liberal and authoritarian. (A similar scheme has been evolved by Mr Gordon Rattray Taylor to cover sexual *mores*.) Logic, ultimately, is irrelevant to the opposing parties: they are temperamentally irreconcilable, and their bias operates in every sphere of human conduct. The authoritarian treats history as regressive, a falling-off from some hypothetical Golden Age; the liberal sees it in evolutionary terms as progressive social development. The authoritarian envisages human laws as divinely sanctioned, and man's condition as essentially static; the liberal treats laws much as Rousseau did, in terms of a social contract, and considers man in essence an evolutionary being. The authoritarian automatically opposes the liberal's attempts to develop scientific discovery and independence of thought—and this, for Professor Havelock, is the true meaning of the Prometheus myth: it symbolizes the eternal struggle of *homo faber*, even *homo technologicus*, against the repressive traditionalism of *homo metaphysicus*, for whom morals rank considerably higher than pragmatic truth.

This point is worth emphasizing, since the myth of Prometheus is one that has exercised a very powerful influence on the post-Renaissance European imagination. Not until Freud gave the Oedipus legend a new and hitherto unsuspected universality had any other classical myth appeared quite so relevant to modern, progressive, technological, anti-authoritarian, upward-striving *homo sapiens*. We have only to see what Shelley and Goethe made of it to realize its explosive potential in socio-political terms. Shelley's *Prometheus Unbound* is a prophecy of revolution; and Goethe, although more personally involved in the myth—he makes Prometheus the son of Zeus, and seems to be attacking some authoritarian father-figure as well as the clerical conformism of his day—nevertheless stands broadly in the same clear tradition. As Professor

Kerényi says in his *Prometheus: Archetypal Image of Human Existence*:

> Goethe's Prometheus is no God, no Titan, no man, but the immortal prototype of man as the original rebel and affirmer of his fate: the original inhabitant of the earth, seen as an antigod, as Lord of the Earth. In this connexion he seems more Gnostic than Greek, but he surely is in no way related to the childlike Gnosis of Goethe when he was still younger. He belongs rather to the more recent history of ideas and anticipates the Nietzschean or Existentialist view of man. *Or perhaps he goes even further* [my italics].

That last sentence is worth noting; it is the nearest Professor Kerényi gets, at any point in his book, to one of the most obvious, and central, facts about the Prometheus myth—its almost classic adaptability to Marxism. Prometheus, it was once said, is the patron saint of the proletariat; and any attempt to evaluate his significance, either in antiquity or today, must (whether the writer accepts the Marxist thesis or not) at least subject the myth to some fairly searching scrutiny in social if not economic terms.

This Professor Kerényi is, evidently, unwilling to do. It is no accident, I feel, that his bibliography omits the name of Professor George Thomson—though Thomson's edition of Aeschylus' *Prometheus Vinctus* is an essential handbook for anyone working in this field. However, the point of the omission is, surely, not that Professor Thomson happens to be a Marxist (continental scholars are much less worried by this kind of thing than their English or American counterparts) but that *any* interpretation of myth in political, social, or historical terms stands diametrically opposed to Professor Kerényi's own theories on the subject. Though Professor Kerényi expressly disclaims either Jungian or Existentialist affiliations, it is plain that both (the former in particular) have had a profound influence on his thought: Prometheus is indeed defined, in his sub-title, as the 'archetypal image of human existence'. It follows that his pursuit of the Prometheus myth will tend to be conducted, if not exactly *sub specie aeternitatis*—though as we shall see, there is a touch of this too—at least well outside the historical process as we normally understand it. The use of archetypal symbolism to explain ancient myth can be most profitable in limited doses, as we have already seen; and there is a great deal in Professor Kerényi's book which is both true and valuable. But of recent years there has developed a marked inclination among certain students of myth to float their subject free of history altogether; and this suggests a wilful blindness to the workings of the primitive mind, ineradicably rooted, even at its most inventive or fantastic, in a solid bedrock of remembered or observed fact. Prometheus is the most down-to-earth, as well as the most genuinely heroic, figure from Greek mythology, and takes less well to this symbolic treatment than most.

It may be as well, before proceeding, to remind ourselves just what we do know about Prometheus from our ancient sources. Professor Kerényi has some sensible remarks to make about the danger of conflating disparate traditions (as is so often done in handbooks of mythology) and we may therefore begin with the earliest surviving witness, Hesiod. Prometheus, according to Hesiod, was a son of the Titan Iapetus by Clymene, and thus brother to Atlas, Menoetius, and Epimetheus. (There are a great many alternative claimants as his mother, but Iapetus remains a constant factor.) When Zeus hid fire from men, Prometheus went to Olympus and stole it, carried it down to earth concealed in a giant fennel-stalk (a practice still in use on certain Greek islands) and gave it to mankind. Hesiod prefaces this tale with an explanation of why Zeus had turned against mankind in the first place. One day, he says, when gods and men were at loggerheads during the reign of Zeus, Prometheus killed a bull, cut it in two halves, wrapped the choicest portions (hidden under the stomach) in the hide, and made a second heap of the bones, artfully covered with fat. He then invited Zeus to choose which he preferred.

Zeus chose the bones and fat—though Hesiod is careful to say he saw through the stratagem. In revenge, Zeus chained

Prometheus to a rock in the Caucasus and sent an eagle to gnaw at his liver every day, the liver being miraculously restored overnight; he also caused Hephaestus to mould a virgin from earth, Pandora, and sent her to Epimetheus, Prometheus' brother, who accepted her despite Prometheus' warning that he should have no truck with any gift from Zeus. Pandora opened the box in which Prometheus had shut all human ills and miseries, and out they flew. Prometheus himself was finally rescued by Heracles, who shot the eagle: Zeus permitted this in order to let Heracles win fame, and eventually had a reconciliation—though of a somewhat uneasy nature—with Prometheus. There are various other later sources which add details to our picture. Apollodorus, Ovid, and Horace, together with the travel-writer Pausanias, all refer to Prometheus having fashioned men from earth and water before Deucalion's flood. One tradition states that his torment in the Caucasus was due to his having seduced Athena, with whom his cult was, in fact, always closely connected.

But the most important, and one of the earliest, alternative sources is, of course, Aeschylus. The *Prometheus Vinctus* gives us a very clear picture of Prometheus, and is, perhaps, the one that has, more than any other, influenced modern thought. Here Prometheus is not a half-Titan of doubtful status, but an immortal god, 'the friend of the human race, the giver of fire, the inventor of the useful arts, an omniscient seer, an heroic sufferer, who is overcome by the superior will of Zeus, but will not bend his inflexible mind'. He originally helped Zeus in the Battle of the Titans, but turned against him when Zeus, flushed with victory, planned to destroy the entire human race. Prometheus armed men with hope, and taught them all manner of crafts, arts and sciences: above all, he gave them fire. Since all this had been done in defiance of Zeus, Prometheus was chained to a rock in Scythia, where Io appeared to him and he prophesied her wanderings. (Note that for Aeschylus his sin was the theft of fire, not, as in Hesiod, sacrificial chicanery.) He then was visited by Hermes: Zeus felt anxiety concerning a certain prophecy known to Prometheus, by which it appeared that Zeus was liable to beget a son who would dethrone him. By what woman, Hermes demanded (diplomatically skirting round the lack of omniscience in Zeus which such a request implied) would this child be born? And just what, in detail, was the decree of fate? Prometheus, seeing a superb opportunity for blackmail, refused to talk; whereupon Zeus, with understandable irritation, blasted him, rock and all, into Tartarus. Eventually Prometheus was brought up again, and pegged out for eagle-treatment in the Caucasus: a punishment which would only end if some other god offered to take his place in Hades. This the incurably wounded Chiron did. Another version, preserved by Servius and Apollodorus, and hinted at by Aeschylus, states that Zeus himself released Prometheus, Prometheus having revealed to Zeus that the woman he must avoid was the sea nymph Thetis.

What are we to make of this curious congeries? One or two points at once suggest themselves. There are signs that the core of the myth is extremely ancient: if one consults Stith-Thompson or any other standard comparative study of world myths, parallels at once come to hand. The theft of fire is a common motif (see Stith-Thompson A 1415) and Prometheus may originally have been some sort of fire-god and metal-worker. It is interesting, though not conclusive, that the Sanskrit word *pramantha* means 'swastika' or 'fire-drill', and that in the *Bhagavata Purana*, a Sanskrit epic, we find the two brothers Pramanthu and Manthu. More suggestive still is the name 'Iapetus', which so sober a mythologist as Rose is seriously inclined to identify with that of Japhet: among Japhet's children were Magog, who is uncommonly like Atlas in his functions, and Tubal, whose metal-working links him with Prometheus. Without pressing any of these parallels too far, we can at least say that the myth in its earliest form probably had a wide Indo-European provenance, and that even by Hesiod's day it had reached a distinctly self-conscious stage.

Now here we come to one of the great difficulties in elucidating classical mythology, or, indeed, the legends of any nation.

A point is always reached at which, while unwilling to jettison a corpus of cherished tradition, men have become sophisticated enough in their morals and institutions to realize that some of the stories handed down to them simply will not do as they stand: they are offensive anachronisms, gods not being so good at keeping up with the new civic morality as are their worshippers. At this point the aetiological myth comes into play: the variation, that is, which *explains* the offensiveness, even if it cannot quite explain it *away*. On top of this there comes a quite deliberate reworking of mythological tradition by creative artists. Both elements find full play in the Prometheus story.

Modern reactions to the idea that myths were consciously remodelled to suit new social conditions vary from over-enthusiastic acceptance to over-cautious rejection: here Professor Thomson and Professor Kerényi stand at either pole. The latter, indeed, says that 'anyone who chooses to find in this material purely poetic inventions or innovations such as are customary in modern poetry must, in every instance supply special proofs.' At this point, rather out of patience, one feels tempted to ask *him* to supply 'special proofs' for the following passage, which shows the cosmic, anti-historical method at its worst:

> And so Prometheus stands before us: a moon-like being, but not a luminous one [*sic*], embodying the darkness of the dark moon, and also bearing marks of human existence; one compelled by his own shortcomings to offend against his environment and his companions in growth; who in so doing employs devious, crooked thinking (for in the world of growth the pathways are naturally crooked); inevitably, a wounder and a wounded one. These are among his human characteristics. The cosmic situation of a dark moon-like being of this kind is that of the new moon, whence rises the sickle—in mythical tales also taking the form of an axe (we shall see it in the hand of Prometheus). The women who are associated with Prometheus in various traditions delimit his situation in the heavens.

Despite the occasional shrewd point, most of this is moonshine, and moonshine, as we know, has a way of proving intangible when one pokes a stick into it. But there is a good deal to suggest, and a good many scholars who think, that even by Hesiod's, let alone Aeschylus' day, the Prometheus myth had come in for heavy aetiologizing: that the story of Prometheus tricking Zeus with the sacrificial bull was a way of explaining why the gods always got short shrift (bones and fat) when distribution time came round after the ceremony, and—less probable—that the Pandora legend was a mere anti-feminist squib. It is significant that Hesiod also makes Zeus *see through* the trick, though behaving as though he had not—thus at one stroke cleaning up the ritual and preserving the theology of divine omniscience.

But Professor Kerényi will have none of this: no aetiologizing for him. 'How,' he asks rhetorically, 'could this wild, abstruse story of Prometheus trying to deceive the gods with his sacrifice carry any force of conviction for the Greeks?' Very easily, one is tempted to reply; there is nothing more inherently unlikely about it than there is about the bullying and blackmail which go on throughout the *Prometheus Vinctus*, and we have learnt from *The Greeks and the Irrational* (another title conspicuously absent from Professor Kerényi's bibliography) that fifth-century Greeks were not half so Apollonian or reasonable as their modern admirers try to make out.[1] To Professor Kerényi the meaning of the myth is that 'sacrifice offered up by men is a sacrifice of foolhardy thieves, stealers of the divinity round about them—for the world of nature that surrounds them is divine—whose temerity brings immeasurable and unforeseen misfortune upon them'. And later he repeats this surprising assertion, apropos a discussion of Hesiod: 'Men are exactly as they showed

[1] There is obviously a danger, in all these counter-reactionary trends, of over-compensation. The corrective lenses which scholars such as Professor Dodds or Professor Havelock supply for classicists' astigmatism may in the end produce an image hardly less distorted than the one they set out to replace. Greece—and this point cannot be emphasized too strongly—was not *primarily* a country of economic upheavals, ecstatic irrationals, or anti-totalitarian scientific thinkers, nor can Greek philosophers or historians be held responsible in some mysterious way for the misapplication of their ideas.

themselves to be in their sacrifices: deceived deceivers.' But what people, in any country at any time, can ever have approached the altar of their god in so wildly improbable a frame of mind? Professor Kerényi seems on occasion to forget that he is dealing, not simply with a pattern of mythologems, but also with the religious impulse.

The crucial element in the Prometheus myth, is, of course, the Titan's championship of mankind, in a practical technological sense, against the arbitrary authoritarianism of Zeus. As Professor Thomson rightly remarks, 'fire stands for the material basis of civilization. That is the one constant element in the myth'. At one level Prometheus may have figured as a folk-type trickster or simple tribal benefactor; but with the development of a more organized society, elaboration became necessary. To quote Professor Thomson again: 'The primitive form of the myth, which simply registered the pride of the community in the success of its collective struggle against its material environment, was no longer adequate, because out of the struggle between man and Nature had now emerged the struggle between man and man.' It is not hard to see how the Aeschylean version of the conflict could be applied to the Age of Enlightenment or the Industrial Revolution. Prometheus can be made the symbol of open-minded, inquiring (his very name means 'forethinker') scientific progressivism, labouring for the people—and suffering for the people—in the teeth of entrenched authority, with its technological dogmatism, its reactionary distaste for science, its censorship, and its oppressively static view of government. So Professor Thomson takes him: in his opinion Aeschylus was a revolutionary poet.

But once again the myth escapes neat classification, because in fact Aeschylus was nothing of the sort; and research on the *Prometheus Vinctus* has been bedevilled by the fact that those who undertook it were always hell-bent on declaring themselves for one end or other of the egg. Some, like Professor Thomson, wanted a revolutionary Aeschylus, blasting away at authoritarian religion and government (a view only tenable by largely ignoring the other plays in the canon); others, more numerous and more conservative, followed the Victorian tradition of conflating Aeschylean with Hebrew or Christian monotheism, and therefore found themselves resorting to really desperate measures when glossing the *Prometheus* itself, which depicts Zeus as an arbitrary tyrant. 'Some indeed,' to quote Mr David Green's pleasant phrase, 'seeing Aeschylus as a pious conservative, an awe-struck Zeus-man, have sometimes been so troubled as to deny that Aeschylus wrote the play at all'. But what is, or should be, clear to any commentator is that *both* these views are true. Aeschylus *does* attack Zeus, radically, in the *Prometheus*: and he is, in all his writings, concerned to reconcile traditional theology and myth with the requirements of a new order, the emergent quasi-democratic society of the Periclean Age. The *Oresteia* concludes by absorbing the whole concept of the *miasma*, ritual blood-guilt followed by vendetta, into a constitutional setting. Similarly with the *Prometheus*, which, we should remember, is the second play in a trilogy of which the concluding play is lost: what Aeschylus emphasizes, again and again, in his portrait of Zeus as the traditional despotic tyrant is that he is *new to the job*. In the last play, one suspects, maturity will have brought reconciliation and mildness. This is the very reverse of a revolutionary attitude; Aeschylus, in fact, in his role as 'awe-struck Zeus-man' is simply tackling an embarrasing episode in his divine hero's past.

Indeed, it could be argued that the *Prometheus* is an *anti*-revolutionary play, that it is aiming to cure by 'reform from within'. The myth was certainly susceptible of a revolutionary interpretation: there is a fascinating, though obscure, papyrus fragment of the comic playwright Cratinus which means, if the late Sir John Beazley's reading is right, that 'Zeus expelled Cronus and imprisoned the Titans; Demos, the Populace, has now expelled Zeus, and the Titans have been liberated; they hasten at once to their old brother Titan, who is Prometheus'. Here is yet another fragment of evidence to add to what we have, and all pointing in the same direction: that the

Prometheus myth was, in the broadest sense, a socio-political symbol. As such, with moral overtones of one sort or another, it has been viewed by ancients and moderns alike. (Professor Thomson quotes an amusing list of famous names apropos the Zeus-Prometheus struggle in Aeschylus, showing who favoured which side, and adding, tartly: 'It is interesting to note that the only poet on the side of Zeus is the fascist D'Annunzio.') There is simply no evidence whatsoever to suggest that anyone in antiquity—least of all Aeschylus—looked at Prometheus in the very sophisticated way that Professor Kerényi does. That fact does not make his book any the less useful or suggestive; and indeed his moral analysis of Prometheus, as a god who put himself in the position of man, who by his gift of fire 'made human existence human', and whose fate 'is an immeasurable consequence of a mistake committed with a clear conscience' has much to commend it. Yet even at his best moments he (like so many other writers who share his approach) tends, as so often to forfeit our patience by a parade of irksome parallels—here through dragging in crucifixion, redemption, and other Christian notions wholly alien to the mythologem he is trying to reconstruct. Not even Frazer, the arch-addict of this sort of game, ever imagined Heracles' rescue of Prometheus as analogical with the Descent from the Cross. The symbolic method has a genuine contribution to make to mythology; but such flights of fancy will hardly, one imagines, help to dispel prejudice against it. The myth of Prometheus smoulders on, like his own fire in the fennel-stalk, with more than one lesson for our science-dominated age: perhaps it should be left to the poets to revise it, while the scholars stick, as they have always done in the past, to looking unto the pit whence they were digged.[1]

[1]It was only in the summer of 1971, during a brief visit to England, that I obtained access to a copy of Professor G. S. Kirk's remarkable study, *Myth: Its Meaning and Functions in Ancient and other Cultures* (1970), and also heard the brilliant and memorable lecture which he delivered at the Triennial Conference in Cambridge. His investigations constitute the first serious attempt to come to grips with the subject on a comprehensive and rational basis known to me. He rightly emphasizes the *multiple* nature of myth, and carries out an extremely damaging critique

of all universalist or monadic theories, in particular of the myth-as-ritual school. While rightly sceptical of Lévi-Strauss' excessive addiction to abstract generalizations, he sees clearly that structuralism is the only approach to have provided a new *aperçu* on mythology and myth-making since Freud and Jung. He emphasizes the importance of the comparative approach for any understanding of myth as an instrument of communication, and makes a close examination of ancient Near Eastern mythology as a preliminary to evaluating that of Greece. Perhaps his most interesting conclusion is that Greek myth has been badly contaminated with creeping rationalism, and is in fact deficient in those fantastic or inconsequential elements which form so important a part of truly primitive myth, as of dream-symbolism.

The Individual Voice

ARCHILOCHUS AND SAPPHO

I

After Homer, darkness. Then, towards the close of the eighth century, a glimmer of light, a faint and fragmentary dawn. But as the sun climbs, illuminating first Boeotia and then Paros, we see that something very odd has been going on during the night. Gone, as though they had never existed, are the Homeric virtues of honour and hospitality, the glorification of battle, the chivalrous aristocratic ideals, and, above all, the bardic convention of anonymity. In their place we find identifiable and all-too-articulate individuals: a surly, puritanical, aphoristic peasant-farmer, an illegitimate colonist with a talent for foul-mouthed invective and a thoroughly disillusioned attitude to war. If Hesiod and Archilochus resemble any character in the *Iliad* or the *Odyssey* it is, surely, Thersites: the voice from the ranks, the snarling apostle of self-help and common sense, the deft puncturer of epic pretentions—and, for that matter, the first class-caricature in European literature. They are realists, concerned with their own lives and emotions, odd cases thrown up by the great disruptive (and liberating) wave of colonization which swept Greeks in their thousands from one end of the Mediterranean to the other during the eighth and seventh centuries B C. We know they had read Homer, because both of them take uncommon pleasure in parodying his language and attitudes; and today, more than ever, we can appreciate the enormous psychological gulf which separated them from him. Homer might cater, as a poet, to the petty princes of Ionia; but he—like they—looked back always, through the grim chaos and penury of the Dark Ages to a golden Mycenae which only gained in lustre as it became more remote in time. The essential point about the *Iliad* and (to a lesser degree) the *Odyssey* is that they are retrospective; they look back from the great watershed of Mediterranean colonization to a lost era, that of the Bronze Age, the Age of Heroes. The genuine historical memories and social details might get blurred with much telling and adapted to anachronistic usages, so that the result was a kind of complex palimpsest; but the gaze was over the shoulder, and the fall of Troy, ultimately, celebrated the night the old nostalgia burnt down.

With the decipherment of the Linear B tablets, and the archaeological work done on Homeric sites in recent years (notably by Professor Blegen at Troy and Pylos) a very different, and far less heroic, background to the Trojan War is beginning to emerge. The mighty city of Troy visualized by Homer (a synchronistic blend, it now seems clear, of Blegen's Troy VI and Troy VIIa) has been reduced to a patched-up, peeling fortress, with squatters—or at the very least, decidedly un-Homeric warriors—leading a hand-to-mouth existence, under siege, amid the ruins of former greatness. The Mycenaean overlords whose names roll so proudly through the Catalogue of Ships suddenly undergo a metamorphosis into niggling bureaucrats. As Professor Page so aptly remarked, in *History and the Homeric Iliad*, 'one would suppose that not a seed could be sown, not a gram of bronze worked, not a cloth woven, not a goat reared or a hog fattened, without the filling of a form in the Royal Palace'. It is amusing to visualize, say, Odysseus' homecoming in the light of this new evidence: the interrogation by countless scribes of Penelope's household as to his age, occupation, parentage, and source of income, the triplicated application for a Grade Two (Lower Rate) Mendicant's Ration Allowance. No wonder the poor man was so proficient, spontaneous, and imaginative a liar[1]; he had to be. At this stage in the argument many scholars have observed, with some justice, that what concerned the royal household scribes was not necessarily fit matter for the bard who

[1]Unless, as I have sometimes liked to believe, the cover stories are in fact a true bill (they fit together with remarkable plausibility) and the period between leaving the Ciconians and returning to Ithaca from Scheria the real fantasy. I hope to develop this hypothesis further elsewhere.

sang after dinner, and that the absence of Homeric panache from the Linear B tablets is a poor argument against its existence: the greatest writer or soldier (Mr Edmund Wilson being, as usual, a law unto himself) does not show at his best when filling out an income-tax form.

Yet despite this caveat, it seems pretty clear that the historical Greeks who—very inefficiently—fought the historical Trojan War were a far cry from Homer's supermen (a point which Archilochus both knew from personal experience and never missed a chance of emphasizing); and that neither the historical truth nor the myth which supplanted it bore much relation to that latter-day Ionian society of chieftains, who affected names like Agamemnon, and for whom Homer and the Homeridae recited their traditional epic poems. This, surely, is the crux of the matter when we come to compare Homer with Hesiod or Archilochus, the first two post-Homeric Greek poets whose work (patchily, alas, in Archilochus' case) still survives. Homeric epic is not personal in its scope or presentation; it does not seek to reflect—except incidentally, through extended similes—the manners, beliefs, background, or deeds of the audience for whom it was composed. (And it might well be argued that the similes were in fact the thin edge of the realistic wedge, produced to give a baffled audience some slight area of comparison with the world they knew.) Antiquity saw Homer not as a historical source-book so much as the great teacher of moral universals, the fountain-head of *areté*, or *virtù*; and the fact that the social pattern behind the precepts had been obsolescent for centuries, finally collapsing altogether under the centrifugal stresses of colonization (and the centripetal pressures of tyranny), made no difference to the reverence with which the precepts themselves continued to be regarded.

The contrast which Hesiod and Archilochus present to Homer, then, (leaving aside for the moment those aspects in which they differ from each other) is one with which we are well acquainted, seen here in its earliest manifestation, its *Ur*-form. They offer the first clear instance of that perennial swing in

European literature, between formalism and realism, mandarin and vernacular, the ideal and the individual, myth-making and direct observation—the antithetical list could go on for ever. As such, the phenomenon should hold peculiar interest for us, not least because one of these poets happened to be a blazing original whose reputation in antiquity stood as high as Homer's own. 'We hear in him,' Professor J. A. K. Thomson once wrote, 'a voice as personal, as poignant, as in Villon or Heine or Burns; it is a revolutionary voice. Modern literature has nothing to teach Archilochus. One can see that in the miserable scanty fragments of his astonishing poetry that have come down to us.' Yet, by a piquant paradox which Archilochus himself would have been the first to appreciate, for every hundred people today who have dipped into Hesiod (or every thousand with at least a smattering of Sappho) there will probably be no more than a handful for whom the bitter, humorous soldier-poet from Paros is even a known name. To some extent this deficiency has now been repaired by the racy, slapdash translation of Mr Guy Davenport, which is, apparently, becoming something of a cult on American university campuses—though when some of the fragments appeared in magazines, they were generally assumed to be the work of a 'new and ingenious American poet' sheltering behind a classical pseudonym and making literary capital out of papyrus scraps, rather as eighteenth-century folly-builders went in for artificial ruins.

Mr Davenport, despite his erratic scholarship, certainly deserves our gratitude for putting Archilochus up in a place where he—or at least his fragmentary modern reincarnation—can be studied at leisure.[1] As he so rightly says, 'to exist in

[1]A late epitaph on Archilochus bids the unwary traveller pass by, and not arouse the wasps that cluster on the poet's tomb. Mr Davenport has undoubtedly poked his own head into a regular academic hornets' nest; but he should take comfort from the fact that more speculative rubbish has been written about Archilochus, by scholars who should know better, than about almost any other ancient Greek poet, with the exception of his near-contemporary Sappho. It would indeed be surprising if some of this textual and contextual moonshine had not filtered through into *The Fragments of Archilochos*.

fragments and in Greek is a doubly perilous claim on the attention of our time'. With Archilochus, indeed, we almost seem to see some kind of malignant historical jinx operating through the centuries. As though it were not bad enough to have lost the vast majority of his work, we are constantly turning up papyri neatly split down the middle, thus leaving us with a maddening row of half-lines. Does a new inscription concerning his life come to light? Then it will, inevitably, break off just when it is becoming interesting. The sources contradict one another, and the editors follow suit. It is not even certain how far we can trust Archilochus' own fragments as an autobiographical guide. Critias (Plato's cousin, and the notorious leader of the Thirty Tyrants imposed on Athens, with Sparta's backing, after the Peloponnesian War) may assert that, unless the poet himself had publicized such matters, we should not have known about his illegitimate birth, his quarrelsomeness, his adulterous escapades, his cowardice on the battlefield, or various other discreditable characteristics. Yet we know from Aristotle that on several occasions Archilochus adopts a first-person *persona* not his own, without the reader or hearer being warned that this is so. As Professor Dover wisely (if somewhat dauntingly) remarked, 'How far are we today right when we assume, unless we have positive evidence to the contrary, that whenever a fragment of an early Greek poet contains a first person singular it comes from a genuinely autobiographical poem?'

With this warning in mind, let us see how well we can reconstruct the poet's life and times.[1] Archilochus—the name means 'captain of a company' and may thus have been no more than a sobriquet—was born in the village of Myrrhine, on Paros, about 716/5 B C. His father's name was Telesicles, and his mother was a slave-woman named Enipo. Thus he began his life with an understandable grievance, since though bastardy was not then

[1]For a detailed justification of the chronology adopted here, see my Appendix, 'The Date of Archilochus'. Most scholars now argue, following Jacoby, for a later birth-date, either 704 or even 680; few would agree with Blakeway in his attempt to put this date back as early as 730.

the moral stigma it later became, it precluded inheritance at the expense of any son born in lawful wedlock. Paros as an island was still very poor, its fine marble as yet undiscovered, its inhabitants—then as now—dependent largely on fishing for a livelihood. The soil was stony (even though under the personal protection of Demeter) and the island's red figs enjoyed a poor reputation. No future there. Like his modern counterpart, Archilochus must from childhood onwards have seen emigration as the one viable solution to his problems. Nor was there much doubt, during those years, as to where young Parians should seek their fortunes: not westward, but in the north. Close to the Thracian coast there lay the offshore island of Thasos, then known (with good reason, as those who have visited it in winter can testify) as Eërië, or 'the place of mist'.

Now Archilochus' own family had close connexions with Thasos, from a period dating back at least to his early childhood. Perhaps in the period 708/5 his grandfather, Tellis, together with a priestess named Cleoboea, introduced the rites of Demeter from Paros to Thasos. This does not imply colonization but commercial penetration, such as always preceded a colonizing venture. About 697/6 his father Telesicles and another prominent citizen named Lycambes were sent from Paros to consult the Delphic Oracle as to the advisability of colonizing Thasos. The Oracle gave its approval to the venture: 'Announce to the Parians, Telesicles, that I bid you found a far-seen township in the Misty Island.' The other oracle supposedly given to Telesicles on this occasion sounds suspiciously like an *ex post facto* forgery concocted at a time when Archilochus had already achieved fame as a poet; but it is none the less interesting for that. It runs: 'That son of yours, Telesicles, shall be immortal and famed in story among men who is the first to meet and speak to you as you step ashore from the ship in your native country'—that is, on his return from Delphi. This is a traditional oracle of the 'first-met' variety. It is interesting when taken in conjunction with what is known as the 'Mnesiepean Inscription', after a third-century Parian worthy called

Mnesiepes, who about 250 BC built an 'Archilocheion' or heroic shrine dedicated to the poet, with a long inscription commemorating his life and works. Parts of this inscription were recently rediscovered and edited by the Greek scholar Kontoléon; they include one anecdote which deserves wider currency than it has hitherto received.

This is what may be termed the incident of the cow and the Muses. While still a young boy, the story goes, Archilochus was sent out by his father to a field known as The Meadows to bring a cow back into the city. He had to get up very early, while it was still dark. The moon, however, was shining. When he got to a place called Lissides (? the Smooth Cliffs) he saw what he took to be a group of women coming back from work—what sort of work at such an hour we are not informed. At all events, true to his later form, he boldly approached the group and 'made fun of them'. They received him with cheerful laughter, and inquired if he wanted to sell them his cow, saying they would give him a good price for it. When he agreed, they vanished, and the cow vanished with them. In exchange, he found a lyre at his feet. Realizing that they must have been the Muses, he took the lyre and told the whole story to his father. Telesicles was astonished, we are told; he also seems to have known his son, since the first thing he did was to send out a search-party after the lost cow; but it was nowhere to be found on the island. This episode (as we learn from the same passage) took place prior to Telesicles' and Lycambes' mission to Delphi; and the 'first-met' son encountered by Telesicles on his return was, of course, Archilochus himself. That both anecdotes are fabrications we need not doubt, despite the plausible details surrounding them; the only interesting problem is whether they were posthumous inventions, or self-inflating propaganda cooked up —as I would like to believe—by Archilochus himself. We have no means of telling; but this kind of spoof would be entirely in character, and it is pleasant to imagine a wry smile hovering over the hard-bitten old soldier-poet's lined features as, between sips at his never-empty wine-cup, he worked out so charmingly preposterous a tale for the edification of posterity.

About 695/4 the colonizing party sailed for Thasos. It included Telesicles, Lycambes, and their families; in all likelihood Archilochus' close friend Glaucus son of Leptines[1] went with them as well, and perhaps his other comrade-in-arms, Pericles. 'Paros, figs, life of the sea, farewell!' he wrote in one fragment; but he was to like Thasos no better, describing it as rising out of the sea, with its topping of wild forest, 'like an ass's back', and even showing a flash of nostalgia for the mountain glens he had climbed as a boy. The would-be colonists were to have a tough time of it. There was gold on Thasos and in the Thracian hinterland opposite; there were also the Thracians themselves to contend with—great hulking savages, red-haired and grey-eyed, who used terrible broadswords and were reputedly so addicted to liquor that they would sell their own children to get it. Nor were the Thracians their only enemies, or even perhaps their worst. Paros was not the only Aegean island to send prospectors northward, anxious to establish a foothold on Thasos and the Thracian Peraea. The Chians were settled at Maroneia, under the slopes of Mount Ismarus (the source of Maron's wine, with which Odysseus succeeded in getting the Cyclops drunk) while on Thasos itself the Parian colonists were continually at loggerheads with rival colonizing bands from Naxos. It was a harsh, primitive, dangerous existence, to which the nearest modern parallel is perhaps the early period in the opening up of the American West—including the Klondike gold rush. There is the same atmosphere of dirt and lice and toughness minus heroics, the same whoring, boozing, foul-mouthed energy, the same crudely Stoic philosophy of life. All this Archilochus saw, experienced, and turned into verse as spare and muscular and realistic as any war-poetry ever written, anywhere or in any age.

[1]By one of those astonishing coincidences that occasionally happen to encourage archaeologists, French excavators on Thasos recently discovered his tombstone, with the inscription: 'Glaucus son of Leptines am I; the sons of Brentis set me up.' Why the sons of Brentis? Who *was* Brentis? Another enigma to add to the rest.

It was natural, given such circumstances, that the two families of Telesicles and Lycambes should have been thrown closely together; and Archilochus (whose toughness does not wholly conceal a marked romantic streak) fell desperately in love with Lycambes' youngest daughter, Neobule. (The fragmentary line 'O that I might touch Neobule's hand' has become justly famous, even though there is a distinct possibility that what it really means is 'Just let me get my hands on Neobule—'.) The Thracian women, with their habit of sucking beer through straws—a habit, we know, calculated to induce rapid intoxication—and their liking for intercourse *per anum*, perhaps to preserve their virginity for the marriage market (a practice not unknown in modern Greece) seem not to have appealed to him. At all events, he set his mind on marriage, and perhaps about 690, being by now twenty-five, he obtained Lycambes' provisional agreement to the match. One of the conditions, it seems clear, was that Archilochus should prove himself a man of sufficient substance to enter upon matrimony. Granted his illegitimate status, this must have presented the young suitor with something of a problem; and he attempted to solve the problem, as did Hesiod's father in slightly different circumstances, by making a trading voyage. During the great period of colonization—and indeed for long afterwards, as we know from fourth-century law-suits—such ventures offered huge risks, but correspondingly huge profits, sometimes of several hundred per cent on the original outlay. If they failed, however, the loss was total and crippling, since more often than not the initial capital was raised on loan. We need not doubt that this applied to Archilochus' case; the best one can assume is that he raised the loan from his father. At all events, he set out with high hopes to Gortyn in Crete; but at some point shipwreck and disaster struck him, putting paid to all his hopes. A recently discovered papyrus, perhaps the most important addition yet to the Archilochean corpus, describes the event in a moving dialogue:

[1]. . .One rule I honour: *Don't flinch,*
Face up to the worst. So I answered her as follows:
'Woman, you ought not to let this slanderous gossip
Worry you for one moment. Myself, I shall only take notice
Of words uttered in friendship. Try being kind to me.
Do you really believe I've sunk to such a nadir of utter
Misfortune? Was my conduct so cowardly in your eyes?
No: I am not such a craven, nor were my ancestors.
I know the code: *Return friendship with friendship,*
Be your enemy's enemy. Provoke me, I'm dangerous—
The ant bites! If you want the truth, remember that command
I had from the oracle: "Go back to Misty City, which once
Was stormed by you and your men. At the spear-point
You levelled its resistance, and won great renown therefrom.
Go then, rule over it, possess it in absolute power;
So shall you be envied by the whole race of mankind." '
She replied: 'You came home to us with one small vessel
After all that lengthy voyage, back home from Gortyna.
You had survived. Neither fish nor vultures had feasted on you.
Don't think I'm hard-hearted—I rejoiced more than anyone
At your survival, I cried and carried on terribly
When I thought of breaking off the marriage we'd planned:
I was willing to stretch out my hand to you, I hoped
We might part in friendship—but I have to think of that
Cargo you lost; it's put paid to our wedding as well.'
I said: 'What could I have done? I possessed no other
Resources. Once the salt waves had swallowed up

[1]Text first edited by Edgar Lobel, Pap. Oxyrh. 2310 fr. 1 col. I vv. 5-39; subsequently by F. Lasserre and A. Bonnard, *Archiloque*, Paris (Budé) 1958, fr. 35. pp. 11-13, cf. F. Lasserre, *Museum Helveticum* 13 (1956) 226-35. The text is fragmentary at the beginning (which is lost) and throughout its second half, having lost between one quarter and one third of the left hand side of the column. Neither Lasserre-Bonnard, nor Davenport in his translation (*Carmina Archilochi* no. 43, pp. 18-19), succeed in extracting much sense from it. If we assume that the whole poem—or the passage preserved, at least—consists of a dialogue between A and B (whom we can, with some plausibility, identify as Archilochus and Neobule) rather than being a monologue delivered by one person, then many of the difficulties, inherent in the Greek text vanish. At line 13 I have supplied Ἠερίην to fill the lacuna: one supplement which I regard as virtually certain. The rest is no more than plausible conjecture; but at least it makes consistent logical sense of the Greek, which no previous interpretation has even claimed to do.

My fortune, there was nothing left me to offer you.'
She answered: 'Still, you are lucky. No enemy spearman's
Made short work of your youthful good looks. Indeed,
God has preserved you alive in the flower of your manhood.'
I replied: 'The man you see also stands condemned
To solitude, stripped of his hopes. I thought I'd struggled
Through to the light, but I'm lying in darkness still. . . .'

The breaking of the young poet's engagement probably took place early in 689, soon after a near-total solar eclipse. The two occurrences, coming so close together, gave rise to a famous poem in which, as Aristotle tells us, Archilochus 'portrays the father talking about the daughter'. The fragment, clearly, is put in the mouth of Lycambes, and represents a piece of hopeful (and highly characteristic) wishful thinking on the author's part that, in fact, his prospective father-in-law was as shocked, by Neobule's decision as he himself had been. When something like *this* could happen, the poem suggests, nothing was certain any more: if the sun itself could be darkened, why not a young man's hopes?

No event's too much to look for, nothing now can be ruled out
As too wonderful, since Father Zeus of the Olympians
Turned the noonday into darkness, overshadowing the sun's
Lambent brightness, while green terror stalked abroad among
mankind.

After *that* we can't be sure of anything, much less surprised
By mere oddities. Don't wonder if you happen to observe
Cows and dolphins changing places, cattle browsing in the sea-
Pastures, fish upon the hillsides, herds that ride the noisy
waves . . .

But Lycambes remained unmoved by this piece of special pleading so thoughtfully put in his mouth, and backed up his daughter's decision. A penniless, foul-mouthed, quarrelsome poet would be something worse than an embarrassment as a son-in-law, even in this new frontier society.

Archilochus retaliated in the one way he knew: with a torrent of poetic abuse which became proverbial in antiquity, and so appallingly scabrous that, according to one tradition, Lycambes and his daughters are said to have hanged themselves for shame. Again, I can't help suspecting another exercise in wishful thinking. The frustrated suitor worked out a lurid fantasy of what he would like to see happen, and this was dutifully recorded as fact by later generations which (a not infrequent occurrence) had only his own works from which to extrapolate his life. But the works, even those tattered fragments of them which survive, do help us to understand how he got his reputation in antiquity; how Pindar, for example, could speak of Archilochus' shiftlessness and venom and 'heavy-worded hatred'. We find him still lambasting Neobule, in the coarsest physical terms (the violence of his sexual imagery and insults is quite extraordinary: who but Archilochus would have called a woman a 'diner on eyeless eels' —a phrase which baffled classical scholars for rather longer than it should have done?) long after the poor woman had passed into thick-waisted and thick-ankled Greek middle-age. But the most famous extant example of his invective (I find it hard to credit the doubts cast on its authenticity) is the great commination service directed against Lycambes, and, on the face of it, written at white-hot speed as an immediate *réplique* to the action which had provoked Archilochus' rage. I give it here in the brilliant version by Guy Davenport:

May he lose his way on the cold sea
And swim to the heathen Salmydessos,
May the ungodly Thracians with their hair
Done up in a fright on the top of their heads
Grab him, that he know what it is to be alone
Without friend or family. May he eat slave's bread
And suffer the plague and freeze naked,
Laced about with the nasty trash of the sea.
May his teeth knock the top on the bottom
As he lies on his face, spitting brine,
At the edge of the cold sea, like a dog.
And all this it would be a privilege to watch,

Giving me great satisfaction as it would,
For he took back the word he gave in honour,
Over the salt and table at a friendly meal.[1]

Not, one may feel, the sort of stuff to drive a well-connected citizen to suicide, but fairly blistering all the same.

Nor, as Critias reminds us, again on the basis of his own works, did he treat his friends with much more consideration than his enemies. Of those we know, Glaucus son of Leptines perhaps comes off best. He is treated to advice and moral reflections (take life as it comes; don't weep in adversity; only trust a mercenary so long as he's fighting) but also comes in for some merciless guying. In the fairly transparent animal fables which Archilochus wrote, Glaucus figures as the timorous stag. His dandified ringlets, clean-shaven upper lip, and camp long-legged cavalry manner are contrasted with the short, heavy, reliable soldier, bowed in the legs but hard to budge—surely a self-portrait by the poet? But he gets off lightly in comparison with the unfortunate Pericles. *His* animal *persona* is that of a mischievous monkey; Archilochus lampoons him on various occasions for gate-crashing, gluttony, drunkenness, boasting about his ancestors ('a FitzFart on his father's side') while in fact being a *parvenu*; he accuses him of homosexuality, failure to secure political office, and heaven knows what besides. How long, one wonders, did they remain good friends? Other public figures got equally short shrift; there may, indeed must, have been a market and audience for these *Private Eye* assaults, but Archilochus was not, by any stretch of the imagination, a comfortable figure for any social group to assimilate, and neither his own nor his ex-fiancée's family can have relished having him around after the highly public mudslinging connected with the

[1] Scholars will know, and the lay reader should perhaps be warned, that this is an extremely free version; those who want a closer but tamer one may turn to Richmond Lattimore's *Greek Lyrics*, p. 5, and for the Greek text either to Diehl's *Anthologia Lyrica Graeca* or the new and excellent text (with German translation and commentary) by Professor Max Treu. I print Davenport's because he captures the inner *spirit* of Archilochus better than any other translator; and in the present context that is of paramount importance.

broken engagement. If my reconstruction is correct, some sort of whip-round was made at this point (spring 689) and Archilochus found himself packed off back to Paros, a remittance-man in reverse. Here he got up to his tricks once more, and after about five years—by which time he had, as Oenomaus of Gadara tells us, 'squandered his capital on political tomfoolery'—he turned up on Thasos once more, broke and angry as ever, an unwanted returning prodigal who refused to stay away or to keep quiet. This time he was back for good.

Archilochus spent the rest of his life on Thasos or the adjacent Thracian littoral, fighting native tribesmen and rival colonists, cursing ('Hear me swear,' says one tantalizing fragment), drinking, fornicating, cheerfully atrabilious, hammering out a dour yet hedonistic philosophy of life (which might be described as fatalism tempered with sensuality) and—the one factor which sets him apart from many such men—setting his experiences down, distilling the sum of his emotions, in tough, spare, utterly original verse, remarkable not only for its vividness of imagery and its metrical innovations, but also for the unique vision of life which it evokes. Archilochus lets us see, unforgettably, just what it meant to be a Greek colonist in the first half of the seventh century B C. *See*: that is the key word. Again and again the parallel which first springs to mind is a visual one: in particular, Matthew Brady's great photographs of the American Civil War. Perhaps through the accident of fragmentation, Archilochus has an almost *haiku*-like ability to convey, in a few words, all the most real and non-Homeric aspects of warfare—the mess and dirt and pointlessness of it all, the built-in protective nostalgia and the private hells of terror. In perhaps his most famous fragment he described himself as 'a squire to Lord Enyalios [the War-God] and one who understands the lovely gift of the Muses'. It was true; he had two masters, and served both well. Though it was his invective which won Archilochus most fame in antiquity, it is his first-hand knowledge of fighting which comes across most powerfully today: he is almost the only ancient writer of any sort (let alone poet) who makes us *see* a battle, makes us say to ourselves: *Yes: yes; this is how it must have been.* One obvious reason is that he was under no temptation to glorify or romanticize war. Realism and myth-making mix no better than Clytemnaestra's oil and vinegar.

It is all a world away from Homer, this dirty, dangerous, vivid, uncomplicated, often boring existence, with rival speculators fighting for mining rights, and corpses drying to parched mummy in the summer sun, and men who prefer to throw away their shields and live rather than to be carried home dead with honour: a world where the Gods have lost their humanity and appear as vast, impersonal begetters of disaster. Pleasure lies in the immediate senses, the enjoyment of women, the wine-cup passed on watch aboard a ship. The rock of Tantalus hangs over Thasos; all the woes of the Hellenes have come together there. War comes up, ugly, ineluctable and unwanted, like the storm-clouds of the *meltemi* over Tenos. One quality which scholars (bemused by that shield-dropping episode, and perhaps taking Archilochus a little too much at his face value) do not appreciate enough is this practical soldier's underplayed yet undeniable courage and, yes, patriotism. This is a man with a foul mouth but a cool head, a captain who looks after his own; I should have liked to be in his company. How anyone could ever have believed the myth about his being a mercenary I cannot conceive. There is not one scrap of hard evidence for it, and it goes against the grain of all his writing. Whatever Archilochus is in the war-game for, it is not money. He may, as he says, depend on his spear for his bread and wine: he may be always on guard, and drink with the same spear to prop him up, like a shooting-stick. But he does not talk about his spear bringing him a regular income, for the good and sufficient reason that no such idea ever entered his head. For his day he was a very modern figure; we can see him, now, as an early overseas version of *polis* man, who believed in fighting collectively for his own people, and already contained within himself the seeds of that fighting, progressively more xenophobic, Greek imperialism which brought Athens to disaster during the Sicilian Expedition.

'Isn't life a terrible thing—thank God,' said Dylan Thomas' Polly Garter in *Under Milk Wood* (perhaps the most heart-warming remark of the century) and one senses the same spirit at work when reading Archilochus. He grins through it all, one sardonic eye alert for human foibles: Lord, what fools these mortals be, and I too, Lord, am mortal. Pericles and Glaucus, as we saw earlier, must have had a lot to put up with; and if it comes to that, Neobule's side of the story would be worth hearing—like Molly Bloom's. Even in his most tattered and ambiguous fragments we sense that idiosyncratic personality at work: the controlled violence, the savage black humour, the perilous tension between the act and the art which it engenders. Out of the Thracian mists there looms a man, individual and uncompromising, who talks about himself and his personal problems, without any trace of traditional bardic anonymity. In particular, he discusses his own sexual urges and difficulties with all the candour of a turned-on group-therapy exhibitionist. He gives a clinical description of the pangs and agonies produced by unrequited love, thus setting a precedent for Sappho half a century later. He tells us, in engaging physical detail, about his impotence (whether this is due to age, over-indulgence, or psychological hang-ups the context never quite makes clear) and achieves small miracles of *double-entendre* when lampooning ladies of easy virtue, such as Pasiphile ('Lover-to-all'), whom he describes as a 'fig of the rocks, nourishing many crows, an accommodating and easy hostess to strangers'. It looks simple till we realize that *syké*, fig, in ancient as modern Greek, refers to the anus, with a homosexual connotation, while *korona*, or crow, can also be a slang term for the penis. Ambiguities of this sort abound in Archilochus (and for the matter of that in a Roman poet such as Catullus: the famous 'sparrow poems', *pace* the Warden of All Souls, make much more sense when we know that *passer*, sparrow, in ancient Latin as in Florentine argot, likewise can bear a phallic connotation). They form an engaging counterpart to the romantic side of him which rhapsodizes over girls with their duennas, the flowers in their hair, the sweet scent of them (but 'O their cunts', he adds, rather spoiling the picture for *Woman's Own* readers), and can draw a striking contrast between his *inamorata*, so white and virginal behind locked doors, while he is so heavy with infamy, sighing his heart out for frustration, unable to work, while time and the seasons drag on.[1]

It is quite impossible to determine the date of Archilochus' death with any accuracy. We can, very probably place it after 652, since he refers to the 'woes of the Magnesians', a phrase which afterwards became proverbial, and refers to the destruction of Magnesia in that year by wild Trerian tribesmen. But further than that we cannot go. He is traditionally supposed to have been killed in battle, by a Naxian known as Crow (perhaps a distant avatar of that remarkable survival-and-destruction figure evoked by Ted Hughes). If so, he must have been in his mid-sixties at the time; and though we have evidence for elderly front-line warriors, the story arouses one's suspicions—especially since Crow was required to purify himself for having slain a servant of the Muses, which would hardly have been the case had they met on the battlefield. I suspect, in fact, that Archilochus, true to form, died during some crapulous bar-room brawl (a theory not invalidated by Crow's protest to the god: 'Lord, I killed him in fair fight') and that posterity, with understandable *pietas*, rewrote his end in terms considered more appropriate to a soldier-poet. Perhaps, at the higher level, posterity was right. We can visualize him as he chews a last mouthful of barley-bread, cracks a coarse joke with his men, and then turns back, without fuss, to the 'dry racket of javelins', the harsh realities of some long-forgotten campaign which is only immortalized because one man who fought in it was a true poet and the Muses' servant. Cicero and those other ancient critics who bracketed Archilochus with Homer and Sophocles and

[1] See Lasserre-Bonnard, frs. 249—56. Numerous graduate students, asked to identify the author of such sentiments, have nearly always plumped for a Roman elegist, most often Ovid. The mistake is understandable, and does credit to Archilochus' extraordinary capacity for being in advance of his time.

Pindar were absolutely right; even in grammarians' snippets and torn papyrus fragments we can sense something wholly new in Greek literature: the voice of the individual speaking loud and clear. It was not to last: the city-state proved an all-demanding collective master, a dispensation which (as we have seen) regarded the odd man out as an *idiotes*. But during that brief spring an immortal element was added to European literature, and Archilochus—quite aside from his own pure talent—deserves eternal credit as its first, if not its only, begetter.

II

About half a century after his death, Archilochus' fame was equalled—and ultimately eclipsed—by that of a woman, ironic rough justice for one who took so disobliging an attitude to the whole female sex in his own work. (Playwrights of late Middle Comedy got their own back by portraying the woman as a randy and omnivorous nymphomaniac, who—bridging the centuries with careless abandon—numbered both Archilochus and Hipponax amongst her lovers.) The woman's name was Sappho, and even in antiquity men spoke of her as the tenth Muse. Today she still remains one of the most famous lyric poets the world has ever known, a name to be ranked with Heine or Villon or Burns, a flame, a legend. Yet, paradoxically, we possess (as with Archilochus before her) a mere fraction of her actual work; and though the reputation she enjoys rests to a great extent on her personal legend, we in fact know rather less about Sappho the woman than we do about Shakespeare the man—another great collector of romantic or cranky adherents, and for very similar reasons. The safe, or safely surmisable, facts can soon be summarized.

It is generally agreed that her life-span covered the end of the seventh century B C and the beginning of the sixth: the period, that is, during which colonization lost its crude initial impetus, as the blank spots on the Mediterranean map were all filled in, as claims were staked and consolidated, and the frontier pioneers (sometimes painfully) turned themselves into wide-ranging traders and businessmen. We can deduce, with a fair degree of confidence, that she was born in 618 B C, the year of Alyattes' accession to the throne of Lydia. Her father Scamandronymus (whose name suggests an Asiatic origin from the Troad) died when she was six years old, and it is a guess, but a plausible guess, that he died during the aristocratic revolt against Mytilene's tyrant, Melanchros, datable to 612/09. This event may mark her removal from Eresos, where she was born, to Mytilene itself, then as now the chief city of Lesbos. The family was an aristocratic one, and Sappho herself, despite her predominantly personal poetry, was closely enough involved in revolutionary plots against the tyranny to be twice exiled from Mytilene. (The tyranny was represented, latterly, by Pittacus, one of the so-called Seven Wise Men, who were chosen for their statesmanlike rather than their philosophical qualities.) On the second occasion (598), if we are to believe the *Marmor Parium*, she was expelled from Lesbos altogether, and relegated to Sicily. Her fellow-poet Alcaeus also went into exile at the same time. Not too long afterwards, however, she was allowed to return home, and spent the rest of her life (as far as we know) in Mytilene, dying at some point not long after 570.

What do we know about her more domestic circumstances? She married a rich merchant from Andros, called Cercylas, and bore him one daughter, Cleis, whom she named after her own mother. She had three brothers, Charaxus, Eurygyus and Larichus: if there were sisters we never hear about them. Eurygyus seems to have died young. Charaxus became a wine-merchant, trading cargoes to Naucratis, the Greek port in the Egyptian Delta. Here he fell disastrously in love with a prostitute or geisha-girl called, variously, Doricha or Rhodope (the latter in all likelihood her professional nickname, the rough equivalent of our 'Rosie'). With Rosie he drank rather more than cider, and wasted his substance in every conceivable way; he had not, it seems, yet learnt the hard Archilochean lesson that (as the older poet put it) any whore's belly is ideally equipped to drain away a man's gold reserves. He not only made her his mistress; he threatened to marry her. Sappho, much incensed, trounced him publicly for this in several notorious poems, thus of course ensuring the incident maximum publicity at the time and eternal fame thereafter, which may well have been her disobliging intention all along. Larichus, her youngest brother, was very good-looking, and (perhaps in consequence, an ugly Ganymede being something of a paradox) cup-bearer at Mytilene town-hall. Last and most ambiguously, she was the centre of a group of girls in Mytilene. The exact nature of this *thiasos* or *hetairia* is less clear than one might guess from reading the lucubrations of romantic scholars on the subject. All else has been overlaid with endless strata of legend, modern no less than ancient, and obscured by the dust of furious emotional polemic.

I knew, when I decided to write a novel[1] about Sappho, that the task of researching her life was bound to present difficult problems, amongst which unacknowledged emotional prejudice ranked very high. Some historical characters—Alexander the Great is another classic example—seem to invite special pleading almost by definition. Even Sappho's most sensible modern critic can speak of the 'copious but inane biographical tradition'; it is not quite so inane as all that, and all too often in such a context 'inanity' becomes coterminous with what the investigator feels personally disinclined to believe. The interesting thing about the tradition of misrepresentation is the way it has come full circle. Comic poets of the Hellenistic era, as we have seen, caricatured Sappho as a randy figure of fun, indiscriminately heterosexual. Her modern supporters have, clearly, gone to the other extreme: *their* Sappho comes over as a cross between Kingsley's Hypatia (buzz, buzz) and Elizabeth Barrett Browning. (Which interpretation, I wonder, would Sappho herself have resented more?) Yet the two ends of the pole have one very interesting feature in common: they both, though for quite different reasons, imply that Sappho *could not possibly have been a*

[1] *The Laughter of Aphrodite:* London (John Murray), New York (Doubleday), 1965.

practising lesbian. Difficult emotional ground here; and a possible explanation of why that pretty but unauthenticated story about Sappho running a kind of finishing-school for young ladies, or even functioning as the priestess of a cult, has had such a long run for its money. (One cynical historian of comparative religions I know said: 'If you want to clean up a bit of dirt—incest, lesbianism, group buggery, you name it—just stick a ritual label on the practice and everyone'll take it in their stride.') Sappho may have been a cultural leader of some sort, though it would not do to press too closely as regards the nature of such a role. She may even have taken the occasional discreet *quid pro quo* for dispensing literary, musical, or balletic expertise. What seems absolutely undeniable is that this group of girls not only tolerated, but largely existed for, intense and passionate relationships (whether consummated or not seems a fairly academic point) with each other.

Perhaps because of this, my own personal quest for Sappho began elsewhere, in a context where the human element intruded as little as possible—the moods and seasons and physical landscape of the island of Lesbos, on which all but a few years of her life were spent (a fine source, then, for glosses on her basic, one had almost said archetypal, imagery), and the very name of which is a constant nudging reminder of the one thing about her which everybody, literary or not, can be relied upon to know. (It also, I would surmise, provides the local tourist board with a nice problem in conflicting loyalties.) Slowly, as the seasons passed, and I explored more of the island's varied scenery—Eresos in the south-west, with its high crouching headlands, and Sappho's traditional birth-place; the great mountain gorges of the northern coast; the cornlands and glittering salt-flats of the inland gulf, where wild horses still roam, as in the Camargue—I came to see how little its essential features must have changed since Sappho's lifetime, how often a puzzling phrase in her poetry could be elucidated or enhanced from the living world around me. The commentator in his study might make heavy weather of a 'rosy-fingered moon' after sunset, but the phrase would come as no surprise—rather with a delighted stab of recognition—to any islander.

The same is true of the simple, permanent things which require no explanation, yet still touch one strangely, seeing them in this place and no other, remembering the unforgettable words —that lilting rhythm, those broad Aeolic vowels and at times outlandish dialect—which *she* had used to describe them: a grape hyacinth carelessly trodden into the furrow; a peasant, swaying on two rickety chairs, reaching up through the branches of his gnarled apple-tree; spring water, crystal-clear, tumbling down a miraculously lush hillside among beech and plane and rowan. Sappho's eye for natural phenomena, in fact, was extraordinarily accurate—which tells us something valuable about Sappho herself. She saw, as anyone may see today if they choose to look, chickpeas blowing golden along the shore, and the brief miracle of spring on Lesbos during which—no cliché or understatement—'the many-garlanded earth puts on her broidery'. That 'downrushing wind' which shook the oaks in her day is no stranger, in October or February, to the modern islander; and nobody who has heard the *meltemi* roaring through the great chestnut forests above Aghiassos will underestimate the force of Sappho's simile for the passion which racks her trembling limbs. There: back to the central theme again, and in Sappho's case it's hard to stay clear of it for long. Sooner or later the human element, the fog of preconception and prejudice, has to be met and faced.

Mytilene itself is a good point of departure in this respect. The municipal authorities have by no means forgotten their famous poetess. One of the city's largest and newest hotels bears her name. (A visiting woman journalist confided to me that approaching by sea and being confronted by two large neon-lit sky-signs, side by side, both obviously hotels and reading SAPPHO and LESBION respectively, was a somewhat daunting experience.) The latest local English-language guide devotes much space to proving that she had the manners, morals and outlook of a Greek Orthodox schoolmistress—and then rather spoils the effect by printing some spirited translations of her poems (the old *Song of Songs* allegorical argument simply won't work with Sappho, who is nothing if not direct). Two public monuments have been erected, if that is the word I want, in her honour. The older is small, inaccessible, and inoffensive, a small cone of rough-hewn stone up on the cliff-top, most often seen in perspective from the beach below. (At least, I thought it was inoffensive until told by one more than usually outspoken friend, a girl, that it looked exactly like an erect clitoris, and how appropriate.) Lately, however, a new white marble statue—the gift, it would seem, of a ladies' group, or *thiasos*, known as the Friends of Sappho—has been sited, somewhat bizarrely, on a tall plinth in the middle of the main public parking-lot. It resembles nothing so much as a hefty but high-minded gym-instructress, and I can never pass it without remembering Sappho's own remark about those she had done good to being the ones who did her the greatest wrong in return.

So assertive a monument unavoidably posed the first of many problems I had to face; what, in fact did the historical Sappho look like? With a character for whom personal and passionate relationships were of supreme importance (not to invoke the dread names of Kretschmer or Sheldon) this seemed a more than usually relevant question.[1] In this case there were two almost insuperable factors operating against me. To begin with, the realistic portrait as we know it is a phenomenon which, we are told, scarcely antedates the fourth century B C—is, indeed, one symptom of that marked trend towards individualism which characterizes the whole Hellenistic period, and reaches its apogee with Imperial Rome. Therefore, since Sappho most probably died between 570 and 565 B C, the chances of any work of art preserving her actual individual features are more or less non-existent—though, it might be argued, the

[1] One, though, it might be argued, of more immediate concern to the historical novelist than the historian: which may explain why I researched, *qua* novelist, many historical problems I could easily have side-stepped were I writing a scholarly monograph, and raises some interesting questions as to the tacit conventions governing historiography. I hope to return to this problem elsewhere.

discovery in 1939 of the Themistocles-herm at Ostia, a Roman copy of a Greek original arguably made towards the end of Themistocles' own lifetime, has shortened the odds on that particular argument considerably. In addition we are hampered by chronic lack of material on which to base our estimate. Though something like fifty statues or busts have been hopefully identified as Sappho by various modern pundits, on grounds ranging from the flimsy to the risible, there is not one (unless we count a late and blatant forgery) which has survived bearing Sappho's name. Nor, it seems, were there many such in antiquity. Indeed, we hear only of two—a statue which was still standing in the Zeuxippus gymnasium at Constantinople as late as 500 A D, and the fourth-century B C Hellenistic bronze by Silanion, which Verres looted from Syracuse during his notorious term as governor of Sicily (and which, incidentally, lends some circumstantial support to the tradition that Syracuse was the place of Sappho's second exile). Paintings were even rarer: that by Leon is the only one on record.

Other surviving representations include some stylized fifth-century B C vase-paintings, a series of coin-portraits, and a few engraved seals: the negative verdict of that great authority the late Sir John Beazley—'No bronze, marble or gem has the slightest claim to represent her'—seems final. And yet I find myself obstinately doubting it. There is a series of electrum coins, struck on Lesbos between the mid-fifth and mid-fourth centuries B C (and obviously the inspiration for the Albani and Castellani busts) which show a striking and by no means conventionally attractive woman's face (though the later issues are progressively more stylized and prettified): strong-nosed, rather fleshy, with a heavy neck and high cheekbones, the hair bound back in a curious kerchief such as peasant women from the outlying villages still occasionally wear. These features have a decidedly Asiatic cast to them: interesting, when we recall the tradition (confirmed by her father's name) connecting Sappho's family with the Troad. Perhaps we can say no more than that the early tradition depicted a typical woman of Lesbos: though

Pollux, in his *Onomasticon*, clearly asserts that the Mytilenaeans put Sappho's head on their coinage.[1] We do much better when we turn to the literary evidence for her appearance, which is strikingly consistent. From the rubbish-tips of Oxyrhynchus, along with so many tantalizing fragments of her poetry, there comes this uncompromising biographical statement: 'In appearance she seems to have been quite unremarkable, indeed more than usually plain, being swarthy-complexioned and of diminutive stature.' Small and dark: these are the recurring epithets in Ovid, and Maximus of Tyre, and the anonymous scholiast on Lucian, who develops the picture with an unforgettable image: 'Physically,' he observes, 'Sappho was very ill-favoured, being small and dark in appearance, like a nightingale with misshapen wings folded over a tiny body.' We have no real grounds for assuming (as has sometimes been done) that all these statements derive from one unreliable source, which can therefore be disregarded, though the suggestion in itself is (like the firm discrediting of those coin-portraits) highly suggestive in psychological terms. The unacknowledged romantic dream of a dreamily beautiful Pre-Raphaelite Sappho dies hard. But for me this dark, vivid (and perhaps in some way crippled) little nightingale is the beginning of a psychologically credible woman, as far removed as could be from the legend. To fill in the picture—and to dissipate the legend further—we must turn to her own surviving work.

Of Sappho's poetry, the ultimate primary source for any understanding of her, less than a twentieth part survives: excerpted phrases preserved by grammarians, to illustrate curious words or usages; torn, semi-illegible papyrus scraps sifted with infinite care from the dry sands of Egypt. Ezra Pound's tiny, enigmatic poem—'. . .spring. . ./. . .too long. . ./ . . .Gongyla. . .' is, in fact, part of one such fragment translated, and typical in its elusive glimpse of a poem, a relationship, a world

[1] I know at least two women today, in Methymna (Molyvos), who could have modelled that coin die; and both of them—the coincidence is at least worth noting—also come of Anatolian stock.

which we can never hope to recover whole and entire. Though some of the papyrus fragments, it is clear, have comparatively little missing, only one out of all Sappho's poems survives intact. It was not always so. Sappho was sung in Cicero's day, and Horace knew her work almost by heart. We find continuing references to the poems during the first three centuries of our era. Then the trail becomes much less clear, though grammarians continue to excerpt them until the eleventh century. What had happened? We may make allowances for the decadence of learning, the difficulties imposed by Sappho's outlandish dialect, and the vicissitudes which all manuscripts underwent during the Dark Ages; but there remains much evidence to suggest—as we might expect, though some very high-powered scholars argue persuasively against it—that Sappho's poems were destroyed by the Church.

Already in the second century Tatian was fulminating against her 'lewd passions', as he termed them; the first public burning would seem to have taken place towards the end of the fourth century, in the time of Gregory Nazianzen (there is a pleasant legend that he used her works, by way of a final insult, as palimpsests for his own pious but enervating homilies). Both the Eastern and Western Churches are said to have been involved. Scaliger, confirmed by Demetrius Chalcondylas, preserves a tradition that the final and irrevocable bonfire (which reputedly lost us most of Alcman, Alcaeus, Erinna, Mimnermus and Bion as well as Sappho) took place at both Rome and Constantinople in 1073, during Gregory VII's Papacy. Yet even granted the truth of this tradition, just how effective such a gesture could hope to be seems open to doubt. *Every* copy? Not even a modern totalitarian government is as thorough as that. The ultimate culprit is, surely, our old friend illiterate Philistinism. No one, I think, has ever accused the Church of making away with the lost decades of Livy.

Those who so fervently maintain Sappho's moral—meaning, it goes without saying, sexual—purity must find it a little hard, if all these book-burning stories are anything more than anti-papal propaganda by disgruntled humanists, that the same Church which twice committed her works to the flames had, apparently, no objection to Martial's epigrams, with their cold, perverted obscenities, or to the sexually prurient and misogynistic tirades of Juvenal. (The latter, indeed, were multiplied in more manuscripts even than the works of Homer.) But then the puritanical mind, as psychologists are well aware, tends to be far more inflamed by open, candid, happy—and, above all, *guiltless*—passion than by even the nastiest sort of arcane filth, which at times, indeed, it seems actually to encourage. Sappho's very spontaneity and innocence, her wholly unselfconscious lack of restraint would alone suffice to explain why her poetry should have been singled out for destruction. *Would that our night could have lasted twice as long*: no hint in these poems that the flesh is inherently sinful, no self-torment except over unrequited passion. As Mr A. R. Burn so wisely observed in *The Lyric Age of Greece* (though he seems to have modified his views somewhat since then): 'To read into the personal sentiments, then being expressed for the first time, the feelings of guilt that would have been inevitable later is anachronistic. The absence of *shame* is a characteristic of Sappho, for which classical Greek moralists were the first to blame her. It was a situation that could only occur once.'

It was indeed. Sappho's lifetime spans of the most fascinating periods in all Greek history, an age of transition—political, ethical, cultural—with a failing aristocratic ideal stubbornly entrenched against the rising flood of mercantilism. What we have here is the second act of a drama on which the curtain rose when Archilochus was a boy. The new-frontier society, with its drinking and whoring, its obsession with gold-strikes and land-claims, its *ad hoc* morality and its grimly cheerful fatalism, had by now changed into something more settled and —almost—respectable; while isolated enclaves such as Lesbos, rich enough to be self-supporting, and out of the mainstream of Aegean colonization, still clung to ancient aristocratic traditions which in some cases may even have reflected the influence of wealthy Minoan refugees, scattered through the islands and along the coast of Asia Minor by the great *diaspora* after 1400 B C. (No accident, I feel, that the armour which Alcaeus describes in one famous poem is *a century out of date* by general Greek standards.) The independence of women in Lesbian society, to which Sappho's poetry bears such striking witness, could very well be explained by archaic survivals of this sort, operating within a closed sphere of influence. It was, as we have seen in the case of Archilochus, an age during which *individuals* flourished as never before or after, a strange spring interlude between the successive (and very different) collectivisms of Homer and the city-state. We do not find such emphasis on private life and personal preoccupations again until the Hellenistic period.[1]

This indifference to public affairs, this preoccupation with one's own emotional life rather than that of the community at large, is the most characteristic quality in Sappho's work. Though she was twice exiled, and an aristocrat, we find no more mention of the class-conflict, the civil strife which convulsed Lesbos during her lifetime than we do of the Napoleonic Wars in Jane Austen's novels. There is one tattered reference to 'enemies', one complaint about not being able to buy the headbands and fine luxuries she would like, in a context which suggests exile, but that is all. The nearest she comes to a formal position vis-à-vis her society is by way of the epithalamium, or wedding-song —though this accounts for a smaller proportion of her work than is often supposed. The line 'Raise high the roof-beams, carpenters' was not invented by J. D. Salinger; it is from the refrain to a Sapphic epithalamium, which goes on: 'The bridegroom's coming, like Ares—*hymenaion!*—far bigger than the biggest of men', while elsewhere she writes (one can hear the jolting drum-and-fife rhythm in the background): 'Seven fathoms long are the doorkeeper's feet/Five hides went to make

[1] It could perhaps be argued that social conditions on Lesbos were such as to permit an early, evanescent phase of realistic portraiture in art—which in turn might increase the likelihood of the early coin portraits being authentic.

up his sandals/Ten strong cobblers laboured to stitch them.' The famous lines on the Evening Star—'Hesper, who gathers back all that the bright Dawn scattered,/you bring the sheep, you bring the goat, you bring the child home to its mother'—probably formed part of a wedding-song like Catullus' *Hesper adest iuvenes*, which we possess in its entirety. The equally well-known fragments about the trodden hyacinth and the sweet apple just beyond reach on the topmost bough both refer to the bride's anticipated loss of virginity, a subject, not surprisingly, on which Sappho achieves some of her most poignant touches, most simply expressed in the fragmentary dialogue (probably based on an old folksong) between a girl and her maidenhead:

—Maidenhead, maidenhead, where are you gone from me?
—Never again shall I come to you, never again shall I come.

But the poem most often quoted as the best example of a Sapphic epithalamium is in fact no such thing; I shall return to this point presently.

The overwhelming majority of these poems and fragments are concerned, in one way or another, with Sappho's own *crises de coeur*, which—even on the five per cent sampling available—would seem to have been about as varied and numerous as those of Colette. This is a world—a hot-house world, some might say—of personal emotions, domesticities, private life aligned to natural phenomena: above all, it is a world of intense, passionate, subtle—sometimes not so subtle—relationships between girls. We know from Alcaeus that there were religiously sponsored beauty contests on Lesbos: this cult of beauty was something which Sappho took with great seriousness. What she dealt in was love: its emotions and imagery and absences, the bright and agonizing world of yearning-keen passions. Even when she introduced a mythical theme, it was nearly always as a gloss on some current private relationship rather than *vice versa* (comparisons with Pindar are fruitful here):

Some say a host of cavalry, others of guardsmen,
And some a fleet, is the finest sight of any
On the dark earth; but I declare the best is
What you love wholly.

Easy enough to make men understand this
Truth the world over: she who so far outshone all
Mortals in beauty, Helen, married to a
Most noble husband,

Yet could leave him, sailing away to Troy, not
Giving one thought to her daughter or her beloved
Parents, lured from the path of virtue by the
Cyprian goddess:

Thus her will was sapped, and all too lightly
Her heart responded to a lover's advances:
So my mind now turns, recalling Anac-
toria's absence,

Whose enchanting gestures, whose gait, whose radiant
Face with its changing moods I would still far sooner
See than all Lydia's chariots, all her empanoplied
Warriors and squadrons.

Here a purely feminine scale of values is set, with conscious deliberation, against Alcaeus' military ideal. The story of Helen is only used to illustrate Sappho's passion for Anactoria, and Helen herself, far from being an awful warning, becomes a classic example of love's irresistibility. As Bowra so well put it, 'what Sappho wants is the physical presence of Anactoria, and this marks the climax and the crisis of the poem'.

Sappho takes the language of love developed by Archilochus and radically transforms it. When Archilochus exclaimed: 'Wretched I lie in longing,/lifeless, with bitter pains piercing/ My bones by the will of the gods', or 'such was the passion for love that twisted under my heart,/thickly misting my eyes, and/ stealing the fragile sense from my breast', he was still using Homeric language, even if for non-Homeric ends; but Sappho speaks for herself. She is a whole-hogger over passion, too; no caveats or qualifications for her. In his so-called 'Delian epigram' (if it is indeed by him) Theognis writes:

> Fairest of things is justice, and best to enjoy good health, but the
> Sweetest delight's to obtain whatever you love.

Contrast this declaration with that of Sappho, who plumps without question for *to kalliston*, beauty, and puts down the panoply of heroic glory (note the use of Lydian cavalry, here as in Mimnermus, to symbolize irresistible military power) with some effectiveness. Yet her choice, we realize, is by no means a soft option. Love, for Sappho, is by no means always (indeed, very seldom) an easy, romantic, enjoyable thing, a mere consumer pleasure. Passion is liable to be disastrous and disruptive: even at her most radiant we are only a hair's-breadth distant from the general notion in classical antiquity that desire is a plague, to be weathered and got through and shaken off as best one may. 'Love shook my heart and wits [*phrenas*] like the wind downrushing on mountain oaks', it is a force as fierce and arbitrary as nature itself: 'Love the looser of limbs shakes me again,/that creature bittersweet, inescapable.' Expectation sharpens delight: loss is softened by the golden recollections of nostalgia. Sappho has a passionate concern for small touch-stone details, the vital minutiae of private life.[1] A fluttering dress can set her heart aflutter; and the nostalgia in her work, the sense of transience, the memory of lost love all the more vivid for being gone, coexists with an intermittent but unmistakable death-wish. This comes out most strikingly in one fragmentary poem of parting which does not always make the anthologies (Lattimore for one omits it) and, when it does, tends to be over-romanticized (as for instance by Bowra in the *Oxford Book of Greek Verse in Translation*) and thus to lose its central point.

Now the crucial key to this remarkable piece is, precisely, its non-romantic, prosaic, conversational language: it reads for all the world like a monologue by some love-lorn schoolgirl ex-

[1] Ancient literary critics, including ps-Longinus, made very heavy weather of Sappho: Demetrius, trying to isolate the literary *charis* in her work, can only describe the whole body of her work, in his impatient, schematizing, masculine way, as dealing with 'maidens' gardens, wedding songs, love poetry'.

pressing herself in fifth-form slang, because (however overwhelming her emotions) that is the only vocabulary available to her. If Sappho went for this effect deliberately (and I believe she did) it shows us another side to her character: wryly self-critical, mockingly amused by life's destructive passions, a butterfly giggling like Dorothy Parker in the very act of being tortured on the wheel of sex: 'No kidding [*adolos*], I wish I was dead. She was crying when she left me, crying a lot, and she said "Oh dear, Sappho, what an awful business this has been for both of us—really, it's not that I *want* to leave you—" And I answered, "Go, and Godspeed, and remember me, for you know how much we loved you. If you don't, if you've forgotten, I want to remind you of all the sweet lovely things we did together . . ." ' Here the text begins to get hopeless, but we find mention of putting sweet-scented flower-garlands round their necks, and lying together on soft-cushioned couches, and putting away desire for other girls, and dancing and singing and ceremonies at the shrines of the gods. Nor is this the only time that Sappho says she wants to die. 'A longing for death possesses me,' one tattered fragment declares, 'and to see the lotus-thick dewy shores of Acheron': a little way farther on in this torn papyrus come the enigmatic words—'spring . . ./. . .too long. . ./. . . Gongyla'—which prompted Pound's poem, referred to above.

Self-mockery and a waspish sense of humour are not two of the qualities which most people would first mention in connexion with Sappho; but they add an extra dimension to her poems and her personality alike. Even her justly famous Ode to Aphrodite is not quite the solemn invocation it is all too often made to appear, although it follows (perhaps parodies would be a more accurate description) the formula for a personal prayer—invocation followed by sanction, and ending with entreaty. It is, of course, true that everyone tends to find in such a poem something reflecting their own special interests—Dionysius of Halicarnassus said its grace lay in the skilful variation of vowel-sounds and the use of soft consonants—and I would not claim to be more immune from such preoccupations than the next man; but at least on this occasion, if I err, it is in distinguished company. First, however, the poem itself:

Throned in splendour, immortal Aphrodite,
Daughter of Zeus, enchantress, I beseech you,
Do not let my heart be crushed by anguish,
  Lady, and torment:

But hither come now, if in time past you ever
Heard my cry from afar, and marked my plight and
Quick-responsive, leaving your Father's mansion,
  Yoked up your golden

Chariot, and came: ah, lovely and swift the sparrows
Bearing you down from heaven, a whirr of wings, down
Through the mid-realm of air, above the darkling
  Realm of this earth, and

Here in a flash! Then you, Lady most blessed,
Smiling with your immortal face upon me
Asked, what was my trouble now, why had I
  Now called upon you,

What new object had my unruly passions
Fastened on this time—'Whom must I now persuade to
Share your affections? Which of them is it now, my
  Sappho, that wrongs you?

'Soon, too soon, your quarry will be your huntress,
Lavishing gifts where now she scorns to take them,
Cold indifference turned overnight to irre-
  sistible passion.'

Come to me now as then, grant me release from
Burdensome worries: all that my heart most yearns for
Bring to fulfilment, and yourself beside me
  Stand as an ally.

What are we to make of this? And what, in particular, is Aphrodite treating as so delectable a joke, a problem which has long bedevilled Sappho's more solemn-owlish admirers and commentators?

It was Professor Denys Page, in *Sappho and Alcaeus*, who pointed out, with exemplary common sense, that the Goddess is described as smiling, not because archaic images always do smile, or even by way of greeting, but because she is *amused*. Nor is the reason far to seek. Sappho has got herself into an emotional tangle once more, and, as usual, is appealing to Aphrodite to sort it out. Professor Page paraphrases the Goddess's speech as follows: 'Why do you keep calling me? Who is it this time, Sappho? It has all happened so often before, and the end has always been the same. Today it is you who love and she who is reluctant; tomorrow it will be she who chases, you who run. So inconstant is your passion, so transient your suffering.' Now this is by no means the Sappho of recent legend: the high-minded teacher, the too-solemn cult-priestess, a kind of early Isadora Duncan, twanging her lyre in a ladylike manner and encircled by yearning but chaste late-Victorian girl-sophomores. To leave the erotic problem on one side for a moment, it is at once clear that the Aphrodite Ode displays precisely the same qualities as the fragment I discussed immediately before it: that is, a capacity for detached self-criticism, and a devastatingly wry sense of humour. Again, Dorothy Parker is the parallel which springs to mind. Even in the depths of her hopeless passion one part of Sappho can stand aside and see how funny it all is, how ludicrously predictable her behaviour. Yet the passion remains real, life is no less intractable for being comic: we laugh wryly, but we are hurt all the same. At the same time, though Sappho mocks herself, she does not mock the Goddess. Indeed she may well have believed, literally, in the epiphanies she describes: whether we explain them ourselves as dreams or waking hallucinations is irrelevant to the fact of her manifest faith. This is the loving familiarity which can spring only from deep devotion, a phenomenon better known to us in its mediaeval context. It is not so far a cry from the Aphrodite Ode to Chesterton's splendid aphorism: 'God has a sense of humour, and Christ our Lord is full exceeding merry.'

But there are more sides than one to a passionate personality, and Sappho has no hesitation about revealing her less dignified characteristics: indeed, one sometimes gets the impression that her whole life was carried on in public. Nothing is too intimate to supply the spark for another poem. She suffers, openly, from humiliating fits of jealousy. When roused, which is a great deal of the time, she can be waspishly vituperative, writing tart moral tracts to her wretched brother in Egypt (but where did she feel *she* stood when it came to washing dirty linen in public?) and lambasting her own rivals in love with icy contempt. 'Fancy falling for some countrified hoyden who can't even arrange her dirty skirt round her ankles properly!' she snaps. Andromeda, we learn from another fragment, will soon be known as Gorgo's wife: Gorgo, it goes without saying, was a girl. In modern parlance, for so fem a character, Sappho displays a remarkable mastery of the butch insult. Would-be rival poets get short shrift, too: 'When you die and are buried, that'll be that—no one's going to remember *you* hereafter, *you* have no share in the roses of Pieria, you'll be ignored by everyone in Hades just as you were on earth. . . .' One can almost see the mischievous, self-mocking expression on her face as she writes: 'Mine is not one of your spiteful temperaments: I have a tender heart.'

A tender heart she certainly had; and a rare embarrassment it has proved to her modern idealizers, who display the most remarkable talent for arguing that, where the touchy subject of love is concerned, Sappho meant almost anything except what she actually said. One great German scholar asserted—and he was by no means alone in his belief—that she could not possibly have been in love with other women, because she was '*eine vornehme Frau, Gattin, und Mutter*', circumstances which (to put it mildly) do not seem to have deterred many of her successors; presumably Wilamowitz was generalizing from his own wife, always a risky procedure. That most passionate of all physical declarations, the ode quoted by pseudo-Longinus in his treatise *On Elevation in Style*, has been described as a wedding-song so often that the obscene grotesqueness of the appellation may not be at once apparent. Let us remind ourselves of the text:

Peer of immortal gods he seems to me, that
Man who sits beside you, who now can listen
Private and close, so close, to your sweet-sounding
  Voice, and your lovely

Passionate laughter—ah, how *that*, as ever,
Sets the heart pounding in my breast; one glance and
I am undone, speech fails me, I can no longer
  Utter a word, my

Tongue cleaves to my mouth, while sharp and sudden
Flames lick through me, burning the inward flesh, and
Sight's eclipsed in my eyes, a clamorous humming
  Rings through my eardrums;

Cold sweat drenches down me, shuddering spasms
Rack my whole frame, a greener-than-grassy pallor
Holds me, till I seem a hair's-breadth only
  This side of dying.

Yet all must be ventured, all endured, since . . .

And there, tantalizingly, our text breaks off. A *wedding-song?* We are, it would seem, required to believe that a complacent bridegroom (backed by a full Greek-style congregation of both families, down to the remotest aunt and cousin) would sit by and listen enthusiastically while Sappho proclaimed to all the world that his bride's physical charms reduced her, Sappho, to a condition of near-orgasm when she so much as looked at her—a theory not only ludicrous, but a good deal more indecent, to my way of thinking, than the obvious and simple truth which it replaced. The real point, as always, is Sappho's capacity for self-observation and self-analysis, the way in which (as pseudo-Longinus pointed out) she expresses the overmastering power of her emotions with both concentration and economy. The scene is simple: a man sitting with a girl. (What were the relations of the sexes on Lesbos? Could they mix freely, and on what occasions? We don't know.) Sappho watches them: envies the man, is turned on by the girl. She shows no jealousy, merely employs the man's state of exaltation as a guide or criterion to her own physical symptoms.[1] Professor Page hardly exaggerated when he wrote of the popular hypothesis: 'There was never such a wedding-song in the history of society; and there should never have been such a theory in the history of scholarship.'

For centuries now it has been a favourite pastime, among scholars and others, to prove that Sappho could not have been a Lesbian, in the modern sense of that word; could not have committed suicide by jumping from the cliffs of Leucas; and could not, for good measure, have embarked, in late middle-age, on a heterosexual affair with a Mytilene boatman. Sappho, more than most ancient writers, has suffered (in antiquity and modern times alike) from misapplied moralizing and misconceived romanticism. One motive, and one only, has dictated the ingenious casuistry applied to the scant evidence concerning her life: the desire to bring it into line with some preconceived picture of post-Christian purity, delicacy and rectitude. Axiom follows definition. Lesbianism is morally abhorrent, *therefore* Sappho cannot have been a practising Lesbian; suicide, apart from its illegality, indicates reprehensible lack of moral fibre, *therefore* Sappho could not have taken her own life; socially, she was from the highest class, a delicate and sensitive lady, *therefore* she could not possibly have had anything to do with a coarse and lecherous lower-class boatman. (One casuist attempted to prove the last of these doubly dubious propositions by claiming that her tastes lay in a quite different direction, which is to have it both ways with a vengeance.) It is perhaps worth pointing out that syllogisms of this sort, though patently absurd as expressed here, are rather more common among classical scholars than the intelligent layman might suppose.

Now anyone who brings a reasonably open mind to Sappho's work will have to concede her passionate and violent emotional involvement with other members of her own sex. (This is not

[1] Not all modern readers take this poem quite as seriously as it was intended; one student of mine suggested that the symptoms described were more appropriate for cholera than for passion.

the place to discuss the complex phenomenon of bisexuality, except to point out that it is far more prevalent a condition than old-fashioned psychologists seem to suppose.) Whether this orientation was taken to its logical, physical conclusion is a point that can never be proved one way or the other—and which, surely, matters very little. (My own feeling, based on a close study of every fragment, is that it was, and that the idea that it should *not* be would simply never have crossed anyone's mind; even the girls' parents were solely concerned to preserve their daughters' technical virginity for marriage, and a homosexual relationship would effectively help such an aim. Again, modern Greek parallels suggest themselves.) The emotional and psychological structure of Sappho's personality is the truly important issue at stake; yet year after year, like criminal lawyers battening on a juicy sex case, scholars and other apologists who should know better have expended learning, passion, and ingenuity on attempts to demonstrate—as though this, *per se*, were of some special, mystical significance—that Sappho did not *go to bed* with her girl-friends. Rose's comment is typical: 'That this is an abnormal condition is very clear; but that it involved any uncleanliness [*sic*] is an idea wholly without support from our evidence [*quite untrue*] and contradicted by the respect with which the best ages of antiquity uniformly mention Sappho.' You can think it, feel it, let it shape your character and dictate your entire life; but so long as you don't *do* it, no one can cry 'Unclean!' In such circumstances, it would appear, Sappho's sublimated passions were at liberty to express themselves more or less as they pleased. It is sad to find such petty police-court treatment being handed out to so rare and splendid a character.

When all else fails, a curious last-ditch argument—familiar to all classical scholars, even if they do not themselves employ it—is regularly brought into play: awkward or unwelcome facts are written off as misunderstood mythology. This is especially true of Sappho's supposed *affaire* with Phaon of Mytilene, and the tradition that she jumped to her death from the white cliffs of Leucas, a western Greek island just outside the Corinthian Gulf.

An identical objection is made to both incidents: they are, it is said, pieces of mythology, misread as fact (just how, we never learn) by ancient biographers, who probably found the first of them, at any rate, in Sappho's own work. This last claim is plausible, but it cuts both ways. Sappho, as we have seen, shows a marked penchant for viewing personal relationships in a divine or mythological context; it is by no means unlikely that she thought of herself as playing Aphrodite to Phaon's Adonis, or the Moon to his Endymion, and enshrined these fancies in poems. Those who insist on a mythical Phaon have to scrape the bottom of the classical barrel for him and make what play they can with Aelian's dubious reference to the younger Marsyas and the comic playwright Cratinus. No one else seems to know of the poor creature—not even Sir James Frazer, who found some far less likely consorts for Aphrodite when compiling *The Golden Bough*.

The social prejudice which militated against any thought of a great aristocratic poetess conducting (at a somewhat undignified age) a violent and scandalous affair with some proletarian ferryman is evident in the ancient world no less than the modern. A tradition arose fairly early that there were *two* Sapphos on Lesbos, the one a lyric poet, the other a courtesan. (The height of confusion is reached by that amiable Byzantine lexicon which it is fashionable nowadays to call the Suda, where we read: 'Some authorities declare that the other Sappho was a lyric poet, too.') Curiously, the same people who dismiss Sappho's affair with Phaon as a variant version of the Adonis-Aphrodite cult make no bones about accepting the exactly parallel story of her brother's infatuation with a Naucratis courtesan at about the same period. Perhaps they might have done did there not exist incontrovertible references to Doricha and Charaxus in the papyrus fragments.

As for Sappho's leap from the cliffs of Leucas, the main argument against this seems to be that a somewhat peculiar (to put it mildly) apotropaic ritual used to take place here annually: it was the custom, Strabo tells us, to cast down some guilty person as scapegoat, having previously tied large numbers of birds to him to break his fall, and there being a crowd waiting below in small boats to rescue him. Which of the two stories is less credible, or how the one may be said to have influenced the other, I leave to the reader's imagination—though, as I remarked earlier, it is extraordinary how much nonsense gets by in this supposedly scientific age if it bears the label 'Ritual Custom'. It may just be worth pointing out that the account of Sappho's suicide, in this particular place, agrees very neatly with the tradition that Phaon abandoned her and went to Sicily, since Leucas lies on the direct sailing-route thither from Greece, via the Isthmus. We are told that he got up to his old adulterous tricks again in Sicily, and was murdered by a jealous husband. Perhaps—it is no more than a guess—Sappho took ship in pursuit of him, and learnt of his death from some Corinth-bound sailor when her vessel made its last landfall before the long voyage across the Adriatic.

This Sappho, it seems to me, is at least a recognizable and consistent human being, individual and alive, not too flagrantly at odds with the evidence that her own poetry affords us. All study of her work is, must be, a frantic raking over scrapheaps whence some verbal splinter may shine out golden before the darkness closes in once more—'the herald of the spring, the sweet-voiced nightingale'—with that genius for economy and the *mot juste* ('whiter than eggs'), those adjectives expressing tenderness, slenderness, brightness which form her private stock-in-trade, the glimpses she offers us of a small, suffering, beautiful, sunlit, intense, hedonistic world, more real than so much of the heroics, and so much more enduring: if it resembles anything in antiquity it is, significantly, a Minoan fresco. I must confess to having developed a strong affection for her while writing my novel; I hope I have done some sort of justice to that brilliant, wayward, small, vital, ugly creature, with her transfiguring smile, her storms and rages and egocentric tirades, her infinite capacity for self-surrender in love, her sharp and crystalline talent. 'Somebody, I tell you, will remember us hereafter,' she once wrote. She could scarcely have foreseen the strange vicissitudes her reputation would undergo down the ages: a pity, because it is hard to conceive a joke which she would have enjoyed more.

The First Sicilian Slave War

THE Roman slave revolts of the second and early first centuries B C were unique. Nothing like them had ever happened before, and after the final suppression of Spartacus in 70 B C no comparable rising ever took place again. The first Sicilian outbreak is little studied by historians; yet it contains some unique features, and its leader, Eunus, was in his own way as remarkable a man as Spartacus. We are also fortunate in that our literary tradition does not here, as so often, stem wholly from pro-Roman sources. Our main evidence for the revolt and its background is to be found in Diodorus Siculus. As his name implies, Diodorus was a Sicilian, from Agyrium; and his account post-dates the revolt by less than a century. He may well have drawn material from the Greek philosopher and historian Posidonius, himself, like Eunus, a native of Apamea; Posidonius was widely travelled and had an interest in the problem of slavery. It has also been suggested that he might have viewed the insurrection from a sympathetic viewpoint, but since one of his main objects in his *Histories* was to justify Roman imperialism, I am inclined to take this hypothesis with a grain of salt. He was also writing some fifty years after the event. Both Diodorus and the epitomators of Livy—our only other narrative source for the slave wars—contain many vivid details that suggest, at second or third hand, an eyewitness account. This could conceivably be provided by the lost *Annals* of L. Calpurnius Piso, who fought against the rebels with some success as consul in 133, and may have earlier served in one of the less successful campaigns, as praetor. Neither Posidonius nor, *a fortiori*, Piso would have been liable to see any moral justification in servile revolutions as such. Yet our tradition undoubtedly reflects a pro-servile element at certain points; and despite scholarly criticism, I am still inclined to believe that this may be traceable to a lost monograph on *The Servile Wars* by a Jewish freedman, Caecilius of Cale Acte.

Diodorus paints a graphic if not always accurate picture of the conditions which led up to the revolt—the brigand herdsmen, the administrative anarchy, the insolence and brutality of wealthy slave-owners. The landlords of Sicily had enjoyed sixty years of uninterrupted peace, which they clearly took advantage of to abuse and exploit their position of authority. At the same time they seem to have largely ignored the island's internal security and administration, presumably regarding such matters as the governor's responsibility and nothing to do with them. Brigandage was obviously a commonplace: at intervals the island seems to have been half-dominated by savage robber-herdsmen, who terrorized travellers and disrupted communications. It was also the habitual refuge for runaway criminals and slaves from the mainland. Bickering guerilla campaigns between the governor's troops and roving *franc-tireurs* were a normal part of Sicilian life in the second century B C. This both provided favourable conditions for a large-scale revolt, and in all likelihood, as we shall see, blinded the Roman authorities to the true nature of that revolt until dangerously late in the day. Strabo confirms the diagnosis of Diodorus: according to him, again, the revolt was the work of slave-herdsmen who had run wild up-country. Appian adds a sociologically interesting point to the same thesis: the rich landowners, he observes, bought slaves instead of employing free labour—a problem which was, about the same time, bothering Tiberius Gracchus.

For over half a century now, however, it has been generally accepted that the glut of slaves in Sicily during the first outbreak could not possibly be accounted for by the ranches alone. Cattle-farming simply does not use man-power on such a scale. Agriculture, on the other hand—in particular the intense cultivation of wheat and similar grain—can absorb almost any amount of labour. Various passages suggest that the majority of Sicilian slaves were field-labourers, the chain-gangs housed in those horrible barrack-huts known as *ergastula*. During the slave-revolt harvests were lost, even though (Cicero claims) the farms were not permanently written off. Valerius Maximus records an acute grain-shortage in Rome for the year 138, and this must surely be linked with the Sicilian insurrection. It is noteworthy that the revolt was centred on the eastern half of the island, where the richest arable land lay, and where, therefore, the rebel leaders could find most recruits. Many of the slave-owners were not Sicilian Greeks but Roman *equites*, who (according to Diodorus) committed the worst outrages against their labourers; Livy, too—as preserved in the epitome by Florus—connects the Roman estates directly with the revolt, and emphasizes the *ergastula* as a likely source of rebel recruits. The evidence, however, is sketchy, and the picture it presents not wholly consistent. Diodorus at least once glosses over the field-gangs: 'They used the young slaves as herdsmen,' he remarks, 'and the others *as their requirements dictated*.'

There is some disagreement as to when the rebellion actually broke out: the most likely date is 135 B C. Diodorus remarks that to the majority the rebellion came as a complete surprise, though intelligent observers had been expecting some sort of explosion for quite a time. There is, in fact, a good deal of evidence which suggests that trouble, in the form of guerilla raids against the local levies, had been brewing for three or four years before the revolutionaries showed their hand openly. P. Popilius Laenas, consul in 132, recorded that during his praetorship in Sicily (probably 140/39) he had sent back no less than 917 runaway slaves to their masters on the mainland. No more likely material for rebellion than such fugitives could well be found: those whom Popilius caught can have formed only a fraction of the whole. Sicily was, as we have seen, the habitual refuge for all criminals on the run from justice across the water: the sweep which Popilius made through the island suggests that he knew there was something in the wind. Amongst those who reached the island there were, almost certainly, a number of Jews and Chaldaeans, evicted from Rome by a praetor's edict during the same year. The account of their expulsion suggests that they had been spreading politically inflammable doctrines.

It must have been soon after 139, too, that a certain Syrian slave from Apamea, known as Eunus—'the Benevolent One'—was persuaded to become the figurehead of the rebellion. (Florus remarks, with revealing acidity, that only the trouble he caused makes us remember his name.) His behaviour prior to the outbreak is suggestive in the extreme. Eunus belonged to one Antigenes of Enna, from his name clearly a Sicilian Greek. Antigenes had bought him from an earlier employer named Pytho. The Syrian was widely known in Enna as a magician and wonderworker. He claimed to have visions of the gods both while asleep and during his waking hours, and to learn the future from their lips. Diodorus admits that Eunus duped many people by his prophecies; and Florus tells us which deity he mentioned in particular. It was, as we might expect, Lucian's 'Syrian Goddess', Atargatis, the consort of the Sun-God Hadad. It seems very likely that Eunus, too, boasted of being the Goddess' consort. Some of his prophecies came true—our sources, which do their best to write him off as a complete quack, are forced to admit this—and his reputation grew and spread accordingly. After a while, moreover, he began to conduct his prophetic sessions while breathing fire through his mouth—with some kind of *enthousiasmos*, Diodorus says, which suggests a trance-like state. The purpose of this demonstration, Florus adds, was to prove his divine authority; and both of them give a detailed account of how the trick was worked, by means of a pierced walnut filled with burning sulphur and tinder, and concealed in his mouth. At some time before the revolt he declared that Atargatis had appeared to him in a vision, and had told him he would one day be a king. This information he imparted (says Diodorus, with obvious surprise) not only to his fellow-slaves, but also to his master Antigenes. Antigenes, far from being angry at the slave's presumption, was amused in a patronizing fashion: he turned the whole thing into a joke, and took to producing Eunus at his dinner-parties to entertain the guests. On these occasions he would question the slave concerning his future kingdom, and ask how he would treat those present. Eunus, quite equably, replied that he would treat the ruling class with moderation, and went into a detailed, colourful forecast of his social and political programme. Highly amused, the guests rewarded him with choice portions of meat, and begged him to remember these favours when he should come into his kingdom (the quasi-Messianic foreshadowing of St Luke, xxiii. 42, is both startling and, I think, significant).

The possibilities of Eunus as the spiritual, symbolic leader of a slave insurrection were obvious. It seems likely that plans for revolt had long been discussed, but had hitherto lacked coherence. The various brigand bands were scattered; there was a bewildering variety of nationalities among the slave population; and the very nature of their subjugation prevented their having any effective central organization—though they do appear to have possessed a first-rate grapevine system. Probably in early 138 an approach was made to Eunus by a group of slave conspirators, seeking, in the first instance, divine approval for a plot to murder their masters. The original narrative of this crucial episode by Diodorus does not survive. Instead we are dependent on a condensed version by Photius, and various excerpts, all clearly derived from the same original account, but leaving a certain residual doubt as to whether the basis for the revolt was local or more widespread. In general the motives are shown as being private and domestic. A group of house-slaves (including, apparently, some tirewomen) have been driven to desperate action by the ill-treatment they have suffered at the hands of their master Damophilus and his wife Megallis, a pair of rich *parvenu* Siceliots whose wealth is derived from ranching. There are hints that these slaves may represent a larger and more general body, but it would be dangerous to build too much on this from the evidence at our disposal. In any case, the question at issue which they pose to Eunus is simple enough. Do the Gods approve an uprising against the ruling classes? Eunus, we gather, piecing together the various excerpts, informed his visitors, 'with his usual hocus-pocus', that the Gods approved, provided the conspirators acted at once—an eminently sensible piece of advice, as was his warning that divine favour depended on their committing no excesses. By way of encouragement, an optimistic prophecy (duly fulfilled in the event) now followed: 'It was fated that Enna, their native homeland, should fall to them, and be the capital of the entire island.'

If the slave liberation movement was first conceived in 138, and open insurrection did not break out until 135, it follows that there must have been the usual period of underground softening-up activities. Furthermore, considerable organization would be needed to co-ordinate the scattered forces available, sound out prospective recruits, and conceive an efficient plan of campaign. The use of the phrase 'native homeland' in Eunus' reply to the visiting deputation suggests that the original conspirators might have envisaged a nationalistic basis for their rebellion. But this was a very tricky line to take. Sicily had no real tradition of national sovereignty; she was the exploited island *par excellence*, continually ravaged or occupied by some external conqueror. In any case, as we have seen, the other potential rebels were a highly mixed lot. There were runaways from Italy, the wild herdsmen from the hills, and other native-born Sicilian slaves. There were probably some Chaldaeans and Jews, who could provide a ready-made apocalyptic ideology for just such a struggle as this: there may even have been men among them who had fought with Simon Maccabaeus. Almost beyond doubt, too, many Spanish guerillas must have fled from Lusitania after the nationalist leader Viriathus was treacherously murdered by Q. Servilius Caepio in 140. But above all there was the strong contingent of Syrian and Cilician slaves, who provided the movement with both leadership and organization. Perhaps no one single factor did more to bring the crisis to a head than the presence of these men in Sicily. Most of them were victims of that organized slave-piracy which had developed in Cilicia with the encouragement of Diodotus Tryphon and Rome's tacit blessing, and which reached a new peak of activity about 145 B C. This infiltration of educated men (formerly in many cases free citizens) into the vast servile plantation which Sicily had become could hardly fail to have disruptive and far-reaching effects. The liberal assumptions of free men were grafted on to the slave's condition at its worst: nothing could better have served to spark off a really dangerous movement against the *status quo*.

It must have amused Eunus to disseminate subversive propaganda and be rewarded for it by his master's guests. Meanwhile minor campaigns were being conducted against the praetor's local levies—probably well away from the towns—and these, besides giving the rebels valuable experience in the field, could (if successful) be scored up as notable victories to boost the underground movement's morale. To the Roman praetors themselves these engagements, though irksome, probably had no more than casual significance, and certainly did not merit an emergency appeal to Rome. There was, they may well have argued, always liable to be brigandage in Sicily; and in any case, as Diodorus reminds us, no praetor dared to burn his fingers by needlessly provoking the rich landowners. It was better not to press these licensed profiteers and bullies of the *latifundia* too hard. Full-scale punitive expeditions were expensive and would only cause trouble; it was safer and easier to practise a policy of 'containment', and turn a blind eye to the excesses of guerilla enthusiasts.

It was in the early spring of 135 that the plan to capture Enna was carried out. The insurgents had chosen their time well. The new praetor, L. Plautius Hypsaeus, had not yet arrived from Rome, where disturbing rumours were already beginning to circulate about Tiberius Gracchus. A large body of Roman troops was held down in Spain, with the siege of Numantia yet to be concluded. There had been an unusually violent eruption from Mount Etna, with lava, smoke and ashes spreading wide over the surrounding countryside; this was locally believed to portend great events in the immediate future. It also probably meant that the retiring praetor, if he had not actually left, was away on a tour of inspection along the East coast.

The attack was launched at midnight. Four hundred slaves gathered in a field outside the city,[1] where they bound themselves by solemn oaths and sacrifices, and armed themselves as best they could. Then, with Eunus at their head belching flames in the darkness, they 'stormed through' Enna, leaving a trail of carnage behind them: Diodorus gives the usual catalogue of child-murder and rape.[2] Soon the original commandos were joined by other slaves from the town itself, and began to turn about for further victims, their own masters and mistresses being already murdered. Damophilus and Megallis, who had hidden in a country house just outside the town, were brought back to face a packed mass of slaves assembled in the theatre. It seems as though some semblance of democratic procedure was adopted by the rebels: Damophilus was allowed to make a speech in his defence, but two of Eunus' leading colleagues, Hermias and Zeuxis, tired of waiting for what they must have regarded as a foregone conclusion, butchered him 'without waiting for the people's due verdict'.

Immediately after this Eunus was proclaimed absolute king by the assembly: liberty, equality and fraternity had, apparently, been tried and found wanting. He assumed the diadem and regalia; he took the name of Antiochus and declared that his subjects were all 'Syrians'; he had the Syrian woman with whom he lived invested as his queen. Then he formed a Royal Council, composed of his most intelligent fellow-conspirators,

[1] Enna is situated on a rocky outcrop some 2,000 feet high, with steep fortified cliffs, and a somewhat shallower approach up defiles from the north and south. The plateau is not, as most historians have assumed, level, but a series of smaller hills. The field was thus probably, in fact, on the plateau itself, at the waste land to the north-west where the modern cemetery now stands.

[2] Diodorus' account will trouble anyone familiar with the actual terrain (see esp. xxxiv–v, 2,11–12,24). To 'storm through' Enna would be rather like storming through a labyrinth on the side of a cliff. It seems clear that Eunus and his troops had strictly limited objectives: the modern configuration of the town (which by its very nature can have changed little since antiquity) suggests that the attack was launched against the south-east part of the rock from the north-west section, with the active or passive connivance of the poorer inhabitants there. In any case there would be no need to scale the rock and storm the gates: the whole operation must have been internal.

amongst whom were Hermias and Zeuxis. Eunus' first royal decree was for the extermination of all surviving slave-owners; but, true to his word, he spared those who had given him meat at table as Antigenes' guests. Another prisoner who received generous treatment was Damophilus' daughter, a girl as kind and compassionate as her father had been brutal, and who had always done her best to alleviate the sufferings of the family slaves, with food or medicines. She was granted safe-conduct to relatives at Catana, and escorted away by a posse under the command of Hermias. At this point another Asiatic slave, named Achaeus, stood up in bold disapproval of the excessive atrocities which had been committed, and predicted that they would bring speedy retribution. Eunus, far from being angry, welcomed Achaeus' plain speaking, and nominated him to the Council; he distinguished himself thereafter both as an excellent military commander and by the wisdom and shrewdness of his advice.

The next three days were extremely busy ones. The *ergastula* around Enna were broken open and the occupants released: soon Eunus found himself with an army of six thousand men. But the men had to be armed. Every prisoner held, except for the armourers, blacksmiths, and similar tradesmen, was now executed (Eunus might praise Achaeus, but clearly felt under no obligation to take his advice); these specialists were set to forced labour in the forges and smithies. Such arms as could be found the slaves reinforced with mattocks, axes, billhooks, slings, sickles, even wooden billets. Thus equipped, they set out to despoil the countryside. We may be fairly certain that food rather than vengeance was their first concern. While, later, they were besieging Syracuse, some came so close to starvation that they ate the sacred fish of Atargatis; and Eunus, though he had no objection to their looting country houses, expressly forbade them to touch farm-workers or agricultural products. It is true that they needed supplies themselves; but Sicily was a fabulously rich island, and Eunus may well have been planning, as a long-term bargaining counter, some sort of grain deal with the authorities in Rome. Much more damage was done by the non-servile small freeholders, who considered this an ideal opportunity to vent their spleen on the lordly occupants of the millionaire ranches. There is no sign of any co-operation between these free 'poor whites' and the slaves, which argues strongly against the revolt having been a generalized proletarian revolution.

Eunus' rag-tag army successfully survived its first brushes with what levies the authorities could muster: these encounters brought the rebels' numbers up to 10,000 or more, mostly agricultural slaves from the *ergastula.* We know little of the battles themselves, except for the fact that the slaves regularly cut off their prisoners' hands. (This practice need not have been due to pure wanton cruelty. The insurgents obviously had no facilities for dealing with captives on a large scale; at the same time they needed to ensure that those they took and subsequently released could not bear arms against them in the future. This way at least their lives were spared.) Meanwhile a second insurrection had broken out in the western part of the island, near Agrigentum. Its leader was a Cilician bandit named Cleon, born in the lawless country below Mount Taurus, and now a herdsman in the Sicilian hills, with a profitable record of murder, brigandage, and highway robbery on the side. Hearing news of the capture of Enna, Cleon too rode down at the head of his gang into Agrigentum, captured it, and laid waste the surrounding countryside. The Roman officials regarded this as a godsend. It was clear, they argued, that the two rival slave armies would destroy each other. But nothing of the sort happened. A mere word from the *soi-disant* King Antiochus was enough; Cleon came east, with his brother Comanus and his five thousand mountaineers, and joined Eunus as one of his most devoted lieutenants. (It seems very likely, in fact, that the two of them had been in communication long before, and that Cleon made his attack on Agrigentum at a prearranged signal.) It was a month almost to the day after the fall of Enna when Cleon and Eunus joined forces; and almost immediately afterwards the new praetor, Lucius Hypsaeus, arrived from Rome, probably in May 135. Clearly Rome was not even yet fully alive to the danger. Hypsaeus raised a levy of 8,000 Sicilians—presumably for the most part Siceliot Greeks and their retainers—and met the rebels in open battle. His men were cut to pieces, and the insurgents' numbers swelled to at least 70,000. Nothing, as they say, succeeds like success.

By now 'King Antiochus' was pretty firmly established: firmly enough, at any rate, to issue his own coinage, with Demeter on one face and a corn-ear on the other, appropriate emblems for a new capital of which Cicero was to say: '*Urbs illa non urbs videtur sed fanum Cereris esse*'—'It looks not so much like a city as one great temple of Ceres.' But Enna alone would not suffice; other strongholds must be captured. The first to fall was Tauromenium, the modern Taormina; three years later its commander, Quintus Fabius, was returned home under something of a cloud by his ruthless father-in-law Publius Rupilius. He had, indeed, been guilty of negligence. Perhaps relying on the *pax Siciliana* no less than Tauromenium's naturally strong position, he had allowed the walls to fall into disrepair and the garrison to become dangerously depleted. The town was in no fit state to stand a siege. Eunus amused himseif and his men by staging a kind of tattoo, just beyond bowshot: a re-enactment of the first uprising, and the bloody fate which befell the ruling class. The citadel fell, and Fabius was lucky to make his escape.

How much of Sicily actually passed under the slave-king's control? Diodorus says that the whole island was in grave danger of subjection: perhaps this need not imply that the greater part of it, in the event, actually fell. Agrigentum, Enna and Tauromenium we already know to have been captured. Strabo adds to this list Catana 'and many others', though without naming them: perhaps they were no more than villages. Syracuse was besieged, but the siege had to be broken off for lack of supplies—which suggests that the supply-lines may have been cut by enemy action. Messana certainly, and in all likelihood other large cities, did not join the rising. It has been plausibly suggested that relative servile contentment can be co-ordinated with the lighter, more constructive work involved in viticulture or olive-production: skilled labourers are far less likely to revolt than agricultural serfs. The only other city we know the slaves to have held (if we accept a highly convincing textual emendation) is the high, lonely hill-fortress of Morgantia. By now, at all events, even the Senate in Rome could see the writing on the wall; and in 134 the Sicilian command was transferred to one of the consuls, C. Fulvius Flaccus, an ineffectual man of pro-Gracchan sympathies. Despite his consular status, Flaccus did nothing to remedy the situation: the rebels captured towns with all their inhabitants, and destroyed several armies (more hapless local levies, one presumes) which he sent against them. The gravity of the situation was now patent and unmistakable.

But the Sicilian *coup* had wider repercussions still. News of the rebels' success travelled fast; and on the strength of it a hundred and fifty slaves formed a conspiracy in Rome. This, however, seems to have been stamped out almost at once, as we might expect. The well-garrisoned capital was a far harder nut to crack than a provincial hill-town like Enna, and contained far more people with a vested interest in the preservation of the *status quo*. The same is probably true of the four hundred and fifty who revolted at Minturnae. A further outbreak at Sinuessa was much more serious: at least four thousand slaves took up arms, and the veteran consular Q. Caecilius Metellus, a severe disciplinarian with previous experience in quelling rebellions, was called on to suppress it. But he was desperately short of troops, and it was not until 132 that, with very great difficulty, the rebels were finally brought under control. Further afield, in the Laurium silver-mines and on Delos, the great slave-mart, large numbers of slaves also revolted. The thousand or so miners were rapidly subdued by the Athenian general Heraclitus; the movement on Delos eventually yielded before a concerted attack by the free citizenry, though it may have lasted till 133/2. Rome, however, took the Delian affair very seriously. Just as

Macedonia had become a Roman province immediately after the suppression of the royal pretender Andriscus, so Rome now discreetly moved in on the affairs of Delos. Political revolution required drastic counter-measures.

The following year the Senate showed they meant business in Sicily. Their choice fell on the ex-praetor L. Calpurnius Piso Frugi, who had already served in this theatre. He was a strong pro-aristocrat and anti-Gracchan,[1] something of a *sine qua non* in that particular year. He took his son with him on his staff, and arrived in a flurry of disciplinary measures, a new broom sweeping very clean. He delivered rousing speeches and decorated distinguished soldiers right and left—not excluding his own son. It is perhaps permissible to deduce from these symptoms that discipline was not all it might have been. Yet Piso, too, for all his discipline, at first got very little further than Fulvius Flaccus had done. He attempted to storm Enna, and failed: his sling-stones have been found outside the walls. Achaeus, Eunus' commander-in-chief, also inscribed *his* sling-stones; but in addition to his name he added—with some justice—the word *Victoria*, and the burning corn-sheaf of Ceres which seems to have provided the slave-kingdom with its national emblem. But at length Piso's dogged persistence was rewarded; he stormed and captured Morgantia. In his fury he slaughtered eight thousand of the defenders, and any who survived he afterwards had crucified. It was the beginning of the end.

In Rome Tiberius Gracchus was murdered; and the consul for 132 who took on the campaign in Sicily was a tough, capable general named Publius Rupilius, who had no love for radicalism in any form. He was, among other things, supposed to have once been a tax farmer's clerk: I suppose a modern Marxist would label him a running dog of the capitalists. With him as

[1] Doubts have been cast on this statement: see W.G.G. Forrest and T.C.W. Stinton in *Past and Present* 22 (1962) 88-9. Their arguments are highly speculative, however, and even they admit that Piso was probably anti-Gracchan in sympathy as early as 132. As they would like to use Piso's *Annals* as a (comparatively) pro-servile source, one can see why they would like to have their author a pro-Gracchan in 133.

deputy commander went Marcus Perperna, soon to celebrate a crushing victory against another rebel leader, Aristonicus of Pergamum. To begin with the two new commanders suffered some reverses. But after a while they rallied, and systematically set about reducing the rebel strongholds. First came Tauromenium, which only fell after the most stubborn and protracted siege, during which the slaves were reduced to cannibalism; and even then it was betrayed from the inside, by a Syrian named Serapion. Comanus, Cleon's brother, was captured while trying to escape—presumably to beg help from Enna. Members of the surrendered garrison were first tortured and then thrown down to their deaths from the battlements. Next it was Enna's turn. Rupilius tried to extract information from Comanus, who very courageously committed suicide during interrogation. Then he and Perperna set about starving the garrison out, helping the process forward by some discreet fifth-column work. Cleon, in desperation, attempted a sortie and fell, covered with wounds. Plague and famine ravaged the remainder, and, once again, the town was betrayed. There followed another wholesale massacre, with crucifixions and hangings in chains; more than twenty thousand rebels, it was estimated, perished during these two operations. The First Sicilian Slave War was over.

'King Antiochus' fought his way out, protected by his bodyguard of a thousand picked men. But the situation was obviously hopeless, and the guards committed mass suicide. Eunus himself went on into the hills, accompanied only by his cook, baker, bath-attendant and court buffoon: even servile royalty, it would seem, aped the most fashionable models of the day. Here he was found, in a cave, by the Roman legionaries, transported to Morgantia, and left to rot away for the rest of his life in a prison cell. Rupilius followed up his victory with a quick sweep through the island, stamping out pockets of resistance wherever he found them. This done, he turned to the problems of administrative reform. To begin with, he called off his mass-executions. It was the merest common sense that an island so wholly dependent on a slave economy could not be run without slaves.

As it was, the shortage had already become so acute that owners were forced to take back known rebels into their service. Ten commissioners came out to help Rupilius draft a new constitution, the so-called *Lex Rupilia.* Most of this constitution's clauses, to judge from our scanty evidence, were concerned with regulating litigation between Greek and Roman, or members of different self-governing cities on the island. The assumption that Rupilius went out of his way to favour the *publicani* stems from a misinterpreted phrase in Valerius Maximus: almost certainly he did nothing of the sort. Nor is it very likely, as Scramuzza supposes, that he broke up the large estates, a move which would have gone flat against local vested interests, and might well have precipitated a second revolt, this time on the part of the landowners. This theory in fact depends solely on a statement that no single slave gang numbered more than thirty men in the Second Slave War, whereas a grazier such as Damophilus had owned four hundred. Even if such a measure were implemented (which is unlikely in the extreme) it certainly did not stop the Second Slave War from taking place.

We can now survey the episode as a whole, and attempt to assess its significance. In doing so we must bear in mind several important generalities. To begin with, the conditions were quite exceptional, chiefly on account of the unprecedented glut of cheap slave labour which became available in the second century BC after a series of successful wars. From Spain, Gaul, Greece, Asia, Africa and Macedonia countless captives came streaming in, and their numbers were augmented still further by the proceeds of slave-piracy, a trade run with the active support of Roman political and business interests. (Strabo makes it quite clear that this was a matter of deliberate policy rather than mere indifference.) The turnover at Delos could exceed 10,000 head a day; in 167 BC no less than 150,000 Epirots were sold into slavery in a single operation. The Roman attitude to slaves may have been much more callous than that of the Greeks—Cato, in his *De Agricultura*, recommends selling old, worn-out slaves with the rest of one's broken harness or farm equipment—

but the contrast was more apparent than real. The Greeks might palliate their slaves' living conditions; Aristotle and many other masters might manumit some of their personal servants; but they all alike believed, *au fond*, that slavery was an institution not only necessary but justifiable, whether on social, moral, or genetic grounds. Aristotle's concept of the slave as an 'animated tool' lies at the root of all subsequent ancient thought on the subject. Whatever *concessions* he might be granted, the slave had no *rights*, and was in essence a mere conveyable piece of property. Good relations were, therefore, entirely dependent on economic conditions and the temperament of the slave-owner. In colonial conditions, as in Sicily, where a plentiful supply of slaves was combined with a demand for high profits and quick production, there were no *moral* sanctions to prevent all the horrors of the *ergastula* from springing up overnight.

There is, contrary to the general belief, no real evidence whatsoever to suggest any organized moral opposition to slavery as such in the ancient world (and precious little in Christendom, at least outside Europe, until the Industrial Revolution suggested a viable alternative). Stoic teaching, frequently associated with such a belief, in fact restricts its speculation in this field to achieving a *correct definition* of slavery and freedom, rather like modern philosophers arguing about ethics. Again and again we find large-sounding liberal theory resting upon an open or implied foundation of slave-labour. 'Every Greek revolution,' wrote Sir William Tarn, 'except perhaps the Pergamene, conveys a sense of unreality, as it never included slaves.' The literature of social protest, from Hesiod to Cercidas, from Crates to the egalitarian Phaleas of Chalcedon (who applied his principles to education and property), all confirm this view. Political revolution, liberty and equality in the modern sense, these are invariably the free man's prerogative. The few apparent exceptions to such a rule will not bear close examination. The Utopian Sun State of Iambulus, for instance, presents an ideal community who do not possess slaves; and in the second century B C a somewhat similar community in real life was to be found among the Essenes. As we shall see, both these factors may have had some influence on the slave-risings; but they did not suggest a revolutionary social programme for the abolition of slavery as such. Nothing could be more profoundly anachronistic; but the idea has proved popular in this century, and has tended to obscure the very real driving motives behind the revolt, which were neither communistic nor merely anarchic in origin.

It is quite clear that we are not concerned here with any kind of primitive socialism; Eunus-Antiochus' royal pretensions should alone suffice to scotch such a notion. The slaves had no economic programme except to take over for their own benefit the existing institutions and natural amenities of an exceptionally fertile island, and presumably to hold it against all comers. Those who argue a purely economico-political basis for the revolt must rest their case almost entirely on a comparison with the Pergamene rising a year or two later, and a careful scrutiny of the latter makes it plain that Aristonicus, like Eunus, was a stranger to the communist ideal. His followers called themselves 'citizens of the Sun State', *Heliopolitani*, which hints at a religious motif, based on the Syrian Heliopolis, Baalbek on the Orontes, with its sun-cult and joint worship of Baal-Hadad and Atargatis. This supposition agrees exactly with the kind of evidence offered by the Sicilian rebellion. The most immediately striking fact about Eunus-Antiochus is that, beyond any doubt, he modelled his kingship in detail on the Seleucid monarchy he had known in Syria, before being sold into slavery. He took the name Antiochus, which several great Seleucid monarchs had borne. He had a royal bodyguard of a thousand men. His court protocol tallies exactly with that practised by the Seleucids. It is even possible that the name 'Eunus' was assumed as a title, comparable to 'Eupator' or 'Soter': *eunoia*, benevolence, was a quality intimately associated with Hellenistic kingship. Most remarkable of all, the names of his leading fellow-conspirators —Hermias, Zeuxis and Achaeus—are also the names of three distinguished ministers of state under Antiochus the Great. It looks as though the slave-king deliberately set out to establish a Seleucid Kingdom of the West which would recall the great days of Antiochus III: it is significant that he called his new citizens 'Syrians'.

Whether Eunus was, or believed himself to be, a legitimate or bastard Seleucid we cannot tell—though nothing would have been easier than for an unwanted royal bastard to be sold into slavery and shipped across to Sicily by way of Delos. That he believed in his own kingship seems certain: a calculating charlatan seldom gets the hold over men which Eunus quite clearly did. And the claim was at least plausible: Eunus could, in theory, have been a brother of Antiochus VI, Alexander Balas' son; or a child of Demetrius I, and thus the brother of Antiochus VII Sidetes; or even one of Antiochus IV Epiphanes' sons, supposedly executed by Demetrius' soldiers in 162. On the other hand, the fact that he was supposed to have died of *phthiriasis* (long regarded as a legendary disease, but now convincingly identified with advanced arterio-sclerosis) fairly soon after his capture in 132 suggests that he was somewhat older—old enough, in fact, to have been a son of Antiochus the Great himself, who died in 187: and this would agree well with the naming of his counsellors. But such speculation cannot be given any final substance. What is certain is that royal claimants, with or without the backing of blood, were peculiarly frequent in this period (again, this suggests a lack of alternative and acceptable systems of government for the potential rebel). There was the Macedonian fuller's son, Andriscus; there was the curious case of Saumacus in the Tauric Chersonese (the modern Crimea); there was, in Syria itself, the example of Diodotus Tryphon, an ex-slave who first played the king-maker and then assumed the diadem in person. Nearer home we find a Roman knight, one T. Minucius Vettius, assuming the royal purple and proclaiming himself king, with the backing of 3,500 armed retainers. The praetor for 104, L. Licinius Lucullus—not Sulla's famous lieutenant—managed to defeat him, but only after suborning his second-in-command.

Considered purely in a political light, these outbreaks must have struck the Roman authorities as peculiarly dangerous. The concept of Hellenistic kingship was the one valid and current ideology which in the second century B C still might provide an effective opposition to Roman rule. It was doubly dangerous on two counts: it offered a programme in which slaves could participate, and it contained a ritual element of religious *enthousiasmos* capable of swaying the most diverse devotees. Antiochus IV Epiphanes ('The God Manifest') celebrated a ritual marriage with the goddess Atargatis, and Eunus will almost certainly have followed his example. Thus he appeared to his Sicilian followers in a guise which they could readily understand, and which carried interesting social implications. He was Abd-Hadad the priest-king, the consort of Atargatis, the god-king of Oriental tradition, giver of good things, the Benevolent One. Sicily provided promising soil in which this kind of seed could grow. Atargatis could without difficulty be assimilated to Ceres of Enna in a characteristic syncretism; she would be equally at home on Mount Eryx, where the great temple with its ritual prostitutes, the *hierodouloi*, hinted at Phoenician Astarte rather than Roman Venus or the resident *dea loci*.

That the island cults—in particular those of the Palici, Ceres, and Jupiter Aetnaeus—were pressed into service by the rebels seems pretty certain: the second uprising was fought under the aegis of the Palici, and it is, I feel, no accident that Palice, the site of the shrine, was founded by another great Sicilian rebel, Ducetius. This receives confirmation from the curious embassy which, in 133, the Senate dispatched to Enna. After the Sibylline Books had been duly consulted, ten Commissioners for Religious Affairs (*decemviri sacerdotales*), were ordered to placate Ceres of Enna, since Enna was thought to be the earliest seat of the goddess. (One French scholar suggests that the *patres* were defending Ceres against her rival the Syrian Goddess, as well as making a placatory gesture to the Roman plebs.) This commission they carried out as instructed. According to Cicero and Valerius Maximus, who probably took their facts from Piso's

Annals, the whole project was brought into being as a result of the Senate's superstitious terror and guilt (*deisidaimonia*) after Tiberius Gracchus' death; though what direct connexion there was between the dead tribune and Ceres of Enna, apart from a common interest in agriculture, is hard to imagine. Diodorus presents a significantly different version of the incident. Here we find no mention of Gracchus, or, indeed, of Ceres; instead the Commissioners make a tour through the island visiting the various shrines of Jupiter Aetnaeus. At each one they not only make due sacrifice, but erect a wall around the precinct and ban all access to it, except for the priests and their acolytes. It has been suggested that this was a move to deprive the slaves of local religious encouragement. But in another sense expiation to Ceres of Enna was an all too appropriate gesture, since Roman greed for Sicilian corn lay, ultimately, at the root of the revolt: how much uneasy, if unacknowledged, guilt did this odd official mission represent?

We must not forget, either, that just as the Greek *koiné* provided a *lingua franca* throughout the Mediterranean world, so the Oriental cults and eschatological Mysteries linked the slaves of many nations in a common bond. A temple to Hadad and Atargatis was erected on Delos in 128/7; and Syrian slaves are known to have carried the cult of Atargatis to Aetolia. The mystery-cults, like nineteenth-century Freemasonry as portrayed by Kipling, obliterated social distinctions: bond and free worshipped together. These cults provided the truly revolutionary spark which was later transmuted into political action. All their emphasis was on *soteria*, salvation: on material blessings in this world and even better rewards in the next. The cult of Zeus Helios suggested a kind of egalitarianism 'under the sun', and Hadad was *par excellence* the god who showed himself *epēkōos*, ready to listen to suppliant prayers. (A parallel situation is provided by the politically dangerous 'cargo cults' in New Guinea.) Widespread syncretism also let in a host of foreign, and especially Jewish, accretions. The indirect influence of Jewish thought and action on the rebellions of the second century was incalculable: among other things, it explains the curious but unmistakable flavour of Messianism discernible in Eunus-Antiochus' career. By 140 B C the Sibylline Books could claim that every land was full of Jews. Messianism was flourishing; a King of the World—again, according to the Sibylline books—would appear from the East; the Maccabees were fighting in Judaea, and a flourishing apocalyptic literature foretold the epiphany of a Messianic warrior-king.

There is a great deal about Eunus-Antiochus which suggests this Jewish, Messianic tradition. His symbolic fire-breathing trick reminds us of the belief that God spoke through His prophets' lips with tongues of flame; in the Apocalyptic Book of Ezra we read of the Messiah breathing fire and sparks to destroy his enemies. Like John Hyrcanus, the Jewish nationalist, Eunus was a blend of prophet, priest and king: he exactly fitted the Messianic role of the national king who would deliver his people from their enemies. It is interesting that Iambulus, whose Utopia may have been conceived about this period, was, so far as we can tell, a Jew. The Sun State itself (in its ethical essentials as presented by Iambulus) bears many striking resemblances to the practice of the Essenes, who first appear in history during the second century B C—notably, sharing the necessities of life, not marrying but maintaining children in common, practising the simple life, worshipping the sun, and taking turns at mutual help.

These suppositions are oddly confirmed by the attitude of our ancient authorities to Eunus. Robert Eisler has pointed out the special Graeco-Roman use of words such as 'miracle-worker', 'quack', 'banditry' or 'brigandage' in a politically euphemistic sense, to describe national or religious insurrections (the habit still appears to be flourishing in most countries today). 'To the Pagans,' Eisler wrote, 'Jesus was a magician, who through sham miracles and with subversive words had incited the people to rebellion and as leader of a desperate gang of men had attempted to seize the royal crown of Judaea.' *Mutatis mutandis*, this is a precise description of Eunus' career as seen through Roman eyes. Josephus mentions similar episodes during the Jewish Wars; he speaks of people being deceived by a 'wizard' who offered them—exactly as we would expect—*soteria* and release from their afflictions. Both Greeks and Romans were curiously ignorant of Jewish doctrine and literature (this applies even to Tacitus and Juvenal, who display some familiarity with the externals of Jewish ritual); the most they recognized were certain cult-practices or observances which they at once connected with subversive activity. This suggests a possible solution to one slight but teasing problem which has not hitherto aroused comment. Why, when at least twenty thousand of his followers were crucified, and when, with the revolt broken, he had no further use as a hostage, was Eunus himself merely kept in prison? The answer is not far to seek. The idea of resurrection had been gaining considerable ground in the second century B C, and the main emphasis of Messianism was, as a result, gradually shifting from this world to the next. Now Rupilius, to judge from our evidence, maintained an active fifth-column; and if he knew exactly what Eunus-Antiochus meant to his followers, he may well have felt that to crucify him would be most impolitic. At best he would create a legendary hero; at worst, a highly dangerous eschatological myth. It is intriguing to speculate whether he may not have acted a little more shrewdly than did a certain Procurator of Judaea, nearly two centuries later.

The First Sicilian Slave War, then, was not an *Urkommunist* revolution against slavery, or, indeed, any kind of socialist or left-wing economic revolt. It was sparked off by the presence on the *latifundia* of intelligent Syrians and Cilicians—often free men by birth—who (and this cannot be sufficiently emphasized) *had nothing against slavery as an institution, but objected violently to being enslaved themselves.* No one seriously maintains that Antiochus' kingdom, while it lasted, was classless or non-servile in its constitution: quite the reverse, in fact, rather like those extraordinary secret 'kingdoms' formed (in not dissimilar circumstances) by eighteenth-century negroes transported as slaves to America. Eunus himself had an imposing retinue of domestics, and no doubt his associates strove to emulate his conservative example. The harsh colonial conditions on the island provided any rebel leader with a willing army from among the downtrodden field-gangs; and these were reinforced by brigand-herdsmen and fighting refugees, in many instances from the mainland. At the same time we should note that large numbers of skilled slaves, whose own conditions were better, held aloof from the revolt, as did the free smallholders (though these took advantage of it to work off a few private grudges of their own). What, in fact, provided the essential unity for action was the international symbolism offered by Hellenistic dynastic ritual and various syncretic mystery cults popular among slaves everywhere throughout the Mediterranean world. Otherwise, despite the obvious genius for organization and training which some of the slave-leaders possessed, it would have proved quite impossible to weld this hopelessly heterogeneous body of men into a political, military and spiritual unity. The workers of the world had not yet learnt to unite. Indeed, there is something infinitely ironic about a revolutionary movement launched under the twin auspices of those most notoriously reactionary institutions, kingship and religion. The tragedy and moral of the whole episode is that no conceivable alternative existed.

Juvenal and his Age

I

IN THE whole of Roman literature there is no more personally elusive character than Juvenal. His work—in marked contrast to the satires of his predecessors Horace and Persius—contains almost no autobiographical material. Of his contemporaries, only the epigrammatist Martial ever refers to him. It has been argued that he was a pupil of Quintilian's, and that the *Institutio Oratoria* alludes to him among 'contemporaries of promise', but this is pure speculation. After his death—it is unlikely that he survived for long after the accession of Antoninus Pius in A D 138—the *Satires* drop out of sight absolutely for about a century. Since both the vices and the literary fashions which Juvenal castigated became increasingly popular with the Imperial Court towards the close of the Antonine period, this neglect is understandable. Marcus Aurelius would scarcely have relished Juvenal's xenophobic attitude to all things Greek any more than his son, Commodus, would have tolerated a satirist who attacked nobles with a penchant for appearing as gladiators. No critic or grammarian in the second and third centuries A D, though they make frequent references to other Roman poets, ever mentions Juvenal.

Ironically (since Juvenal's view of foreign religions was something less than respectful) his earliest rediscoverers seem to have been the Christian apologists, who raided his arsenal of moral invective for their own sectarian purposes. Tertullian (*c.* A D 160—220), though he does not mention the satirist by name, had clearly absorbed some of his more pithy tags. The first direct reference to Juvenal by a Christian writer comes early in the fourth century AD. Lactantius quotes with approval the last lines of Satire X ('Fortune has no divinity, could we but see it: it's we/We ourselves, who make her a goddess, and set her in the heavens') and foreshadows the traditional view of Juvenal as a distinguished pagan moralist with a genius for crisp epigrams. The first non-Christian interest in the *Satires* hardly predates the fourth century, and may have been stimulated by the work of two Christian poets, Ausonius and Prudentius, who adapted and imitated them. Perhaps soon after 350 the first ancient commentary was produced; by 390 the historian Ammianus Marcellinus could observe that certain contemporary aristocrats, who had no time for literature in general—Juvenal's attraction has always been at least as much moral and political as artistic—were devouring him with some enthusiasm. At the same period Servius, the great commentator on Virgil, was at work in Rome: he alludes to the *Satires* on more than seventy occasions, thus breaking the complete silence of his predecessors. The bitter old poet from Aquinum had reached a wide public at last, after centuries of neglect; from then on his fame never wavered.

But the years of darkness left a legacy of ignorance and neglect behind them which still bedevils any attempt to establish exactly what Juvenal wrote, let alone the details of his life. When the *Satires* were resurrected, it was natural that those who studied and admired them should want to know something about their author. But if as seems probable, they had nothing to go on but one manuscript lacking its final pages, biographical details could only be sought from the *Satires* themselves. There are some thirteen late Lives extant, mostly derived from that preserved in the commentary by Probus; with the exception of the first sentence, all the details look as though they were manufactured after a study of Juvenal's own text. The first sentence tells us that Decimus Junius Juvenalis was either the son, or the adopted son, of a wealthy freedman, and 'practised rhetoric till about middle age, more as an amusement than as a serious preparation for teaching rhetoric or pleading in the courts'. The Lives generally agree that his birthplace was Aquinum, a hill-town near Monte Cassino, some eighty miles south-east of Rome; that he was exiled for attacking an actor with influence at court; and that this exile was spent in Egypt, though some Lives opt for Scotland. The emperor who banished him is variously given as Trajan or Domitian. There is one incredible tradition that his exile to Egypt took place when he was eighty years old, and was combined with a military command. Apart from the actual fact of exile, there is nothing here which could not have been invented in the fourth century by some scholar who simply read the *Satires* and then looked through his history books for an appropriate context.

Only one of these Lives attempts to supply the date of his birth, and none tells us when he died. The year A D 55 may be only a guess at his birth date, but it is a plausible one and fits the rest of our evidence; moreover, if the compiler of the Life had intended to fabricate evidence of this sort, he would in all likelihood have added a supposititious date of death as well. There is a tradition that he survived, worn out with old age, for some time (but we are not told how long) after the death of Hadrian in A D 138. Some sources believe that he died in exile, others that he returned to Rome, but pined away because his friend Martial had returned to his native Spain in A D 98. (This last assertion is obviously based on the evidence of Martial's poem to Juvenal from Bilbilis [12.18] and reinforces the suspicion that the biographers were making bricks with such straws as they had.) One, unfortunately, asserts that he 'amplified his satires in exile and made many changes in them,' a claim which may well have derived from the confused state of the text, and which has provided a splendid loophole for adventurous modern editors. The biographies do not tell us whether Juvenal ever married or had children; indeed, apart from the persistent tradition of his exile, and its cause, there is hardly anything in them—such as his military service, or his supposed presence in Britain and Egypt—which could not have been inferred from his own words. The variants on the story of his exile suggest that even this was preserved without any explanatory facts, and that Egypt or Britain may have been chosen as its locale simply because he shows knowledge of them both in the *Satires*.

An examination of Juvenal's writing tends to confirm such a view. The biographical or chronological evidence which the *Satires* yield is singularly small. The first Book, consisting of Satires I–V inclusive, contains allusions to the banishment of Marius Priscus, a corrupt provincial governor, whose trial was held in A D 100 (I, 40-50); to the death of Domitian in 96 (IV, 153); and perhaps to the publication of Tacitus' *Histories*, between 104 and 109 (II, 102-3). Satire II contains further allusions to Agricola's campaign in the Orkneys and his plan for reducing Ireland (159-161), and to Domitian's assumption of the office of Censor (30, 63, 161). Both of these events can be dated to A D 84/5, and yet Juvenal treats them as recent and topical. The impression conveyed by this Book as a whole is that some of the material (especially Satires II and IV) may well have been composed in private draft during the reign of Domitian, and circulated more freely after his murder in 96, when Nerva called off the Terror and brought back the political exiles. If the reference to Tacitus is upheld, the publication of Book I will have taken place about 110/12.

Book II consists entirely of one work, the gigantic and virulent Sixth Satire directed against women. Here we find (407ff.), as a specifically topical allusion, mention of floods and earthquake in the East, and a comet 'presaging trouble/For some eastern prince, in Armenia, maybe, or Parthia'. Just such a comet was visible at Rome in November 115, the year before Trajan's Parthian campaign; and in December of the same year there was a famous earthquake at Antioch, which endangered the life of the Emperor himself. This provides us with a plausible *terminus post quem*. Once again there are earlier datable references which suggest that parts of the draft had been written, or sketched, some time before: the mention of Trajan's German and Dacian victories in 97 and 102/3, the allusion to the Capitoline Games founded in 86, the lovingly accurate description of a complicated hairstyle which had vanished for twenty years when Satire VI appeared.

Book III consists of Satires VII-IX. Satire VII begins with

some twenty lines praising 'Caesar' as the one hope for the arts, the only patron writers and literature can depend on in these troubled and philistine times. The introduction has every appearance of an afterthought or revision, tacked on to an already existing draft; the bulk of the satire is devoted to a survey of the poverty and humiliation which not only writers, but lawyers, rhetoricians and schoolteachers have to endure. There is, moreover, a distinct flavour of ironic ambiguity about the compliment Juvenal pays his Imperial patron. On every count it seems likely that the Emperor in question was Hadrian, and that the publication of Book III took place between his accession in 118 and his departure for a tour of the provinces in 121. Satire VII is the first occasion on which Juvenal refers to an Emperor in anything but disparaging terms; Satire VIII, even more surprisingly, is dedicated to a young nobleman just going out to govern a province, and is a lecture on the theme of 'Virtue the one true nobility'. Satire IX, the sad tale of a discarded male gigolo, looks very much as though it had been rescued from Juvenal's bottom drawer and added as a makeweight.

Book IV (Satires X-XII) contains no evidence which would enable us to guess its date of publication with any accuracy. In Satire XII there is a description of the inner harbour basin which Trajan constructed for the port of Ostia (XII 75-81). We know that this basin was built in 104; the knowledge, however, does no more than give us an obvious *terminus post quem* for the date of the satire's composition. But in Satire XI Juvenal speaks of himself as an old man with wrinkled skin—too old, indeed, to stand the noise and dust and heat of the Games—who prefers to sit quietly at home and sun himself. Also, his material circumstances have clearly changed. The nightmare obsession with poverty and degradation that permeates his earlier work has disappeared, and much of his lethal invective with it: now, he reveals, he is the owner of a modest competence—a farm near Tivoli, at least three slaves. It is not much, and he is conscious that snobbish guests might despise his bone-handled cutlery and frugal menu (XI 129ff., 203ff.); but he is no longer the snarling, indigent, chip-on-the-shoulder flayall of the First Book. Indeed, Satire XII, a poem which celebrates the safe return of a friend after near-shipwreck, suggests that he has begun to take on a few of the characteristics he previously despised. When he slips into the grand manner one is no longer always quite sure that he is parodying it; and his periphrastic mythological allusions become less mocking, more turgidly Alexandrian.

With Book V we are on slightly firmer ground. This contains Satires XII-XVI, and seems to have been the last work Juvenal published. Satire XII can be dated to A D 127 by a reference to the addressee, who is described as sixty years old, and whose birth took place in the consulship of Fonteius Capito, A D 67. The events described in Satire XV are dated by Juvenal to the consulship of Aemilius Juncus—that is, to 127; and are described as having taken place 'lately', though the word *nuper* was capable of much stretching. Highet further argues, very ingeniously, that the reference in Satire XIV (96–106) to young Romans becoming Jewish converts and undergoing circumcision provides us with a *terminus ante quem* for Book V's publication. In 131/2, largely as the result of Hadrian banning the practice of circumcision, a violent Jewish rebellion broke out. 'Therefore', Highet argues, 'Juvenal could not have brought out a book complaining about the custom as being too easy and too common, if it had been made illegal and difficult before the book was published'. There is, then, a fair presumption that Book V appeared between 128 and 130. If this is so, we have a consistent and plausible chronological sequence of publication, as follows: Book I, *c.* 110-12; Book II, *c.* 116; Book III, *c.* 118-20; Book IV, ? *c.* 123-5; Book V, *c.* 128-30.

Now this picture assumes an unnaturally short creative span, and thus confirms the late biographical tradition that Juvenal only began his career as a satirist when already middle-aged; he himself, in the programmatic First Satire (25), speaks of his youth as something over and done with. If the birth-date of A D 55 represents something fairly near the truth, as I believe it does, then Book I would not have appeared till Juvenal was in his mid-fifties, and Book V when he was well over seventy. If he was still alive after Hadrian's death, he must have been about eighty-three or eighty-four when Antoninus Pius assumed the purple. Such a life-span fits in very well with his special pre-occupations. Born a year after Nero's accession, he would have been an impressionable fourteen during the terrible 'year of the four emperors' (A D 69), when, after Nero's assassination in July 68, Galba, Otho and Vitellius were successively toppled and murdered, leaving Vespasian the undisputed occupant of the Imperial throne. Twenty-six at the time of Domitian's accession in 81, he would have just turned forty when a palace conspiracy finally removed the tyrant in 96. The pattern is not susceptible of complete proof; but it makes consistent sense.

At some time during this period Juvenal made the acquaintance of the epigrammatist Martial, a man some fifteen years older than himself, whose first eleven books of *Epigrams* appeared between A D 85/6 and 98, at which point he left Rome for Spain. There is at least a possibility that Juvenal himself was a Spaniard. Sir Ronald Syme has pointed out that there were a large number of Junii in Spain, and that many of them settled—like our Juvenal—at Tivoli; the cognomen 'Iuvenalis' suggests either foreign or lower-class antecedents, and in fact two owners of it were freedmen from towns near Aquinum. (There was also one consul during the period, in A D 81, who had this cognomen: I have sometimes wondered whether 'Iulius Iuvenalis' should not in fact be 'Iunius Iuvenalis'.) Martial twice refers to Juvenal in Book VII of his *Epigrams*, published in the autumn of 92; then there is a gap of about ten years, until 101/2, when Martial sends his old friend a rather gloating little sketch of Bilbilis and its rural pleasures (XII 18), prefaced by a contrasting picture of what Juvenal himself may be assumed to be doing; pushing through crowds in the noisy Subura, or trudging uphill, sweating under the folds of a full-dress toga, to kick his heels in the ante-rooms of the great.

The earlier poems had described Juvenal as *facundus*, or 'eloquent', a term regularly applied to barristers and speech-makers, and one which confirms the tradition that he practised *declamatio* as a young man. The later epigram, composed during the gestation of Book I of the *Satires*, agrees in detail with the picture Juvenal draws there of the squalid and humiliating life endured by the 'client', or retainer, of some wealthy patron. Now the passage I have quoted from the Life specifically emphasizes that Juvenal's practice of rhetoric till 'about middle age' was not dictated by the necessity of earning a living; it was an *amusement*, the pastime of a *rentier* living on a gentleman's income. The tone of Martial's two earlier epigrams are quite consistent with such a supposition: Juvenal is a man to whom he sends little presents, whose friendship he is determined not to lose. But the note from Spain contains an unmistakable note of spiteful triumph: one gets the impression that Fortune (Juvenal's favourite bugbear) has reversed their positions.

There is one more piece of evidence, tantalizingly fragmentary, which both confirms the tradition that Juvenal's family came from Aquinum (we have his own word for it, too: see III 318–21) and suggests that the poet, in his youth, may have been relatively well-off. Two inscriptions (recorded in the eighteenth century but now lost) were found near the modern Aquino, both dealing with a certain [Ju]nius Juvenalis. The first commemorated his gift of an altar or shrine to Ceres, the second was a vote of thanks from the citizens of Aquinum to 'their benefactor', and a resolution to set up a tablet and statue of him to put his generosity on record. This Juvenal was a man of parts: commanding officer of a cohort of Dalmatian (Yugoslav) auxiliaries, joint-mayor of Aquinum during the census year (which implied extra responsibilities) and 'Priest of the deified Vespasian'. We cannot be certain—since the stone was broken, as so often with inscriptions, at the crucial point—whether this [Ju]nius Juvenalis was, in fact, the author of the *Satires*; but if he was not, he must have been a close relative, since he came from the poet's home-town, and was similarly associated with the cult of Helvine Ceres. (Ceres, incidentally, as Highet acutely points out, is almost the only Roman deity whom Juvenal consistently treats with anything like respect.)

The auxiliary command recorded here could be held either by a veteran centurion before retirement, or by a young man of the Equestrian Order, as the first step in 'the regular pattern of upper-middle-class service by which a man with some money could, without entering politics, make his way up through army appointments and governorships and administrative jobs until, with luck, he might become one of the most powerful officials in the empire' (Highet p. 34). The plum jobs in this field were the Prefecture of Egypt and the command of the Praetorian Guard, Rome's Household Brigade. If the man who dedicated this offering had been a veteran, he would surely have mentioned the fact; it seems reasonable to assume that he was a young *eques* (and thus of reasonable means) at the outset of his career in the Imperial administration. He was joint-mayor of Aquinum, a person of some standing: the office tended to go to men of about twenty-five, with some commissioned army service behind them. Vespasian died in 79 and was deified in 80—but his son Titus also died and was similarly deified in 81: it seems a fair assumption that this Juvenal became Priest of the Deified Vespasian in 80, though the dedication itself may have been made later.

There is nothing here that is inconsistent with what we know about Juvenal the satirist, and much to suggest a very close connexion between the poet and the municipal careerist. If [Ju]nius Juvenalis of Aquinum was twenty-five when he was appointed Priest of the Deified Vespasian, he would have been born in A D 55, the precise date given in the Life. If he saw active service with his Dalmatian cohort, it was almost certainly during Agricola's campaign in Britain, between 78 and 84. Now one curious fact about the *Satires* is the number of times Juvenal alludes to Britain. Besides such public events as the campaign to capture the Orkneys, or the border warfare against the Brigantes, he brings in various odd incidental details: the short northern nights, the oysters of Richborough, whales off the Atlantic coast, the spread of civilization among the natives (a point also picked up by Tacitus in the *Agricola*) and chariot-fighting techniques. It is at least a possibility that he saw service in Britain during 78-80, and was appointed to his honorary priesthood on his return, dedicating a shrine to Ceres for having brought him safely through the campaign in which he fought.

There still remains the enigmatic problem of his exile. The ancient commentators, and the Lives which follow them, agree that Juvenal was banished—'on the pretext of military promotion', one remarks—to a military station in Upper Egypt, either at the Great Oasis or the frontier post of Syene. The reason for his relegation is always the same: three lines which are preserved in Satire VII (90-92):

What nobles cannot bestow, you must truck for to an actor.
Why bother to haunt the spacious ante-rooms
Of the great? Colonels and Governors, the ballet appoints
Every man jack of them.

These lines form the climax, in their present position, to a swingeing diatribe against Domitian's favourite, the ballet-dancer and actor Paris, who seems to have had enormous influence in the distribution of honours and appointments. It is generally assumed that what sent Juvenal into exile was his specific reference to Paris; but there are weighty objections to this, the most telling of which is Domitian's pattern of behaviour during the last four or five years of his life. In 83 he had had Paris executed on suspicion of being the Empress' lover, and had divorced his wife. Ten years later he was still brooding over the affair. He executed one young aristocrat, Helvidius Priscus, merely for producing a farce in which Paris of Troy deserted the nymph Oenone, thus obliquely reminding Domitian of the Imperial divorce. He put a young ballet-dancer to death because of a supposed facial resemblance to his former favourite, and even killed those who dropped flowers on the site of Paris' execution. It is inconceivable that Juvenal's gross attack could have been punished with the lesser penalty of exile. As Dr Michael Coffey points out (with a horrific list of examples) 'the pattern of punishment especially in [Domitian's] later years suggests that death not exile was the fate of those who seemed to smirch the imperial dignity'.

But did Juvenal in fact refer to Paris at all? The lines described as having brought about his banishment are general, they name nobody. It is lines 87-9 that would have earned him instant execution, and would surely have been quoted by any scholar trying to manufacture a good case. No commentator mentions them in this context, and there is no proof that they even existed when Juvenal's original lampoon was in circulation. Now since Martial's two flattering epigrams were composed in 91/2, Juvenal's disgrace must have come later: as Highet rightly says, 'Martial was so subservient to Domitian that during the emperor's reign he would never have expressed affection for a condemned man'. If Juvenal was exiled, it would have been during the years of terror between 93 and Domitian's assassination in 96—a fact which has led some scholars to dismiss the entire story of exile as a late fabrication. But if Juvenal made no specific reference to Paris at all, and was in fact (since Paris had been dead for a decade) merely expressing irritation at some obnoxious jack-in-office of the moment, the story of exile becomes much more plausible. We know from various sources —including Juvenal himself in Satire IV—that Domitian had a peculiarly macabre sense of humour. It would have been very much in character for him to inform this importunate and indiscreet person that he was being transferred to some command in the Oasis as a mark of promotion—and for Juvenal to discover, the following day, that what this meant was *deportatio*, the harshest form of exile, involving loss of civil rights, confiscation of property, and severe limitation on movement.

If we accept this theory, Juvenal would have been exiled to Upper Egypt in 92/3, and returned to Rome in 96/7, after the accession of Nerva and the recall of the political exiles. We know, on his own testimony, that he had visited Egypt, and that he loathed the Egyptians, with a xenophobic ferocity which eclipses even his distaste for the Greeks. His knowledge of the country is extensive and peculiar: it includes, again, vivid details—the negresses of Meroë whose breasts are bigger than their babies, the earthenware skiffs used on the Delta canals, the chap-fallen, wrinkled, elderly female baboon. But even three years of exile here could leave its mark on a man. Gregory Nazianzen saw Hero, the philosopher, when he was released after a four-year sentence in the Oasis, and said he looked like Lazarus come back from the tomb. And this exile was only the culmination of fifteen nightmare years under Domitian. The psychological effect on such men was brilliantly described at the time by Tacitus, in his *Agricola* [§5, Penguin trs. pp. 52-3], in terms which recall Dostoyevsky's *House of the Dead*:

> Now at long last our spirit revives.... Public security, ceasing to be merely something hoped and prayed for, is as solid and certain as a prayer fulfilled. Yet our human nature is so weak that the cure lags behind the disease. Our bodies, which grow so slowly, perish in a flash; and so too the mind and its interests can be more easily crushed than brought to life again. Idleness develops a strange fascination of its own, and we end by loving the sloth that at first we loathed. Think of it. Fifteen whole years—no mean fraction of our human life—taken from us. Many have died a natural death, all the most irrepressible have fallen victims to the cruelty of the Emperor. Even we few that survive seem to have outlived, not only our fallen comrades, but our very selves, in those years stolen from our manhood that have brought us from youth to age, from age to the far end of life's journey—and no word said.

Penniless, his position and career smashed, seared by exile and the Terror, Juvenal came back, turned forty, to a Rome of jumped-up guttersnipes and decadent aristocrats: too proud to work, conditioned by his upbringing beyond any hope of adaptation, resigned to the humility of a client's life. Who in such circumstances—as he himself asked—could help writing satire? And who could refrain from making the various instruments of his downfall the main targets for his invective?

We can now summarize the main outline of Juvenal's life—always bearing in mind that most of the evidence is circumstantial, and that very little is susceptible of proof.[1] He was probably born in A D 55, the son of a well-to-do Spanish freedman who had settled at Aquinum, and who was determined to see that his son had a successful career in the Imperial civil service. (I have often thought that XIV 190ff., with a father getting his son out of bed early to study law-books and generally prepare himself for an official career, might be an autobiographical reminiscence.) Perhaps in 78 he got his foot on the first rung of the ladder by obtaining the command of a cohort of Dalmatian auxiliaries, and serving in Britain under Agricola. In 80 he was welcomed home with honour by his fellow-townsmen, made joint-mayor of Aquinum, and dedicated a shrine to Helvine Ceres in thanksgiving for his safe return. His career was proceeding very much according to plan. He was made an honorary priest of the Deified Vespasian. But in 81 Titus died, and Domitian came to power. For the first two years of his reign preferment lay in the hands of an odious Greek actor, and even after the actor's downfall Juvenal's promotion continued to hang fire. For ten years he divided his time between the capital and his home-town, practising declamation, cultivating influential friends, and—very privately—trying his hand at satirical sketches to relieve his feelings. He made the acquaintance of another literary Spaniard, Martial, and was much influenced by his outlook and subject-matter. If he married, there is no evidence for it. His published work suggests that he was fond of children, but disliked smart society women and coterie homosexuals.

Late in Domitian's reign, probably about 93, a lampoon of his on the sale of commissions became known to the authorities, and he was exiled to the Great Oasis (or Syene) in Upper Egypt, with loss of property and civil rights. Recalled by Nerva after

[1] With various modifications and additions, the pattern of this reconstruction more or less follows that worked out by Highet in *Juvenal the Satirist.* Much criticism—especially over the matter of Juvenal's exile—has not succeeded in denting its general outlines, or in proposing any more plausible alternative. Even where I differ from Highet's findings, my debt to his research is incalculable, and I am glad to acknowledge it here.

Domitian's assassination, he fell into the squalid and humiliating life of a *déclassé* hanger-on—an existence which supplied incomparable material for the first three books of the *Satires*. Soon after his return, in 98, Martial abandoned the urban rat-race and went back to Spain (borrowing his fare off the Younger Pliny) from where he sent Juvenal a short poetic epistle of the *suave mari magno* variety, contrasting his own rustic relaxation with Juvenal's own barren and obsequious daily round. During this period Juvenal was working at, and polishing, what he finally issued (*c.*110-12) as Book I of the *Satires*. Book II followed about five years later, and Book III shortly after the accession of Hadrian. From now on the tone of Juvenal's work underwent a marked change, and this may well have been due to the improvement in his material circumstances. He seems to have had a small farm at Tivoli, and a house in Rome where he could entertain friends to a modest but pleasant meal. It is very likely that he benefited in some way by Hadrian's patronage of the arts; perhaps the Emperor gave him a pension and a small estate, as Augustus had done for Horace. If so, it is not hard to see why Juvenal thereafter dropped his stringent attacks on bad literature; Hadrian's taste was far from impeccable, and his touchiness over aesthetic matters notorious. Two more books of *Satires* appeared, in 123/5 and 128/30. By now Juvenal was a septuagenarian, who must have recalled, with some irony, his own vivid descriptions of old age in Satire X. He probably survived Hadrian by a year or two, to die, leaving few friends and little reputation, about AD 140—in the middle of what Gibbon described as 'the period in the history of the world during which the condition of the human race was most happy and prosperous'.

II

'On the death of Domitian,' the Younger Pliny wrote, with characteristic candour, 'I reflected that here was a signal and glorious opportunity to punish guilt, to avenge misfortune, and to bring oneself into notice.' The reader of Juvenal's *Satires* cannot help but feel that their author (who may have been on bad terms with Pliny) envisaged an identical programme. Satire I, his manifesto, and probably the latest composition in the First Book, announces *indignatio* as his driving motif, and the world at large as his subject-matter:

> All human endeavours, men's prayers,
> Fears, angers, pleasures, joys and pursuits, these make
> The mixed mash of my verse.

But in fact this programme is never carried out. Juvenal writes from a very limited viewpoint, and the traverse of his attack is correspondingly narrow. Throughout his life, so far as we can tell, he never once questioned the social structure or the moral principles of the regime which had treated him so shabbily. (Any crypto-Republicanism one can detect in his work is no more than a reflection of the fashionable Stoic shibboleths current throughout his lifetime.) All that he asked of the Imperial administration was that its rulers should behave according to the dictates of virtue and morality; as for the upper classes, he seems to have hoped for no more from them than that they should set a good public example and avoid activities liable to tarnish their image with the plebs. His approach to any social problem is, basically, one of static conservatism. He may have thought that the client-patron relationship was fundamentally degrading, but he never envisaged its abolition. He attacked wanton cruelty to slaves, but did not query the concept of slavery itself (another characteristically Stoic attitude). His most violent invective, whether borrowed from the common rhetorical stockpot or the fruit of his own obsessions, is reserved for those who, in one way or another, threaten to disrupt the existing pattern of society, to inject some mobility and dynamism into the class-structure. It follows, *a fortiori*, that he will display especial animus against those who have robbed him, and his kind, of their chance to achieve what they regard as their birthright *within that framework*. This is one of the main keys to an understanding of the *Satires*.

Satire I is rightly regarded as a programme-piece: in it Juvenal deploys most of the main themes which he afterwards reiterates—vapid, cliché-ridden literature and rhetoric; various kinds of social and sexual obnoxiousness; above all, the corrupting power of wealth. But the attack is both calculated and highly selective; in each case there is a special, and revealing, motive behind it. Juvenal's main point about mythological platitudes, acute enough in itself, is that they served as a handy refuge for writers anxious to avoid dangerous contemporary issues: that their unreality is due to deliberate escapism. The reader must draw his own conclusions. Juvenal neither attacks the rhetorical system of education *en principe*, nor the civilization which produced it. Instead he works through a cumulative list of significant illustrations. But his main thesis, developed with passionate intensity through the first three books, is (to put it in economic terms) the appalling influence which mobility of income can have on a static class-structure.

The actual figures whom Juvenal presents on the stage, both here and in subsequent satires, fall into three broad stylized categories. First, and most interesting as a pointer to Juvenal's own preoccupations, there is the decadent aristocrat—of either sex—who has in some way or other betrayed the upper-class code whose conduct fails to reach those well-defined social and moral standards imposed on the governing classes as a complement to their privileges. This scapegoat figure is accused of many things, from extortion to miscegenation, from outrageous homosexuality to public appearances in the gladiatorial arena: what is common to each case is the *abrogation of responsible behaviour* which it implies. A governing class that lowers its standards and neglects its traditional duties constitutes a positive danger to the social structure over which it is set. This is what lies behind Juvenal's occasional blurring of social and moral criticism, as when the consul who demeans his office by driving his own gig in public is bracketed with forgers and adulterers, while Nero's crimes rise from mere murder to the climactic horror of his appearances on the stage. The rhetorical anti-climax is a device which Juvenal (like De Quincey in 'On Murder as one of the Fine Arts') employs to some effect; but it is hard not to feel the real and passionate animus behind examples of this sort. Juvenal flays upper-class shortcomings all the harder because he sees his world in peril: his terror of social change makes him treat infringements of accepted manners or conventions on a par with gross major crimes. In a sense his instinct was sound. Collapsing social standards are as sure a sign of eventual upheaval as the ominous drying up of springs and wells which heralds a volcanic eruption. In the famous Sixth Satire against women, what Juvenal really objects to is not so much licentiousness *tout court* as the breaching of class and convention. All his examples are chosen from ladies of high society; and what most arouses his wrath against them is that they contract liaisons with *lower-class* persons such as musicians, actors, or gladiators. (One gets the feeling that he would have no particular objection to a little in-group wife-swapping provided it was done discreetly.) These great ladies are several times compared, disadvantageously, to their social inferiors, who bear children instead of having abortions, and would never indulge in such unfeminine pursuits as swordplay or athletics.

Balancing this picture, and in sharply dramatic contrast to it, is that of the wealthy, base-born *parvenu*, a figure whom Juvenal clearly found both sinister and detestable—with good reason, since as a phenomenon he directly threatened Juvenal's own social position, and that of the whole *rentier* class in Rome. The rise of the freedman class forms one of the most significant elements in the history of the early Empire. These coarse, clever, thrusting ex-slaves, most often of foreign extraction, suffered from none of the crippling conventions and moral beliefs that every upper-class Roman inherited as part of his emotional luggage. What enabled them to amass such gigantic fortunes, and to force their way into positions of immense political power, was by no means only their native ability. They were cashing in on their masters' ignorance of, and contempt for, a world ruled by commerce and industry. Since the middle-class Equestrian Order, to which Juvenal aspired, was mainly a matter of the right property qualification, freedmen and their descendants began to monopolize all the best posts which it offered. It is no accident that Juvenal, in Satire I, draws so blistering a portrait of the Commander of the Praetorian Guard and the Prefect of Egypt. These were the supreme prizes of any Equestrian's career: in Juvenal's poem they are both held by Egyptians—a jumped-up fish-hawker called Crispinus, and a Jew, Tiberius Julius Alexander, whose statue, Juvenal suggests, should be used as a public latrine. He is always referring, enviously, to the capital sum of 400,000 sesterces which was required for admission to the Order. He and his shabby-genteel friends are kept out of the seats reserved for Equestrians while the sons of panders, auctioneers and gladiators are entitled to them. He attacks those who are irresponsible enough to fritter away their capital and become *déclassé*—a charge he also brings against the aristocrats, but for a different reason: since wealth now is the sole criterion of acceptance and power, they are imperilling their position of authority by destroying the *de facto* foundation on which it rests.

Yet though Juvenal regarded enough capital to qualify for Equestrian status as the *summum bonum*, he never indicates in any way that he would consider working to obtain it. He vaguely hopes for it as a gift from God, or 'some godlike human', which presumably is a periphrasis for Imperial patronage. Here we hit on a central and vital factor in his attitude to life. Juvenal was a bred-in-the-bone *rentier*, with all the characteristics of his class: contempt for trade, indifference to practical skills, intense political conservatism, with a corresponding fear of change and revolution; abysmal ignorance of, and indifference to, the economic realities governing his existence; a tendency to see all problems, therefore, in over-simplified moral terms, with the application of right conduct to existing authority as a kind of panacea for all ills.[1] His particular dilemma, like that of many

[1]A fallacy, I might add, in which numbers of his critics, both modern and ancient, have sedulously followed him. Here some remarks made by R. R. Bolgar, in *The Classical Heritage*, may appositely be cited: 'It is a common belief among

another *laudator temporis acti* yearning for some mythical Golden Age, is that he is living by a set of moral and social assumptions that were obsolete before he was born. The only occupations he will recognize are those of the army, the law, and estate-farming. He is as rigidly and imperceptively snobbish about trade as any nineteenth-century rural squire—and with even less justification. As Highet says in *Juvenal the Satirist*,

> Since his ideal is the farm which supports its owner in modest comfort (or the estates which make a man a knight), he does not realize that Italy now lives by imports. And he will not understand that the Greco-Roman world was built up by the efforts of the shrewd, energetic, competent men who made harbours, highways, aqueducts, drainage-systems, and baths; who cleared the forests and set up the trade-routes; who exchanged the products of the far parts of the globe and ventured on innumerable dangerous voyages.

All Juvenal can see in the immense commercial activity of his day is a frantic scrambling after quick profits, stupid luxuries, or wheat to keep the rabble quiet. He is ready to admire Trajan's splendid new harbour at Ostia, but the socially inferior men who built and planned it elicit nothing from him but a quick, dismissive gibe about making money out of privy-contracts—'These are such men as Fortune, by way of a joke,/Will sometimes raise from the gutter and make Top People.' His ideal is not so far from that of Naevolus, the ageing homosexual gigolo: a small country home bestowed by some wealthy patron; 'a nice little nest-egg at interest/ In gilt-edged stock'; a life of cultivated idleness, the Victorian 'genteel sufficiency'. 'What can I do in Rome?' cries Juvenal's friend Umbricius, in a famous and much-quoted section of Satire III, and the reader is so carried away by the rhetorical brilliance of

scholars that a disinterested curiosity has been the main force behind every advancement of learning. This theory, though it contains a measure of truth, is not altogether innocent of wishful thinking. That human curiosity has always existed and has always exercised its own dynamic admits of no doubt; but history suggests that the force of that dynamic cannot really be compared with the violent impulsions of the political and economic needs which are the main determinants of our destiny.'

the passage that it never occurs to him to answer. briefly: 'A useful job of work.' Nor, indeed, does it occur to Juvenal.

It is sometimes said that Juvenal is a very modern figure, and this is true; but in ways he is far more like a nineteenth-century phenomenon such as Dickens. Indeed, it could be argued, without stretching the paradox too far, that George Orwell's essay on Dickens is the most illuminating introduction to Juvenal in existence. The social parallels are so numerous and striking that they cannot be ignored. Again and again it might be the Roman poet rather than the English novelist that Orwell is analysing. Juvenal, like Dickens, 'displays no consciousness that the *structure* of society can be changed.' Like Dickens again, he lived in 'a city of consumers, of people who are deeply civilized but not primarily useful'. He too records 'pretentious meals and inconvenient houses, when the slavey drudging fourteen hours a day in the basement kitchen was something too normal to be noticed'. He too 'knows very little about the way things really happen. . .As soon as he has to deal with trade, finance, industry or politics he takes refuge in vagueness, or satire.' He too sees revolution as a monster, and is acutely aware of the irrational bloodlust and opportunism of the mob, the *turba Remi*. He too has a special compassion for children: like Dickens he attacks bad education without proposing a better alternative. His xenophobia may be closer to Thackeray: but what he shares with Dickens more than any of Dickens' own contemporaries—and for much the same reasons—is that special horror of slums and poverty, that ignorance of, and distaste for, the urban proletariat which stand high among 'the special prejudices of the shabby-genteel'. Like Dickens, he frowns—as we have seen—on social miscegenation: he objects to Eppia running off with her ugly gladiator for exactly the same reason that Dickens objects to Uriah Heep's passion for Agnes Wicklow. He too is a caricaturist; and as we know, it is fatal when a caricaturist sees too much. He too (like every urban Roman of his age) was 'out of contact with agriculture and politically impotent'. He too 'only succeeds with the [landowning-military-bureaucratic] class when he depicts them as mental defectives'. He too (and this is both his strength and his weakness as a satirist) in the last resort 'sees the world as a middle-class world, and everything outside these limits is either laughable or slightly wicked'.

The *rentier* and the caricaturist combine to produce a comic yet nightmarish *reductio ad absurdum* of the dole-queue at some great man's house which in fact is the core and centre of Satire I. It is a vivid and brilliant piece of work, memorable—Dickensian echoes again—for its 'turns of phrase and concrete details'; wildly exaggerated, yet embodying social truths along with the personal fears and obsessions. The *sportula* ('dole' is an inadequate translation) has degenerated from a friendly *quid pro quo* into an impersonal soup-kitchen hand-out: one of Juvenal's most valid points against excessive money-grubbing is the way it corrupts personal relationships. In this Kafka-like crowd of greedy and obsequious hangers-on, impoverished aristocrats on the way down (including a consul and a praetor) jostle for precedence with a Syrian chain-store magnate on the way up, who remarks, unanswerably from his own point of view: 'What's in a senator's purple stripe, if true-blue nobles/Are reduced to herding sheep up-country, while I have more/Stashed away in the bank than any Imperial favourite?' Juvenal's comment is one of dejected and cynical resignation. *So let the Tribunes wait, and money reign supreme*, he remarks, adding that though the Romans—who were much addicted to deifying abstractions—had not as yet raised an altar to Cash, *still it is Wealth, not God, that compels our deepest reverence.*

But this, of course, was just as true of Juvenal and his class of cultured *rentiers* as of anyone else: once again he provides us with that nice touch of moral ambiguity which makes him so enjoyable to read. However much he might inveigh against the corrupting influence of money, he would never have admitted for one moment that it could possibly corrupt *him*. He not only yearned with fervent and frustrated longing for the financial portion that would admit him to the company of the elect, but regarded it as his moral prerogative—a not uncommon phenomenon among individuals or groups who lack the ability to obtain what they want by native talent. The idea that financial acumen should dictate the size of one's bank-balance seemed to him not only outrageous but quite irrelevant. He seethed with impotent fury—as did many of his class—to find himself shouldered aside and outsmarted by the kind of shrewd, vulgar millionaire whom Petronius depicts so memorably in the *Satyricon*; worse still was the sinister political influence wielded over successive Emperors by Greek freedmen, to whom men of parts were forced to kowtow in the most humiliating manner. His introductory Satire, with its forgers, gigolos, informers and crooked advocates, is a threnody on the theme of collapsing social values, on the impotence of the old middle classes when confronted by a ruthless, unprincipled, and commercially talented opposition.

It is significant that Juvenal's programme-satire hinges round the caricature of a patron-client relationship because, fundamentally, it was the only relationship—certainly the only business relationship—that he was capable of understanding. At one level, the *quid pro quo* concept was built into Roman manners as a basic principle; it permeated the formalized structure of *amicitia* (which means both more and less than the English word 'friendship') and was extended to men's relationships with the Gods. Here, as so often, Juvenal betrays his inability to see beyond the *status quo*. This was not really his fault, and Orwell, again, makes us see why: '*Given the fact of servitude*,' he remarks, '*the feudal relationship is the only tolerable one.*' If any single statement can illuminate and resolve the whole social content of Juvenal's work, this is it. He saw the feudal relationship everywhere: between master and slave, between patron and client, between the jobber of army commissions and the hopeful military careerist. Roman society formed a vast pyramid, with the Emperor—the most powerful patron of all—at the top, and the rabble roaring for bread and circuses at the bottom; in between came an interlinked series of lesser pyramids, where one man might play both roles, patronizing his inferiors and toadying to those above him. This is one of the points which Juvenal brings out and exaggerates in his caricature, and refers to again later (V 137-8) when describing Trebius' ultimate ambition—'to be a magnate yourself/and a patron of magnates'.

It is curious that all Roman writers of this period, Juvenal included, should have so despised the *captatores*, the professional legacy-hunters, because, in a sense, legacy-hunting was the sole occupation of the leisured classes: sinecure appointments, the *sportula*, a 'modest competence' on retirement—it all came to the same thing in the end. Petronius recognized this: he remarked that in Croton there were only two sorts of people, the rich and their sycophants. Perhaps the *captatores* were despised—in a way like the merchant-freedmen—for being efficient professionals, in whom the cold and obsessional pursuit of wealth had destroyed all human feeling. This is certainly what Juvenal felt; he regards it as necessary to emphasize, when celebrating the survival of his friend after a storm, that his motives are altruistic—not those of the legacy-hunter (XII 93-130). He believed in the feudal relationship; it was the only one he knew, and he was aware that it had originally expressed, in formal terms perhaps, a personal, human relationship that contained a good deal more than mere reciprocal expressions of obligation. But what he now saw was the systematic reduction of this feudal concept into pure financial huckstering, at all levels, where both parties—without any thought of personal contact, let alone affection—were angling to secure the biggest possible profit. When Juvenal writes, as he so often does, about the corrupting effect of wealth, this notion is never very far from his mind. Money corrodes sexual relationships by encouraging, not only infidelity, but knowing complaisancy in the cuckolded husband; money destroys social stability by turning ex-slaves into titular middle-class gentlemen; money excuses vulgarity, buys favourable discrimination, corrupts true friendship, procures false sycophancy, leads to perjury, murder, fraud; money has become the criterion for winning professional respect; we mourn its loss with more heartfelt tears than we would the death of a friend or a lover.

Once client and patron had a genuine mutual relationship, based on trust, obligation and service; now all we see are 'retainers whose friendship was bought/With the meal-ticket stashed in their wallets'. What is more, the whole idea of altruistic obligation is now actively despised, with dire effect on society as a whole:

When you tell a young man that only fools give presents
To friends, or relieve the debts of a poverty-stricken relation,
It simply encourages him to rob and cheat, to descend
To any criminal act . . .

Juvenal devotes three entire satires to demonstrating the way in which, at various levels, this relationship has become a corrupt parody of its original self. In Satire IV we see it from the apex of the pyramid, where Domitian and his Imperial Privy Council are on show; cold sadist and cowardly sycophants discussing, not the situation on the frontiers, but what to do with a giant turbot. In Satire V it is the same story, but the props have been changed; the sadist is now a wealthy patron giving a dinner-party for his hangers-on, and deliberately torturing them with the contrast between what he is given and their own insultingly cheap entertainment. In Satire IX the principle is applied to the field of sexual relationships (it is also apparent at intervals during Satire VI) and taken to the ultimate point in human degradation, with a homosexual patron who grudges every penny he pays his gigolo, and puts sex on an exclusively cash basis:

'I paid you so much *then*,'
He says, 'and a bit more later, and more that other time—'
Working it out by piece-rates.

The homosexual's name is Virro; so is that of the host at the dinner-party. Whether Juvenal was pointing at a real person or not, he clearly intended his readers to link the two characters —and with good reason. But the pessimism goes further, since—

as Juvenal so clearly sees—it takes two to make, or corrupt, a relationship; and those grovelling courtiers, those greedy free-loaders, that professional male prostitute, have all encouraged the intolerable situation in which they find themselves by abandoning their self-respect, their basic *humanitas*. Vicious host and decadent parasite, both are equally to blame.

The moral dilemma which Juvenal presents, here and elsewhere, lies at the very heart of his position as a satirist, and has a very personal application to his life. Like his friend Umbricius, like all decent, educated *rentiers* of the middle class, who stick by their moral principles and expect certain traditional privileges and monopolies in return, Juvenal finds that the historical process is threatening to sweep him into oblivion. 'There's no room in this city for the decent professions,' Umbricius laments, before retiring to rural Cumae; and a study of Books I-III of the *Satires* shows us exactly why. Lawyers with principles are being ousted by cheap, flashy shysters, as crooked as the clients they defend. Posts in the army or the civil service are handed out by Greek freedmen, and obtained by former Egyptian fishmongers. Writers are at the mercy of ignorant, contemptuous patrons. Teachers are despised, bullied, and paid a miserable pittance. The traditional ruling classes are frittering away their money and their authority, and a new class of greasy and unprincipled upstarts is threatening to replace them. Worst of all, the 'humane professions' have been invaded by a flood of sedulous, slippery, quick-witted Greeks,

All of them lighting out for the City's classiest districts
And burrowing into great houses, with a long-term plan
For taking them over. Quick wit, unlimited nerve, a gift
Of the gab that outsmarts a professional public speaker—
These are their characteristics. What do you take
That fellow's profession to be? He has brought a whole bundle
Of personalities with him—schoolmaster, rhetorician,
Surveyor, artist, masseur, diviner, tightrope-walker,
Magician or quack, your versatile hungry Greekling
Is all by turns. Tell him to fly—he's airborne [III 72-8].

Juvenal's xenophobia is not so much of the old-fashioned nationalist variety as that which we find in a trade unionist who sees his job threatened by immigrant labour. In this new urban rat-race he and his kind had either to compromise their principles, and beat the Greeks and freedmen at their own game, or go under. He could no longer rely on the benefits of Imperial preference.

The classic example of survival by compromise is, of course, Juvenal's elder contemporary Martial, the fashionable social pornographer, Rome's equivalent of a scandal-sheet gossip-columnist. His gross adulation of Domitian was only matched by the neat *volte-face* he performed after that Emperor's assassination, when he flattered Nerva, in equally lavish terms, for being above flattery. Juvenal felt unable to take this way out; perhaps, in any case, his special talent would have made heavy weather of Martial's feather-light political insincerities. At all events, he preferred to endure the grinding and humiliating indigence of a client's life, attending upon great men, stomaching snubs and insults, in return for a bare subsistence dole and the occasional dinner invitation. Perhaps, with luck, a patron might sometimes lend him a peeling hall in the outer suburbs for a public recitation of his work-in-progress. The tragedy was that no conceivable alternative existed for him. He knew, all too well, the degradation involved: but a *déclassé* gentlemen had to make his choice between subservience and the gutter:

> . . . are there no sidewalks
> Or bridges, no quarter-share in a beggar's mat
> For you to make your pitch from? Is your hunger quite
> So all-devouring? Is dinner worth every insult
> With which you pay for it? Wouldn't your self-respect
> Be better served if you stuck it out where you are,
> Shivering cold, on a diet of mouldy dog's bread? [V 8-11]

Pity the poor *rentier*: robbed of his perquisites by clever foreigners, despised and humiliated by the upstart *nouveaux-riches* who have replaced his traditional patrons both in the professions and at court, caught between the twin horrors of beggary and moral self-abasement. What we hear from Juvenal, in the earlier satires at least, is the *cri de coeur* of a doomed class. Later, the tone sheds its hysteria and asperity: once Juvenal has achieved the *rentier*'s 'modest competence' much of the impulse for his satirical invective fades away. Though this does not make it any the less forceful or valid, his moral indignation had highly personal motives behind it; and these—as is inevitable—both modify and illuminate his moral, religious and philosophical outlook.

III

Like so many writers who feel that the world they inhabit is out of joint, Juvenal is continually harking back to the distant past: the Golden Age before Saturn's fall, the semi-mythical period that followed Rome's foundation by Romulus, the early Republic of Livy's zealously Imperial propaganda. He never loses an opportunity to contrast the thrift, abstemiousness, simplicity, patriotism and moral rectitude of the good old days with the selfish hedonism and social flux he sees all around him. This well-worn rhetorical device had been done to death by almost every Roman poet since the close of the Republic; but Juvenal's handling of it deserves attention on at least two counts. To begin with, from his point of view there was a great deal of truth in it. The trouble with literary commonplaces, especially when they are sedulously imitated from one generation to the next, is that we tend to write them off as mere stage-properties. But the two or three centuries before Juvenal's lifetime *had* radically transformed Roman civilization and *mores*; a vast and sudden influx of wealth *had* corrupted former standards of behaviour and promoted reckless ambition; the Republic, however venal and inefficient, *had* been replaced by a despotism, however benevolent and enlightened; the average Roman citizen *had* lost effective political power; foreign upstarts *had* obtained a stranglehold on some of the most influential positions in the Empire; such members of the old aristocracy as had survived the Civil Wars and subsequent Imperial purges *were*, very often, taking refuge in hellraking or philosophical quietism. Juvenal, as they say, had a case.

What he has been most often criticized for (though lately, as we shall see, the pendulum has begun to swing the other way) is the form in which he proposed to present it. Towards the close of the First Satire he remarks that the blunt outspokenness of a satirist such as Lucilius would be impossible today; put the finger on a successful murderer, let alone an Imperial favourite, and you are liable to end up as a human torch in the arena. Therefore the oblique approach must be cultivated:

> It's too late for a soldier
> To change his mind about fighting when he's armed in the battle-line.
> For myself I shall try my hand on the famous dead, whose ashes
> Rest beside the Latin and the Flaminian Ways.

This disclaimer has produced a whole host of interpretations. Juvenal is being flippantly evasive, and refusing to commit himself; he is covering his line of retreat against possible libel actions, and in fact has every intention of attacking contemporary figures; his indignation is the synthetic flourish of the mere rhetorician, and his disclaimer a clumsy imitation of similar stock apologies by Horace and Persius. Such historical instances as he presents—and there are fewer of them than one might suppose—are mostly taken from the reigns of Claudius, Nero, and Domitian. What is more, his *Satires* were published—whatever the date of their original composition—under emperors whose humane and liberal attitude would, surely, have made such elaborate precautions unnecessary. The arbitrary despotism of the Terror, with its police spies and informers, had been swept away. Why, we ask ourselves, does the fellow keep hedging in this pusillanimous fashion?

The answer seems to be, as Kenney shrewdly pointed out, that Juvenal does not so much make specific attacks against the dead (except in Satire IV, which is an isolated, and probably early, anomaly) so much as use them by way of *exempla*, pegs on which to hang a moral generalization. This was a common practice among satirists and rhetoricians, and had the specific authority of Quintilian to back it. It also, unfortunately, provides a field-day for adherents of the new school in classical literary criticism ('new' is perhaps an otiose epithet, since it could well be argued that before the emergence of *Arion* classical studies had no formal literary criticism at all, or at least nothing that would be recognized as such by any serious student of English literature born much after John Addington Symonds). Two fundamental concepts in this modern critical approach are (1) the assumption that an author's writing *persona* can be neatly and completely hived off from his personality and experiences as a historical character (hence much talk about the 'biographical fallacy'); and (2) the belief that ancient literature must be studied in isolation from its historical (and biographical) context, with reference to the literary conventions governing the *genre* in which each work is composed rather than the cultural background supporting it. To readers with a degree in English this may, I fear, all seem a trifle *vieux jeu*; I can only assure them that it is at present roaring through the classical world with the contagious virulence of measles when that disease first hit the Pacific. Pindar would seem to be the latest victim; at the 1971 Classical Conference in Cambridge Eugene Bundy's articles on Pindaric criticism, jettisoning all the background and going overboard for the formulae of encomiastic literature, were being discussed in awed tones, like some new Gospel (though one is glad to report a few sturdily dissident voices). Anyone who wants to see what this questionable *nouvelle vague* can do—good as well as bad—to Roman satire in general and Juvenal in particular, should turn up the volume of essays entitled *Critical Studies on Roman Literature: Satire*, edited by Professor J. P. Sullivan. The longest and most pretentious essay in this collection, 'Is Juvenal a Classic?' has been contributed by Mr H. A. Mason, a former regular contributor to *Scrutiny*, and it may be worth while (as a kind of awful warning) to examine it in some detail.[1]

Mr Mason, as we might expect, believes that the *persona* which Juvenal adopted for satirical purposes bore no relation to his everyday self (how this schizophrenic division is achieved we never learn), is worried by his lack of modern-style moralizing, and praises him chiefly as 'a supreme manipulator of the Latin language'. He states his general attitude very early on. He parts company, he tells us,

> with those of my fellow-amateurs who see Juvenal as a neurotic sufferer from ill-treatment by Domitian; full of pent-up feelings all clamouring for simultaneous expression; with a prophet's diagnosis of the true ills of his time and a prophet's mission to set them right; deeply indignant, morally earnest, passionately sincere; simple-minded and literal on the whole; a man with something of a philosophy, though not a formal philosopher; and at the same time an admirable witness to what was happening on the seamy side of Rome.

Where this is not wrong-headed it is old hat. A number of reputable scholars—most notably Gaston Boissier, in that admirable work *L'Opposition sous les Césars*—had been hacking away at the image of Juvenal the moral prophet long before Mr Mason appeared on the scene, so that there is something decidedly *déjà vu* about his strictures. We do not take Juvenal's assumption of the high moral tone nearly so seriously as our

[1] One critic from the same stable, reviewing my translation of Juvenal, and discussing the Introduction (of which this essay forms a revised and expanded version), remarked that though I listed Mr Mason's article in my bibliography, I showed no signs of having read it in my text. This was not, in fact, the case; I had read it several times, chiefly because an initial perusal suggested that it was for the most part portentous rubbish, and I felt I must have misunderstood Mr Mason's arguments. Subsequent readings led me, however, to realize that my first reaction had been, if anything, somewhat too charitable. I therefore forebore to bother the readers of my translation with otiose matter. When I came to review the book edited by Professor Sullivan, I rectified this deficiency. The resultant row filled the correspondence columns of the TLS for weeks, to everyone's great enjoyment, mine included; but it also suggested to me with some force that I had badly underestimated the readiness of intelligent people to swallow this particular brand of fashionable literary nonsense.

grandfathers did, and we are, perhaps, more ready to appreciate his talent for parody and obscene *double-entendre*. But Mr Mason's own contribution to this reassessment seems to be—as we might expect—an effort to cut his author free from history or personal problems altogether; we see why when we read his section on the Sixth Satire.

'The poem,' he writes, 'can never be presented as the supreme *pièce justificative* when asking whether Juvenal is a classic as long as we are reading it as the outpourings of a frustrated neurotic.' This is really a most odd notion; surely, even on Mr Mason's own terms, the antecedents of the poem are irrelevant to its ultimate value? There is no reason why one piece of great art should not be produced by a howling neurotic and another by a sane man properly 'distanced' from his work; both are equally valuable, even though the first may have been directly stimulated by its creator's neurosis. Mr Mason seems to suppose, in a muddled fashion, that if Juvenal *was* an embittered neurotic who suffered under Domitian (and he may well have been) this somehow detracts from his literary value; so emphasis is laid on Juvenal's unreality, hyperbole, and literary artifice. He is, we learn, 'far less interested in presenting a social reality than in extracting opportunities for witty excursions'. Mr Mason, as one might expect, pounces with an almost audible whoop of delight on the *Quellenforschung* experts (he should see what Housman has to say about *them*) who can show us that almost every idea in Juvenal was borrowed from Martial. If Juvenal's description of a rich man setting fire to his own house, can be paralleled from the epigrammatist, it follows (does it not?) that the actual incident need never have happened at all. The trouble, of course, as all readers of Juvenal know very well, is that verifiable history and social data will keep creeping in (the same applies to Bundy's theories about Pindar). Mr Mason dislikes the powerfully lurid passage about Messalina in the brothel (too well documented to dismiss as rhetorical fantasy) because Juvenal 'has relied on the brute facts. . .to do all the work for him'; and doubtless, if he had been writing before

Ostia was excavated, he would have dismissed Juvenal's multi-storeyed rickety apartment block in the Third Satire as another instance of playful literary hyperbole.

'The royal road to Juvenal,' he asserts, 'is through profound enjoyment of the poetry of Eliot and Pound'—an arsy-varsy pronouncement which suggests that Mr Mason read F. J. Lelièvre's article on 'Parody in Juvenal and T. S. Eliot' and let it go to his head.[1] In point of fact, Eliot in his *Waste Land* mood, and Pound nearly all the time, are the exact modern equivalents of that allusive Alexandrian obscurantism which drove the later Roman satirists to parody or drink. But Mr Mason is so determined to find anticlimactic wit everywhere that he often trips over his own feet. Thus, when Hannibal in the Tenth Satire urges his men to plant the standard of Carthage in the Subura, Mr Mason at once assumes he means the Subura *qua* red-light district. Granted that such an allusion is possible, he ignores the fact that the Subura was also a busy shopping centre and (more important) geographically at the very heart of Rome. But then neither Mr Mason's Latin nor his taste is invariably reliable. One of his main theses hangs on an interpretation of the last two lines in the First Satire,

experiar quid concedatur in illos
quorum Flaminia tegitur cinis atque Latina,

which he takes to mean, in a general sense, 'out of notorious examples taken chiefly from the past, I shall make an original kind of great poetry'. By now the average reader may well be so bemused by the author's brisk air of confidence as not to realize that under no circumstances whatsoever could Juvenal's text be twisted to mean anything of the sort.[2] As for Mr Mason's taste, we get a nice instance of that when he comes to discuss Dr Johnson's *The Vanity of Human Wishes*. That famous line

[1] Mr Mason afterwards publicly denied ever having read this article, and while one must accept his word that he failed to do his homework properly in a field which so closely concerned him, the similarity of thought remains undeniable.

[2] This assertion was challenged by correspondents after the publication of the review in which it first appeared. None of their arguments struck me as convincing, or even worth serious discussion; I stand by my point.

'Turn'd by his nod the stream of honour flows' provokes a gloss that must have the Great Cham turning in his grave: 'It is hard not to see Wolsey as an enormous edifice spouting water now in this direction, now in that.' Like a Brobdingnagian *mannekin-pisse*, one presumes.

But the thing that Mr Mason makes heaviest weather of is, curiously, Juvenal's obscenity. Since he will not have it that Juvenal (and therefore, *a fortiori*, his presumed source Martial also) is concerned to depict real social conditions, he has to explain the obscenity as a *literary convention*; and as a result (to at least one reader's incredulous delight) he takes the winking apologies of Pliny and Martial on the subject at their face value. 'How,' he asks, in self-induced rhetorical puzzlement, 'are we to account for the Romans' apparent relish of the abominable?' Quite simply, one is tempted to reply: they were—especially in the higher social and moneyed echelons—sophisticated people with coarse tastes and immensely dirty minds. Mr Mason need only go round the House of the Vettii in Pompeii to know who bought Martial's epigrams, or his predecessors' in the same field; indeed he could do worse, to begin with, than read Professor Sullivan's admirable study of Petronius, and reinforce it with some discreet inquiries into the state of the modern pornography market.

It is here, I can't help feeling, that Mr Mason's whole approach, despite its incidental virtues, begins to founder at two vital points. In the first place, the assertion that Juvenal is no guide to the social conditions of his day crumbles on a detailed examination, and can only be maintained at all by a careful—not to say artful—selection of *testimonia*. It also involves the strange but (as we have seen) fashionable assumption that satirists can aim at targets *which have no basis in reality*, but are simply traditional literary lumber out of the stockpile—as though this were not, precisely, what Juvenal, Martial, Persius and Petronius were all with one voice attacking! [1] *Hominem pagina*

[1]There has been much argument, a great deal of it quite pointless, as to whether Juvenal's general picture of Rome under the Flavians is truth or rhetorical fiction.

nostra sapit, says Martial, and Mr Mason blandly quotes him; this is to have it both ways with a vengeance. Of course Juvenal exaggerates; so does every political cartoonist. But his hyperbole is always rooted in social or historical truth. Hyperbole which takes off from fantasy rather than into it is the merest paradox.

The second point is this. After a while there intrudes (as there was bound to) what one can only term an element of moral anachronism into Mr Mason's literary judgment. Though in ways he is anxious not to miss the least hint of *double-entendre* (one half-expects him to take *vive bidentis amans* as a cheerful recommendation of rural bestiality) his fundamentally puritanical approach, hinted at by his remarks on Johnson, is stated unequivocally towards the close. Juvenal, he complains, 'is not interested in lust as it presents itself to the individual conscience as a soiling constituent of life.... It is this *absence of interest* that is horrifying in Juvenal....' But of course, the point is that no ancient author of any kind—with the possible exception of Plato, and even this is doubtful—ever thought in such terms at all; what Mr Mason is doing, though he may well not realize it, is introducing a series of concepts which belong more properly to the history of Christianity (and its secular non-conformist offshoots) into a context where they are quite irrelevant.

This type of approach makes it hard to appreciate how much incidental light Juvenal's use of rhetorical *exempla* sheds on his attitude to the Imperial civilization under which he is forced to live. Again, he does not criticize the structure of his society as such; all he sees is a steady decline in moral integrity from the Golden Age to his own day. If his solution—let men pursue virtue and all will be well—seems to us intolerably naive, at least he saw the crucial flaw at the heart of his society, and expressed it

My own feeling is that it is limited, selective, and often prejudiced; that it leaves out a great deal—the happy, virtuous, hard-working majority are not, alas, the stuff which inspires great satire—and exaggerates much of what it includes; but that ultimately it is based on fact, and presents a truly observed if highly partial portrait both of Rome itself and of aberrant upper-class *mores* during Juvenal's lifetime. A satirist may resort to caricature; but he seldom tilts at exclusively paper windmills.

in memorable terms. As Horace had earlier remarked, Rome was suffering from a progressive moral decline; and Juvenal saw no reason to suppose that the rot had stopped in his own day. If anything the situation had deteriorated still further. There was no guarantee that tomorrow's Emperor would be any improvement on his predecessors, and in the circumstances, as Highet well remarks, 'it would be trivial to satirize only the men and women of his own time.... This realization was one of his chief contributions to satire.' It was indeed; despotism has no guarantee of benevolence (though the Stoics tried to make their moral precepts a kind of inoculation against excess) and Juvenal at his gloomiest hardly foresaw some of the Imperial horrors in store for posterity. It is an ironical gloss on his theory of parental influence that such a philosophical paragon as Marcus Aurelius should have produced, in his elder son and successor Commodus, precisely the kind of brutalized gladiatorial thug whom Juvenal most detested. But the satirist's pessimism is prescient: he knows, only too well, that one good emperor does not bring the millennium. The central problem remains unchanged, and must be treated *sub specie aeternitatis*. This realization is one of his major claims to be treated as a classic; but it does not require us to cut him loose from his historical context and treat him as a platitudinous rhetorical fantasy-monger with a gift for memorable phrase-making.

It is also very relevant when we examine his attitude to religion, in particular to the concept of Fortune or Destiny. Stoic orthodoxy identified Fortune with God, and Nature, and Reason: this uneasy compromise reflected a prevalent mood of fatalism, which felt that the world must be ruled either by blind and random chance or else by immutable destiny. At the lowest level this trend was exemplified by the common passion for astrology and fortune-telling; for thinking people, especially those living within the shadow of the Imperial throne; it posed some very disturbing questions on the existence of free will. Tacitus felt the dilemma acutely. Is it true, he wonders, that 'the friendships and enmities of rulers depend on destiny and the luck of a man's birth'? May not our personalities play some part in determining our lives? Under Augustus it had been easy enough to believe in a benevolent Destiny directing the affairs of Rome and her citizens; by the time Lucan came to write his *Pharsalia* Fortune looked far less appealing. Juvenal accurately reflects this ambivalent attitude. At times he portrays Destiny as a capricious, immutable deity, playing hopscotch with our careers; but he also, with great emphasis and some shrewdness, declares at the end of Satire X:

> Fortune has no divinity, could we but see it: it's we,
> We ourselves, who make her a goddess, and set her in the heavens.

Ethically, Juvenal feels, as did most Stoics, that man must pursue virtue by his own efforts: though uncommitted to any specific philosophy, he had mopped up, in a piecemeal fashion, most of the popular intellectual attitudes of the day. These included a briskly flippant cynicism towards the myths and ritual of traditional Roman religion, and a creed of moral self-help which by implication left little scope for divine interference.

What he never seems to have realized is that this detached urban sophistication of his struck at the very roots of the high-minded Republican *pietas* which he professed to find so admirable. Even when lauding his rude forefathers to the skies, he cannot help sneering wittily at their shaggy, acorn-bleching primitivism: all his descriptions of the Golden Age have an unmistakable note of civilized latter-day mockery running through them. There is, in fact, a radical split detectable between Jevenal's moral ideals, and the fashionable intellectual scepticism which he shared with most educated Romans of his day and age. This dichotomy sets up tensions and cross-currents throughout the *Satires*: it is nowhere so obvious as in Juvenal's dealings with Roman deities or mythology. In the old days, he tells us, the numinous power of the gods was nearer to Rome, and no one ever dared to scoff at divine power. It does not seem to occur to him that he never loses an opportunity of scoffing at it himself. He pokes fun at Jupiter's sexual escapades, and

Numa's assignation with Egeria; he mocks Mars for being unable to keep robbers out of his own temple, and offers us a hilarious glimpse of life on Olympus before King Saturn 'exchanged his diadem/ For a country sickle, when Juno was still a schoolgirl'; he pooh-poohs anyone who is naive enough to believe in Hades, and repeatedly debunks traditional mythology, which he sees, in his superior middle-class fashion, as a collection of mildly ridiculous and unedifying *contes drôlatiques*. In short, he falls into an error very common among intellectual moralists, that of proclaiming a social ideal with his rational mind, and then destroying any hope of its fulfilment by the emotional attitudes he brings to it. He, and those like him, who uphold *sapientia*—a word which embodies both the reasoning faculty, formal logic, and moral philosophy— against Fate, superstition, and all the messy irrational magma which bedevils men's minds everywhere, made one cardinal error. They totally ignored the cohesive social binding power of irrational and emotional factors on the human mind; they genuinely believed that men could be made wise and good by taking thought, and needed no other stimulus. There are, in any age, some people of whom this is true: but they always remain a small, if articulate, minority. By mocking religious traditionalism, the Stoics were undermining the very foundations of those antique virtues they sought to promote. Cash may have been a despicable deity; but it was hardly more despicable than the collection of blind, arbitrary, indifferent or bloody-minded figures of fun which Juvenal presents in the *Satires*. Philosophical self-help has always been a dubious substitute for religion; and as a rallying-cry for a national regeneration of morals it is laughable. One suddenly realizes what a tiny proportion of Rome's population Juvenal was addressing, how narrow his terms of reference were.

In this connexion, I think the significance of his, and his predecessors', penchant for satirical parody has received less attention than it deserves.[1] Juvenal uses this device, not only

[1]The volume of essays edited by Professor Sullivan, and referred to above, makes some amends for this deficiency. Mr W. S. Anderson refers to Lucilius'

to point the contrast between heroic past and degenerate present by decking out the latter in borrowed antique plumes, but also as an escape-valve for his own highly ambivalent feelings about the past. The parody kicks both ways. At one point in Satire IX Juvenal makes a male prostitute the recipient of an address which echoes Virgil's exhortation to a similarly oriented, but somewhat more genteel, literary shepherd. 'The unlovely reality of Naevolus,' as Mr Lelièvre demurely remarks, 'placed alongside a romanticized conception of the passion in which he deals, may be felt to represent an astringent comment on the conventions of pastoral poetry.' Perhaps it is even more than that. Juvenal parodies a number of authors—Horace, Ovid, Statius, Homer and Lucretius among them—but I do not think it is accidental that his favourite target should be grandiloquent epic, nor that the author he makes more fun of than all the rest put together is Virgil, the mouthpiece of Augustus, the singer of Rome's imperial destiny. Virgil announced, in the *Georgics*, that mythological themes were obsolete, and that 'Caesar' (that is Augustus) would be his theme; Juvenal makes a similar declaration, but—significantly—chooses as *his* alternative topic vice and crime. Where Virgil glorifies, Juvenal belittles: with symbolic appropriateness, he uses more diminutives than almost any other Roman poet. He delights in transferring a heroic phrase to a mundane context. The cannibalistic Egyptian riot of Satire XV is a kind of anti-epic battle, and I have often wondered whether the spear-flinging ape on goatback at the end of Satire V was not meant to recall the equestrian manoeuvres of the *lusus Troiae* in Book V of the *Aeneid*. Juvenal may think that Rome has been rotted by long peace, but the glories of battle and conquest held singularly little appeal for him either.

'anti-heroic attitude'; Professor R. G. M. Nisbet quotes—with obvious relish—Persius' remark in his introductory poem, '*nec fonte labra prolui caballino*', which we may translate as 'I never gargled in the Muses' horse-trough', *i.e.* Hippocrene. Mr Mason isolates, as one of Juvenal's favourite techniques, 'the belittling remark in the style of epic grandeur', which is quite true, but spoils the effect by adding that 'if Juvenal is a classic, he is a classic of wit...he was more interested in literature than social conditions.'

I have said that he had no concept of altering the structure of his society, and this is true: on the other hand he was often prone to indulge in the backward-looking wish-fulfilment dream—something very different. *If only* is the keynote of his fantasy: *if only* Rome had never acquired an empire, *if only* we were still the small, simple, agricultural community that we were in the days of the Kings, *if only* there had not been that dreadful influx of wealth and clever foreigners to corrupt our morals, tempt us with luxury, give us the appetite for power! When Juvenal looks back to the Golden Age, he is lamenting the loss of innocence. His real hero is not so much Cicero—though the career of that provincial-made-good must have whetted his own ambitions in more ways than one—as Cato the Censor. Cato was a walking embodiment of the old semi-mythical virtues: husbandry, piety, service to the State. His xenophobia was at least as marked as Juvenal's, and as a moral Jeremiah he left the satirist standing. He even, more appropriately than perhaps he knew, went to the length of giving Rome's sewerage system a radical overhaul. (So, in a sense, did Juvenal.) His official post as Censor was one to which every satirist unofficially aspired.

But what made Cato particularly interesting to the intellectuals of a politically impotent age was the fact that he offered an almost unique example of morality, without any strings attached, actually controlling and changing the course of political events. Seneca had argued that only differences of character and behaviour distinguished the king from the tyrant: it followed as necessary corollary that the one safeguard against despotism was the inculcation of moral virtue in the ruler. Under the early Emperors there was an obvious political explanation for this alarmingly *simpliste* attitude. What one cannot abolish, one must take steps to improve. Besides, no one had forgotten the bloody chaos and anarchy which had accompanied the death-throes of the Republic. The Romans might have sacrified their freedom, but they had won peace, prosperity, and stable government in exchange. It was not difficult for the Emperor's supporters to argue that any show of independence, any talk of 'liberty', directly threatened the *pax Romana*. We have seen such arguments in our own day. The only alternative was the complete political quietism of thinkers such as the ex-slave Epictetus, who openly stated that Caesar could be left to guarantee men's social security, but that personal problems and emotions were the domain of philosophy. (This did not stop Domitian banishing him in 89: there were three purges of 'philosophers' at this period, by Vespasian in 71, and by Domitian in 89 and 93.) This was the intellectual legacy which Juvenal inherited. It would, I think, be true to say of him, as Professor Clarke says of Tacitus, that 'his heart was on the side of the republican past, his head on the side of the imperial present'.

If we try to pin down any coherent philosophy in Juvenal's work, we soon find ourselves forced to admit defeat. Juvenal himself (XIII 120-24) expressly denies allegiance to any of the three major groups of his day, the Stoics, Epicureans and Cynics —which does not mean that he refrained from raiding their commonplaces, in an eclectic fashion, whenever it happened to suit his book. His attitude to marriage resembles that of the Cynic, his cultivation of friendship has an Epicurean flavour, his aphorisms on such topics as virtue and fortitude and destiny are forceful expressions of Stoic doctrine, often more striking than anything composed by more professional thinkers. But he had little formal knowledge of philosophy as such, and scant aptitude for sustained rational argument: like A. E. Housman, one surmises, he found abstract thought irksome. His attitude to the whole business, fundamentally, was that of the caricaturist who formed so large an element in his creative personality: he saw life as a series of vivid, static, distorted snapshots. The 'intellectual image', as Mr W. S. Anderson rightly reminds us, does not exist in Juvenal: it would be very strange if it did, since the cast of mind which it implies is wholly alien to Juvenal's method of exposition. Philosophers, for Juvenal, were primarily eccentric individuals, who spent their time laughing, weeping, living in tubs, or avoiding beans. When he came to deal with contemporary upper-class Stoics, it was in the same personal terms. He shows us a group of hypocritical crypto-homosexuals with crewcuts, aping Cato's sternness and shagginess, but in fact corrupt shams, whose knowledge of the philosophers is limited to the plaster busts they have on display in their houses. Juvenal does not work out a coherent ethical critique of institutions or individuals: he simply hangs a series of moral portraits on the wall and forces us to look at them.

IV

Le style, as Buffon said, *c'est l'homme même*; and when we examine the style, imagery, and structure of Juvenal's *Satires*, we find an almost uncanny congruence between the author's personality and the form of self-expression he chose. Satire had, originally, been a literary medley, a loose sequence of isolated scenes. Intellectual exponents of the art such as Horace and Persius had tightened up its structure a good deal; but for a writer of Juvenal's temperament, who worked through images rather than by logic, the old form was far more congenial. He picked a theme, and then proceeded to drive it home into his reader's mind by a vivid and often haphazard accumulation of examples. Juvenal's sense of overall structure—as so often with an artist who dislikes abstract concepts—is sketchy, to say the least of it. Very often his work reads like a series of paragraphs that bear only a token relationship to each other, written at different times and stitched together without much concern for tidiness or coherence. If Juvenal ever read Quintilian's remarks about the need for economy and order in one's presentation of a subject, they cannot have made much impression on him. He announces a topic for later treatment, and then forgets all about it. He is full of abrupt jumps (some of them probably due to lacunae in our text) and splendidly irrelevant digressions. He prowls all round his subject, with the purposeful and disjunctive illogicality of a monkey exploring its cage. The cumulative effect is impressive: at times Juvenal seems to forestall the techniques of cinematic montage, and if he had been alive today it is a fair bet he would be making his living as a disgruntled and dyspeptic script-writer at Cinecittà. This is especially apparent in Satire III, with its fast-moving, well-edited shots—arranged, we may note, in chronological sequence—of street scenes in the City. We can almost hear the cutting-room shears at work as we move from the fatal accident (pedestrian crushed under waggon load of marble) to the victim's house, and from there to Hades' bank, for a glimpse of the brand-new ghost awaiting Charon the ferryman; or from the bedroom of an insomniac and compulsive bully to the dark street where he picks his quarrel with an innocent passer-by.

But since Juvenal was well acquainted with the rules of rhetoric—and since (perhaps more important) classical scholars are themselves tidy-minded intellectuals with a great gift for logical analysis—it has too often been assumed that the *Satires* must follow some *rational* structure and pattern if only we had the wit to see it. 'An abrogation of form,' says Mr W. C. Helmbold, 'is unthinkable for a professional writer of Juvenal's attainment.' This seems a very dubious assertion, besides begging the question of what can be defined as 'form'. Behind it one glimpses that old ghost which still haunts classical studies, however often right-minded scholars may exorcize it: the feeling that ancient authors achieved a perfection which somehow places them above common literary error, that they cannot be criticized, only explained and justified. *Tu nihil in magno doctus reprehendis Homero*? Horace asked—'Tell me, do you, a scholar, find nothing to cavil at in mighty Homer?' Such an attitude, besides betraying a fundamental misconception of the way Juvenal worked, has had unhappy consequences for his text. When the German scholar Ribbeck argued that the second half of the *Satires* was so different in tone from the first that it must be the work of a late forger, he was only half in jest. Any passage which fails to measure up to an editor's preconceived standards of Juvenalian perfection, from the standpoint of aesthetics, rhetoric, structure, content, or even—on occasion—of decency, is liable to be excised from the canon as an interpolation, on the grounds that 'Juvenal could not possibly have written it.' So of recent years the *Satires* have been laid on a Procrustean bed of structural analysis: this has produced some useful insights, and a great deal of disagreement.

In Satire II, for instance, Juvenal has two loosely related themes, homosexuality and hypocrisy, which he develops by something not very short of random association. Our philosophers are hyprocrites because they mask their homosexuality behind a pretence of virtue. They are aristocrats, and therefore doubly reprehensible. Domitian is the arch-hypocrite: despite his, and his relatives', sexual excesses he assumes the role of Censor. In any case, homosexuality is progressive and contagious, a symptom of our corruption: if a man joins the philosophical coterie he will end up at drag-parties and homosexual 'marriages'. Our conquests abroad contrast shamefully with the canker at the core: Rome corrupts all who live there. Now there is no overall logical pattern about this development, but it remains remarkably effective nonetheless: the apparent inconsistencies which some writers have found (for example between the supposedly unrelated topics of hypocrisy and perversion) melt away on inspection. Satire III is so splendidly orchestrated that the lack of logical sequence seems not to have bothered critics as much as one might expect. It falls loosely into two halves, on the vicissitudes of a poor but honest *rentier* and the discomforts and actual dangers of city life; but even so, Juvenal moves from one train of thought to another exactly as the fancy pleases him. As always, he obtains his effects by the piling up of visual effects, paradoxical juxtaposition rather than step-by-step development, a series of striking contrasts between the decent, innocent Roman (a kind of Candide-like observer) and the crooks, Greeks, draymen or other *canaille* who push ahead of him, bang him in the ribs, splash him with mud, beat him up at night, steal his job, drop slops on his head, and leave him to beg in the gutter when his apartment burns out.

If Juvenal can confine himself to a single theme, and then expand it by means of one extended dramatic illustration, his form is neat and logical enough: what Mr Anderson calls a 'frame' presentation, with the *exemplum* topped and tailed by introduction and coda. Two good instances of this are Satires V and XV, where in each case the dramatic illustration—a clients' dinner-party, a grisly fight in the desert—forms a simple core or armature round which the entire poem is articulated. It is no coincidence that the most satisfying satires, structurally speaking, tend also to be the shortest. Juvenal's only idea of structural enlargement is repetition, adding one 'frame' to another until he runs out of material. His dilemma bears some resemblance to that of Russian composers when endeavouring to make use of traditional themes: as Constant Lambert said, 'the whole trouble with a folk song is that once you have played it through there is nothing much you can do except play it over again and play it rather louder.' (Anyone who doubts this should look at Tchaikovsky's Fourth Symphony and see what he does with Little Fir Tree motif.) But—and this is equally significant—there is no correlation between regularity of form and literary excellence in the *Satires*. The most dramatically vivid of them, that little *tour de force* Satire IV, is a broken-backed affair which has defied even the most ingenious attempts to unify its parts. Once again we see the principle of random selection at work, a train of thought which proceeds from one enticing image to another like a man leaping from tussock to tussock across a bog. Juvenal begins with an anecdote about his favourite *bête noire* Crispinus, the commander of the Praetorian Guard. Crispinus has bought a giant mullet for 6,000 sesterces—about £120. But the mention of one giant fish reminds Juvenal of another; he drops Crispinus and sails into a spoof-epic sketch of Domitian and his Cabinet solemnly debating what should be done with a giant turbot presented to the Emperor by an Ancona fisherman. Some scholars have found 'connecting ideas between the two parts in the ways in which Crispinus and Domitian use their big fishes and in the similarities of the two men's characters', which is little more than a ratification of the free-association principle. Juvenal, I cannot help feeling, would have been the ideal candidate for a Rorschach test.

This is nowhere more apparent than in what is arguably Juvenal's greatest, as well as his longest, achievement: the enormous diatribe against women and marriage which forms Satire VI, and was published by itself as Book II of his complete works. There have been innumerable attempts to extract a coherent pattern from this unwieldy monster, but all have broken down on points of detail. Highet describes the overall theme as the futility of marriage, and claims that the poem has a 'good bold simple structure, ending in a powerful climax'. But even he admits that 'the chief difficulty in it is to find some reason for the arrangement of the various types of married women's folly, in 352-591, and here the manuscripts appear to have been badly disturbed.' (When in doubt, blame the text.) Anderson, on the other hand, declares that 'the structure of Satire VI is conclusively against an interpretation of the central theme as that of marriage. The subject of the satire is Woman, Roman Woman, and her tragedy. She has lost her womanhood. . .; in its place she has adopted viciousness.' Both are right, both wrong: the two themes coexist in the satire, and Juvenal moves between them as the fancy takes him. He opens with a semi-ironic portrait of the Golden Age, when Chastity had not yet retired from earth: adultery, he reflects, is man's longest-established vice. Why marry, he asks, when so many handier forms of suicide are available? You'll be lucky to find a virgin, and even a virgin will soon change her ways when she starts moving in the society of young upper-class Roman matrons. From voyeuristic orgasms at the theatre she'll soon graduate to liaisons with actors, musicians or gladiators. Two cautionary illustrations follow: the senator's wife who ran off with a swordsman, Messalina's activities in the brothel.

So far the sequence has been orderly enough. But Juvenal's powers of concentration never seem to extend much beyond a hundred lines, and here, as usual, free association begins to creep in. After a couplet on sex crimes so irrelevant that some critics think they should be transferred to the end of the poem, Juvenal observes that the peccadilloes of rich wives are condoned because of the dowry they bring: the cash-motif has appeared again. There follows a cutting little sketch which illustrates Juvenal's favourite theme, the corruption of personal relationships, and—as in Satires IV, V, and IX—attacks both parties with equal vigour. This episode has never, I think, had quite the attention it deserves. Sertorius and Bibula are a cynical *reductio ad absurdum* of the marriage of pure self-interest. Bibula may be a mercenary gold-digger who takes Sertorius for all he's got; but Sertorius, equally, is a cold sensuous hedonist whose only interest in Bibula is a physical one, and who dumps her, ruthlessly, the moment her charms begin to fade. The marital relationship has been pared down to pure calculating self-interest; no human emotion remains in it. Here we have the same psychological theme which reappears in the commination on *captatores* at the end of Satire XII:

> So long live legacy-hunters, as long as Nestor himself!
> May their possessions rival all Nero's loot, may they pile up
> Gold mountain-high, may they love no man, and be loved by none.

Selfish greed, selfish indulgence are, between them, destroying all human intercourse and affection. The individual now stalks through life as though it were some sort of no-man's-land, in armoured isolation, out solely for what he can get, giving no quarter and expecting none. Even marriage has become the same battleground in miniature. Hell, as Sartre said, is other people; but it is also oneself.

Yet (Juvenal goes on) there is no way out for a prospective husband: if the corrupt woman is a bitch, the virtuous woman is a bore. Who would want to marry such a highminded noble prig as Cornelia, 'Mother of the Gracchi', and burden himself with that insupportable legacy of noble rectitude? (Here, for once, the urban sophisticate shows through the moralist's mask: I suspect that this represented Juvenal's basic attitude to the whole Republican myth.) Virtuous pride is far from easy to live with, and brings its own retribution—look what happened to that sow-like breeder Niobe. With which reflection, Juvenal suddenly switches to an attack on Greek fashions. From this point the *montage* technique comes increasingly into play, and the pace quickens with a kind of hysterical frenzy. Women torment you and run your life, forcing you to discard old friends and make bequests to your wife's lovers. There are quick shots of a wife bullying her liberal husband into torturing a slave, a mother-in-law pandering to her daughter's adultery. A preamble on female litigiousness and quarrelsomeness leads into some vivid glimpses of upper-class ladies practising sword-play. Women nag in bed, we are told, and talk their way out of anything. At this juncture Juvenal stops and asks what produced the decline in morals: wealth, he concludes, and too many years of peace (this is rather like the pre-1914 journalism of Belloc and Chesterton and W. E. Henley). Then he is off again on alcoholism, orgies, and queer go-betweens who turn out to be strongly heterosexual in bed. The final sections of the poem present a series of stylized portrait-sketches: the woman who is mad on the Games, the well-informed busybody who talks back to generals, the hearty drinker with her dog-whip and her obliging masseur, the tyrant in the boudoir, beating the slave-girl who dresses her hair, the astrology-fans and devotees of exotic cults. With some final sulphurous remarks about abortions, aphrodisiacs, and parricide for profit, the satire grinds to a snarling but essentially unresolved halt. The reader has been not so much reasoned into agreement as battered into submission.

This technique may indicate a defect in Juvenal's constructive powers, but it seems to me a fundamental part of his satirical equipment. If it is a weakness, the weakness has been turned to the best advantage, and with considerable ingenuity. Here Juvenal stands poles apart from a naturally architectonic poet such as Virgil or Horace. The writer he far more resembles, not only in his pessimism and sense of moral purpose, but also in style and technique, is Lucretius. Both have the same urgent, nagging, neurotic method of exposition; both use the hexameter as a weapon with which to bludgeon their audience. Both, we may note, share that odd preoccupation with Golden Age of rural primitivism from which they themselves, by temperament and habitat, were so far removed. Source-hunting in literature is, on the whole, an unprofitable game; but Juvenal *was* a noticeably bookish writer, and his debts were more interesting than most, since he turned them to such good use. He must have known Martial's *Epigrams*, for instance, almost by heart, since there is scarcely one of the earlier satires but contains some echo of them; yet Juvenal's borrowings are far from indiscriminate, and reveal a keen sense of judgment. He saw, clearly, that Martial's supreme quality was his gift for direct observation, his *pointilliste* use of the occasional piece to build up a composite, Mayhew-like portrait of Roman life and manners. Juvenal took the technique (and some of the descriptions) but adapted it to his own purposes, changing not only the context but also the phraseology. Furthermore, as Mr Lelièvre has pointed out with some acuteness, Juvenal's deliberate echoes of earlier writers very often serve the same purpose as do those employed by Eliot in *The Waste Land*: they are touchstones to intensify the sense of moral decadence.

Orwell, in the essay I mentioned earlier, remarked that Dickens' genius emerged most clearly from 'turns of phrase and concrete details'. Broadly speaking, the same is true of Juvenal, though temperamentally he was far removed from Dickens, and altogether lacked the novelist's generous scope and warmth. Juvenal is, *au fond*, a miniaturist, and his greatest gift—whether in a dramatized scene, a piece of invective, or a moral statement —is for vivid and memorable concision. His language, however casual and demotic it may appear, has been distilled, refined, crystallized. It is not surprising that his whole lifetime's output barely exceeded 4,000 lines of verse. Seldom can one man's body of work have had less spare fat on it. We see this most clearly and obviously in the famous aphorisms which, even in Latin, have become part and parcel of the Western European inheritance: *panem et circenses, quis custodiet ipsos custodes? rara avis, mens sana in corpore sano*, and many others, such as *maxima debetur puero reverentia*, ('Never forget that a child has first claim on your respect') which are less well known since the decline of Latin as a major pillar of secondary education. This gift of Juvenal's extends to his invective, in particular to his cold, quasi-clinical handling of sexual misdemeanours. He never once uses the Latin equivalent of a four-letter word (in which he provides a striking contrast to Martial); but as Highet says, when it comes to turning your stomach with a couple of well-chosen phrases, there is almost no one to touch him. While lambasting Domitian in Satire II he throws off the following couplet:

> ...*cum tot abortivis fecundam Iulia vulvam*
> *solveret et patruo similes effunderet offas.*
> ('His niece, a fertile creature, had her row of abortions,
> And every embryo lump was the living spit of Uncle.')

I have printed the Latin here because no translation on earth could do full justice to Juvenal's revoltingly skilful use of language and rhythm. The first hexameter, with its predominantly spondaic feet, its repeated *v*s, *o*s and *u*s, moves forward in a series of slow, sluggish heaves that irresistibly suggest uterine contraction; the second begins and ends with an explosive burst (*solveret*, *offas*) which represents the actual expulsion of the embryo. Finally, there is the vulgar term *offa*, which not only *sounds* disgusting, but carries unpleasant associations, since it is most commonly used in connexion with pigs or sows.

This is no isolated instance. Perhaps Juvenal's greatest poetical achievement is his ability to marry sound, sense and rhythm into one organic whole. His ear for the nuances of vowel-sounds and consonantal patterns is acute, and few Roman poets can equal his absolute control over the pace, tone and texture of a hexameter. The garrulous bluestocking in Satire VI (434ff.) elicits the comment: 'Such a rattle of talk/ You'd think all the pots and bells were being clashed together.' In the Latin you can actually *hear* them: *verborum tanta cadit vis,/ tot pariter pelves ac tintinnabula dicas/ pulsari.* With apparently careless ease he catches the crackle of a fire, the cooing of doves on the roof-tiles, an old man greedily gulping his food, the belch and eructation of some gluttonous Palace trimmer, the drunken dancing of Egyptian villagers, a tittering Greek, the heave and lurch of seasickness, the harsh, abrupt, staccato rattle of a bully's questions suddenly fired at his victim, the scrannel, hen-like piping of a counter-tenor. Examples could be adduced from every satire. Verbal dexterity is reinforced by a sparing, but dramatic, use of simile and metaphor: the informer who could slit men's throats with a soft whisper; the lofty but gimcrack tower reared by ambition; the father who is destroyed by the son he has himself trained in vice, like a lion-tamer who vanishes into the maw of his own lion; the senator's wife who drinks and vomits like a big snake that has tumbled into a vat. Sometimes the implications are very subtle. It took Mr Anderson to make us see that 'the metaphors in VII 82ff. transform the inanimate epic of Statius into a very attractive female, whose allure resides entirely in her sex'—the point being, of course, that Statius is prostituting his art by pandering to popular taste (and, we might add, compromising his integrity by selling ballet-scenarios to Paris in order to make a living). We have already seen something of Juvenal's penchant for the diminutive and the anti-climax as devices for satirizing contemporary littleness: here, too, the effect is prepared for with great verbal skill, so that the deflationary punch-line, or even word, catches a reader with his defences down and forces him to *think*:

> Squalor and isolation are minor evils compared
> To this endless nightmare of fires and collapsing houses,
> The cruel city's myriad perils—and poets reciting
> Their work in *August*!

A few shocks of this sort, and we begin to ask ourselves whether, socially speaking, the amateur gladiator of distinguished family, the muleteer-consul, or the stage-struck Emperor are not symptoms of more deep-seated flaws in the body politic than might at first be supposed.

But for the modern reader, whose interest in Juvenal is (*pace*

Mr Mason) to a very large extent antiquarian rather than moralistic, the prime quality of the *Satires* is their ability to project the splendour, squalor and complexity of the Roman scene more vividly than the work of any other author, Horace and Cicero included. This, of course, is particularly true of Satire III, on which J. W. Mackail wrote a paragraph in his *Latin Literature* which I can no more resist quoting than could Duff:

> The drip of the water from the aqueduct that passed over the gate from which the dusty, squalid Appian Way stretched through its long suburb; the garret under the tiles, where, just as now, the pigeons sleeked themselves in the sun and the rain drummed on the roof; the narrow, crowded streets, half choked with the builders' carts, ankle-deep in mud, and the pavement ringing under the heavy military boots of guardsmen; the tavern waiters trotting along with a pyramid of hot dishes on their heads; the flower-pots falling from high window-ledges; night, with the shuttered shops, the silence broken by some sudden street brawl, the darkness shaken by a flare of torches as some great man, wrapped in his scarlet cloak, passes along from a dinner-party with his long train of clients and slaves: these scenes live for us in Juvenal, and are perhaps the picture of ancient Rome that is most abidingly impressed on our memory.

Yet this is only a fraction of the motley scene which Juvenal paints, with quick, bold, economic strokes: the 'smoke and wealth and clamour' of Rome which Horace described are here, and its smells too, and above all its colourful, polyglot inhabitants, caught in one vivid phrase after another, glimpsed for a moment and then gone—the African poling his felucca up the Tiber, with a cargo of cheap rancid oil; the plump smooth successful lawyer riding above the heads of the crowd in his litter; the homosexual fluttering his eyelids as he applies his make-up, or wearing a chiffon gown, near-transparent, to plead a case in court; the ageing gladiator, straight out of Hogarth or Rowlandson, 'helmet-scarred, a great wen on his nose, an unpleasant/Discharge from one constantly weeping eye'; a lady of quality, her large thighs wrapped in coarse puttees, panting and blowing at sword-drill; the downtrodden teacher and his resentful pupils conning lamp-blackened texts of Virgil before daybreak; the sadistic mistress who sits reading the daily gazette or examining dress-material while one of her slaves is being flogged in the same room; the would-be poet giving a recital in a cheap, peeling hired hall, with his claque of freedmen distributed at strategic points through the audience (only Juvenal would have added the realistic touch of placing them *at the ends of the rows*); the fat, horsy consul Lateranus, swearing stable oaths, untrussing his own hay, or boozing with matelots and escaped convicts in some dockside tavern; the contemptible trimmers hurrying down to boot Sejanus' corpse in the ribs ('and make sure our slaves watch us') while sneering at the rabble for its opportunism; the miser hoarding fish-scraps in September; the squad of slaves with fire-buckets guarding a millionaire's *objets d'art*; the court-martial presided over by a group of hobnailed old colour-sergeants; the temple-robber scraping gold leaf from the statues of unprotesting deities; the sizzle of sacrificial offerings, the roar of the crowd at the races, beggars blowing kisses, the carver flourishing his knives, fortune-tellers, whores, confidence-men, politicians—it is an endless and kaleidoscopic panorama. But it was not so much human endeavours that obsessed him—he had always been rather hazy about what people actually *did*—so much as humanity itself, that marvellous anthill which he hated and loved with equal fervour, and from which, even at his most scorbutic, he never wholly succeeded in tearing himself away.

Appendix

THE DATE OF ARCHILOCHUS

THE chronology of Archilochus, like his character, is both ambiguous and elusive. This was not always thought to be the case. Until Blakeway turned his attention to the problem, in 1936,[1] Archilochus seemed to offer one of the very few secure dates in the seventh century B C. A famous fragment[2] describing a total or near-total eclipse of the sun had long been identified with that visible in Greece and the Aegean during the morning of 6 April 648. 'Zeus, father of the Olympians, has made night from midday; Ζεῦς ἐκ μεσημβρίης ἔθηκε νύκτα.' The actual time of the eclipse was 9.28 a.m. over Athens, and some fifteen minutes later in the Cyclades; but μεσημβρίης could, it was argued, signify 'forenoon'. It was also taken as axiomatic that Archilochus' phrase meant a total eclipse in the technical sense; but to the untutored eye there is virtually no distinction between a total eclipse of 12+digits and an annular eclipse of 11·5 digits or above. Thus alternative candidates for Archilochus' eclipse tended to be ignored—as did the fact that the eclipse date itself was closely related to his engagement, an event which tends to occur early in life. The 648 eclipse—reinforced by an allusion to the 'woes of the Magnesians', generally taken to describe the city's destruction by Trerian tribesmen in 652[3]—meant that Archilochus' life-span was pegged firmly within the first half of the seventh century.

Blakeway pointed out that most ancient chronographers placed the poet's *floruit* rather earlier, either soon before or soon after 700, and that such evidence, backed by the *Monumentum Archilochi* on Paros, was not lightly to be dismissed. Various historical allusions in the poems themselves were said to look back to the period between 730 and 700.[4] But Blakeway's trump card was an alternative eclipse, that of 14 March 711, total (more recent calculations show only 0·93 totality) over

Thasos, near-total over Paros. There are, of course, other criteria for dating Archilochus; but despite scholarly disclaimers,[5] it is the astronomical evidence which has continued to dominate later research, and all other testimony has been tacitly chopped or stretched to fit it. Blakeway used the 711 eclipse (which he claimed, oddly, that Archilochus need not actually have seen)[6] to produce a birth date of 740 to 730, a 688/5 *floruit*, and a date for the poet's death, in battle, during the decade 670–60. This meant explaining away the 'woes of the Magnesians', which Blakeway connected, not with the city's final destruction in 652, but its capture by the Ephesians between 700 and 690.[7] The chronology of Archilochus was thus thrown into the melting-pot.

Five years later came Jacoby's magisterial rejoinder.[8] He isolated the *floruit* offered by Apollodorus, 664/3, as the only feasible one, and put Archilochus firmly back in the seventh century, with a tentative life-span of about 680–40. He assumed without question that 'Archilochus saw the eclipse and that it was total or nearly total in the place where he saw it',[9] an argument which has the massive weight of common sense and common probability to support it. He also insisted, less convincingly, that 'the woes of the Magnesians' could *only* refer to the city's destruction in 652. Archilochus, he claimed, went back to Paros in or shortly before the year of the eclipse (648) and *then* had his ill-starred affair with Neobule: such a hypothesis meant tacitly ditching even the Apollodorus *floruit* date, which would have produced a sighing lover in his mid-fifties. From the 'woes of the Magnesians' fragment Jacoby deduced that Archilochus was living on Thasos after Magnesia's destruction; and as he was not an old man when he emigrated thither, he must have been a young man about 652.[10] This kind of circular argument excites more wonder than conviction. Yet Jacoby's article seems to be acquiring canonical status (no one thought of challenging it at the 1963 Geneva colloquium), which is odd, since it suffers from precisely the same kind of special pleading as Blakeway's: that is, both give the unmistakable impression of straining their evidence to fit a date—that of the eclipse—which in one case seems much too early and in the other much too late. Neither Blakeway nor Jacoby could utilize the new Mnesiepean inscription first published by Kontoléon in 1952,[11] and Lasserre (who implausibly reverted to the 711 eclipse combined with a 705 birth date[12]) did not fully recognize its significance. A fresh review of the evidence, then, may not come amiss.

Let us begin with the external chronological sources. Several ancient authorities, including Herodotus and Apollodorus,[13] calculate either Archilochus' *floruit*, or the foundation of Thasos, or both, from the reign of Gyges. Unfortunately Gyges' dates are no longer quite so firm as scholars once thought them: fresh study of the Assyrian annals of Assurbanipal and Assurhadden now suggests that, instead of dying in 652, he may have survived into the 640s, which in turn affects his traditional accession date of 687, calculated from the length of his reign as recorded in our Greek sources. On the other hand, the traditional dates are, precisely those given by Apollodorus, who places Archilochus' *floruit* at 664. We may also note that Xanthus of Lydia makes the foundation of Thasos coincide with the *beginning* of Gyges' reign, and the foundation date selected by Dionysius of Halicarnassus coincides within a year with the accession date, 716, chosen by Herodotus. It is also interesting that Cicero chose Romulus' reign for the *floruit* of Archilochus, since the traditional date of Romulus' death, 716, is also that which Herodotus held to mark Gyges' accession. Dates for the *floruit*, then, include 716 (twice), 700—696, 694, 684, and 664. Can we obtain anything firmer than this?

Internal historical allusions in Archilochus' text are for the most part illusory or unhelpful. The mention of Euboean bowmen is no more proof that Archilochus fought in the Lelantine War (let alone as a mercenary) than the allusion to Siris is that he ever visited Italy. Fr. 15 LB confirms Herodotus' assertion that Archilochus and Gyges were contemporaries; that does not necessarily make them coevals. Fr. 280 LB—'I weep for the woes of Thasos, not for those of the Magnesians'—*may* indicate that Archilochus was still alive after 652, but need not do so. Blakeway's arguments for an earlier catastrophe should not be minimized.[14] The one crucial passage for fixing Archilochus' date still remains fr.82 LB, that describing a solar eclipse, and Jacoby was wrong to belittle its importance. Aristotle preserved the bulk of it in his *Rhetorica* [1418b 24] as an illustration for the dramatized use of insult. Archilochus, he says, 'portrays the father talking about the daughter in his iambics'— ποιεῖ γὰρ τὸν πατέρα λέγοντα περὶ τῆς θυγατρὸς ἐν τῷ ἰάμβῳ. Both, that is, are characters in a poem—nor can there be any doubt of their identity. The father is Lycambes, the daughter Neobule: we have here yet another unmistakable reference to the poet's broken engagement. Furthermore, the only possible *raison d'être* for the mention of an eclipse in this poem, given the context, is that it was local and recent, an allusion as topical as it was dramatic. Find the right eclipse, and we obtain a most valuable peg in the reconstruction of Archilochus' chronology.

At this point it will be helpful, for a moment, to abandon the search for absolute dates, and remind ourselves of the *relative* sequence of events in Archilochus' lifetime, beginning with our evidence for the colonization of Thasos. Pausanias [10.23.3] tells us that the poet's grandfather, together with a priestess named Cleoboea, first brought the rites of Demeter from Paros to Thasos. Such a move would probably have been carried out, not at the actual time of colonization, but earlier, during the softening-up period, when traders and merchants were assessing the island's potential.[15] The true Parian colonizer, the *oikistés*, of Thasos, is agreed to have been Archilochus' father Telesicles.[16] From the Mnesiepean Inscription[17] we know that Telesicles and one other citizen of Paros were appointed *theopropoi* to consult the Delphic Oracle about their projected colonizing mission. This fellow-emissary's name is given; he was none other than Lycambes. Now if Lycambes went from Paros to Delphi with Telesicles, and afterwards to Thasos, several conclusions emerge. First, since Archilochus is described as 'still a young boy' at the time of the oracular consultation, ἔτι νεώτερον ὄντα, that is, under twenty, his provisional engagement to Lycambes' daughter Neobule can be placed, with some confidence at least five years later (Solon and Hesiod, among others, put the average minimum age for a man to marry at about thirty, and certainly not under twenty-five).[18] Nor is it likely that the two families would still have been on speaking terms *after* the barrage of poetical abuse with which Archilochus greeted his broken engagement. The engagement itself, then, must have taken place on Thasos, several years after the colonists had settled there. Archaeological evidence suggests that the original colonization of Thasos took place soon after 700 B C.[19] We can, therefore, assume that Archilochus' estrangement from Neobule was closely linked in time to a total or near-total solar eclipse, visible over Thasos, in the period between 700 and 685; and if we can narrow the field down to one eclipse, we should then be able to use its date as an absolute point on which to hang Archilochus' *curriculum vitae*, in so far as this is determinable.

There is, by great good fortune, one such eclipse, and one only: that of 11 January 689, which was visible in the Aegean area about 10 a.m., and achieved 96 per cent totality over Thasos, as against 92 per cent at Paros and 93 per cent in Athens.[20] The next eclipse to meet all the necessary requirements was not until 27 June 661. Let us work from the hypothesis that the 689 eclipse was the one Archilochus had in mind, and relate this to our other evidence. If his engagement to Neobule was broken in the early spring of 689, it had probably been arranged in 690, before his unsuccessful trading venture to Gortyn in Crete, and when he was at the minimum acceptable age for matrimony, that is about twenty-five. This gives us a hypothetical birth date of 716/5—a figure which twice recurs in the chronographical calculations of his *floruit*, being Gyges' putative accession date and the (traditionally accepted) year of Romulus' death. The coincidence is at least worth noting. Furthermore, if Archilochus was still under twenty at the time of his father's oracular consultations, this dates the oracle itself not later than 697/6. Assume at least a year's preparation for a major colonizing venture: then the party, including Telesicles, Lycambes and their families, will have sailed for Thasos about 695/4—the *floruit* date, it is just worth noting, given by Hesychius. It was then, on Thasos, some four years later, that the engagement took place—between the son and daughter of two families which were clearly on the closest of terms. The repudiation of the betrothal must have produced a painful situation, and it looks very much as though Archilochus now (spring 689) returned to Paros, since the circumstances of his venture to Thasos as recorded by Critias and Oenomaus of Gadara have no connexion with the official expedition under his father's leadership. Critias tells us that he 'left Paros for Thasos on account of his own poverty and fecklessness', Oenomaus that he had 'squandered his substance on political tomfoolery'[21]—both likely enough occupations for him. That the son of the *oikistés* would have accompanied his father's expedition in such circumstances seems barely credible; but if we posit a *second* journey, everything falls into place. This hypothesis is supported by the terms of the oracle supposedly given to Archilochus himself (as opposed to his father). As Pouilloux points out, he is told to *live* in Thasos, not to *found* it; the island is given its historical name (rather than Eërië) and described as 'famous'.[22] If Archilochus went home to Paros in 689, he may well have been back again by 684 (Eusebius' *floruit* date), having spent all his money and got into political trouble—a prodigal son returning, after four or five years' absence, to a lukewarm welcome from his much-abused former friends and relatives. Here, I believe, he spent the rest of his life, a penniless and hard-bitten old colonist, fighting and whoring on Thasos and the Thracian mainland opposite. There is no convincing evidence, however, to show that he was ever a mercenary, and nothing which suggests a latter-day return to Paros (the battles he describes between Parians and Naxians were for colonizing *Lebensraum* in the north, not over each others' barren islands). It was, then, still on Thasos, probably soon after

652/1—though an earlier date cannot be ruled out altogether—that Archilochus was killed, by a Naxian nicknamed Crow.[23] It is quite possible (the killer's need to defend his action and seek purification suggests it) that Crow, whose real name was Calondas, killed the elderly Archilochus during a private brawl rather than in battle—though old men did, on occasion, fall fighting.[24] The ambiguity of Archilochus' end is all of a piece with the rest of his existence. In death as in life, the woes of the Thasians had made themselves his concern.

NOTES AND REFERENCES

1. 'The date of Archilochus', in *Greek Poetry and Life*: Essays presented to Gilbert Murray (Oxford 1936) pp.34-55. I do not propose to discuss Löwy's curious attempt (Anz.Akad. Wien Phil.-hist.Kl.70 [1933] 31ff.) to bring the date of the eclipse down to 557.

2. Fr.82 LB=fr.74 Diehl and Bergk. In this article I shall use the Lasserre-Bonnard (LB) numeration throughout.

3. Fr.280 LB.

4. See, e.g., frs.18,9 and 20–27 LB, together with Bonnard's sensible comments, pp.xix ff.

5. E.g. that of Jacoby (see n.8 below) p.97.

6. *Op.cit.* p. 52: cf LB 27, discussing fr.82.

7. Strabo 14.1.70, C.647; Callinus ap. Athenaeus 525c: Clem. Alex. *Strom.*1 p. 333b, cf.Plin. HN 35.8, 7.38: all cited in support by Blakeway, p.52.

8. F. Jacoby, 'The Date of Archilochus', CQ 35 (1941) 97-109. See his remarks on p.109 in particular, and cf. J. Pouilloux, 'Archiloque et Thasos', in *Entretiens sur l'Antiquité classique*, Vol. 10 (Geneva 1963) p.16.

9. *Op.cit.* p.97.

10. *Op.cit.* pp.105-7.

11. N. Kontoléon,

12. *Les Epodes d'Archiloque* (Paris 1950) p.293.

13. Reff. in Lasserre-Bonnard, with *testimonia*, pp.ciii-cv. For information on the Assurbanipal Chronicle I am much indebted to Mr D. M. Lewis.

14. See above, n.7.

15. Blakeway, p.49, n.1.

16. Oenom. Gadar. pp.55,70 [Vallette]=Eusebius *Praep.Ev.*5.32–3, 6.7.8; Steph.Byz. s.v. Thasos; Anth.Pal.14.113.

17. The relevant passage [E^1II 40-57 Kont.] is reproduced by Lasserre-Bonnard, *Vita* 11a, p.cv.

18. Hesiod WD 695ff.; Solon 19.9f., cf. Lasserre, *Epod.Arch.* pp.50, 293.

19. Pouilloux, *Recherches* 23ff., citing Jacoby.

20. Based on computations by Dr R. R. Newton of the Johns Hopkins Applied Physics Laboratory; cf. also his book *Ancient Astronomical Observations* (Johns Hopkins, 1970) pp. 91-3, F. K. Ginzel, *Handbuch der Mathematischen und Technischen Chronologie* (Leipzig 1911) Vol.2, p.524, and T. Oppolzer, *Canon of Eclipses*, trs. O. Gingerich, (New York 1962), pp.48-54. I am most grateful to Dr Newton, and to Dr J. Derral Mulholland of the Department of Astronomy in the University of Texas at Austin, for technical help over the Archilochean eclipse.

21. Fr.264 LB p.72 [=Critias fr.B 44 D-K, Eusebius *Praep.Ev.* 5.31.1]: Plutarch *De Malig.Herod.*21, cf.Pouilloux, *Recherches*, p.32.

22. *Entretiens*, pp.9-10.

23. Heracl.Pont.*Pol.*8; Plut.*De Ser.Num.Vind.*17=Lasserre-Bonnard, *testimonia* 14b, pp.cvii-cviii.

24. See e.g. Tyrtaeus frs.6-7 Diehl.

Index

INDEX

INDEX

INDEX

INDEX

INDEX

INDEX

INDEX

INDEX

INDEX